The Change Agent's Guide
to Innovation in Education

THE CHANGE AGENT'S GUIDE TO INNOVATION IN EDUCATION

Ronald G. Havelock

*Program Director, Center
for Research on Utilization
of Scientific Knowledge
Institute for Social Research
University of Michigan*

Educational Technology Publications
Englewood Cliffs, New Jersey 07632

Portions of this *Guide* were originally developed as part of Contract No. OEC-0-8-080603-4535(010) with the Office of Education, U.S. Department of Health, Education, and Welfare, under the title "Diffusion of Utilization Research to Knowledge Linkers in Education." Contractors undertaking such projects under Government sponsorship are encouraged to express freely their professional judgment in the conduct of the project. Points of view or opinions stated do not, therefore, necessarily represent official Office of Education position or policy.

Printed in the United States of America.

Library of Congress Catalog Card Number: 72-87317.

International Standard Book Number: 0-87778-039-0.

ISBN for Library (clothbound) Edition: 0-87778-048-X.

First Printing: January, 1973.

Second Printing: December, 1973.

Third Printing: August, 1975.

TABLE OF CONTENTS

ACKNOWLEDGMENTS

A large portion of the development work which led to the production of this *Guide* was supported under contract with the United States Office of Education. Special thanks are due to Thomas C. Clemens and Richard Elmendorf of the National Center for Educational Communication for their support and helpful advice throughout that development project. A very large number of people made substantial contributions to the effort. Janet Huber and Shaindel Zimmerman coordinated all the work which led to the first draft, including identification of quotations, assembling the bibliography and the appendices, writing up case studies and draft materials for chapters, and communicating with our field reviewers. Diane R. Vinokur worked in a similar capacity for the second draft. Elizabeth A. Campbell revised the appendices for the present third version. Joyce Kornbluh, the Center's editor, Douglas Truax of the Institute editorial staff, and Mary C. Havelock provided helpful comments on rough versions of the manuscript at numerous intervals. Special thanks are also due to my secretary, Rita Wiegers, for her endless patience and effort in a project which called for constant rewriting and reformatting.

Finally, credit should be given to the 115 educators across the United States who reviewed the first draft of the *Guide* and provided helpful comments for the development of the second and third versions.

E.J. Albrecht
Herbert H. Baker
Jarvis Barnes
Joseph E. Barrett
Carl R. Beck
L.L. Belanger
Virgie M. Binford
Richard M. Bingman
John R. Bottom
Harry L. Bowman
Marvin Boyer
Anthony Brackett
Stuart R. Brown
E.J. Buchanan
Bruce G. Caldwell
David H. Carlisle
George F. Castore
Charles S. Chandler
John Church
Gabriel Cifor
Warren C. Coffey
Roy Cole
W. Owens Corder
John Coulson
Glenn H. Crumb
Marylyn A. Dolan
Patricia Ann Ellis

Randy F. Elmore
Fenwick W. English
Thomas Fine
Ted B. Freeman
William P. Freitag
Marshall L. Frinks
Don E. Goodson
Delmar Goodwin
Eldon E. Gran
George H. Grimes
Harry J. Groulx
Rex Hagans
Thomas S. Hamill
William U. Harris
Charles F. Haughey
James R. Hayden
Irene K. Heller
Donald E. Hess, Jr.
Henry C. Heusner
Henry J. Heydt, Jr.
Edwin P. Hildebrand
Dean Honetschlager
Paul D. Hood
John V. Hussey, Jr.
Homer L. Jacobs
Stephen Jamba
Lynn Jenks

Ralph E. Kellogg
John J. Keough
Jack R. King
Anne T. Kohler
Jane B. Laskaris
Francis P. Laverty, Jr.
James L. Lovvorn
John MacDonald
James M. Mahan
Adriano J. Marinelli
E.R. McLaughlin
W.R. McNeill
Carl Means
Chester S. Merrifield
Henry A. Meyer
Peggy L. Miller
Troy Mills
William H. Mills
Franklin P. Morley
Edith K. Mosher
Franklin W. Neff
Irvin Nikolai
James L. Olivero
John Orr
Leon Ovsiew
LeRoy D. Owens
Robert W. Parlier
Brank Proffitt
Robert L. Putnam
Robert G. Rainey
Elizabeth S. Randolph

Luton R. Reed
Charles H. Rogers
Anthony J. Russo
Einar R. Ryden
William Sather
Charles Sayre
Robert G. Scanlon
Thomas H. Scannicchio
Carol Schnebel
Tom Schurtz
Duane T. Sermon
Donald K. Sharpes
Bruce E. Shear
Mary Lela Sherburne
Kenneth E. Shibata
Jim Simpson
Henry R. Smith
Asher Soloff
Martin Sorensen
Matt L. Tomasiewicz
Samuel D. Ulsaker
William G. VanHook
Philip Vik
Robert A. Williams
James A. Winter
M. Richard Wolford
John F. Wood
David H. Wright
Robert H. Zeller
Jerome M. Zummach

A SPECIAL NOTE TO ADMINISTRATORS

The executive leadership of an organization has two responsibilities: one is *maintenance* of the system the way it is, and the other is *changing* the system so that it performs better. In other words, the leader is both a change agent and a resister of change. Much of his time and energy must be spent on keeping things going, keeping people motivated, making sure that the work of the organization gets done at least as well as it has in the past. But if he is on top of his job, the good leader will also spend some of his time working to change his system; he will be looking for better ways to do things, new solutions to old problems, and new problems that he and his staff should be concerned about. Hence, he has a real and continuing need to know about change and the process of change.

Even though he is only a part-time change agent, the administrator should have at least six goals in mind for which the material in the *Guide* is very relevant.

First, he should know about the *process of change,* how it takes place and the attitudes, values, and behaviors that usually act as barriers or facilitators.

Second, he should know who in his system has the resources relevant to various change efforts. For example, he should be able to identify the *innovators* in a particular area, i.e., those who are most likely to adopt a new idea and experiment with it before their colleagues. He should also know who is good at *carrying through* on an innovation, applying it systematically and conscientiously, and sticking with it until it works. These "maintainers" are sometimes different from the "innovators." Finally, he should know who in his system are the "defenders" or resisters of innovations. Sometimes these individuals will have a legitimate concern for maintaining standards of "good" practice. The administrator must be able to give these different voices a chance to be heard before final decisions are made.

Third, the administrator needs to maintain a high level of *awareness* of new practices potentially worthy of adoption by his system. This does not mean an encyclopedic grasp of all the programs that are available, but it does mean an *acquaintance* with leading national programs based on a continued scanning of newsletters, press reports, and the broad-readership educational journals and magazines.

Fourth, the change-oriented administrator works to achieve a certain degree of "dither" in his system; he builds a staff with a diversity of views and approaches, and he encourages dialogue among them.

Fifth, the administrator-change agent should always hold a total system view of change and its effects. He should know the social ecology within which innovations take place. This means seeing his organization as an entity of many subparts working toward common goals and at the same time as one of many subsystems in the community. He should also see his organization as a subsystem in the greater national educational enterprise. Some innovations will look good in one "system" context but not in others. The administrator needs to be aware of these intersystem relationships and consequences.

Sixth and finally, the administrator-change agent needs to be working constantly to build the internal self-renewal capability of his staff and of his organization as a whole. He should be recruiting and developing staff members with capabilities as good "process helpers," "resource linkers," innovators, product champions, and evaluators. He should also provide a continuing open forum for advocates of change. Experimentation should come to be accepted as a dominant *norm* of the system. To develop such a norm you must be prepared to reward people for innovating *even when they fail,* and you should encourage outside linking even when the immediate benefits to you or the system are not obvious.

This *Guide* is not written especially for administrators or students or teachers or any other special group within the educational establishment, but it can be used effectively by individuals in all these roles when they want to bring about change. The administrator, however, is probably in a special position to foster or to stifle innovation, and for that reason the material which follows may be especially relevant to him.

A SPECIAL NOTE TO INSIDE CHANGE AGENTS WORKING FROM BELOW

Most of those who will want to use this book will not be in positions of power or authority with respect to the system they want to change. Nevertheless, it is possible to be effective working from within and from below. A few special points are in order for change agents in this situation.

First of all, diagram the organization as a system (see Stage II and Stage V). What are its goals, norms, key subsystems, and key people?

Second, with your diagram in hand or in mind, look for allies and potential allies. If you have a concern, the chances are that many others silently or vocally share your concern. Some of these allies will be insiders like yourself but some will be outsiders, community members, and others who can become part of a *team* working together.

Third, build your own "expert power." Know your "innovation" inside and out, its strengths, and its weaknesses; know what evaluations have been done; what objections might be raised by administrators, teachers, and students, and have answers ready for these objections.

Fourth, *be persistent* if you know you have a good case. Many studies have shown that successful change agents try harder and keep on trying. Your advantage over the outside expert consultant is that you are there and you won't go away.

Fifth, if you have an adversary (usually someone over you or further up the hierarchy than you are), analyze the situation from his point of view. Total up the pros and cons from his vantage point. This exercise should help you to understand how he might be won over or bypassed. It may even show you something about your innovation that should be changed.

Sixth, develop a sense of timing and act strategically; wait for the opportune moment and don't confront the opposition impulsively but only when there are other forces working in your favor.

Last, but not least, be prepared to let others share the credit. People feel rewarded if they feel they have done something for themselves; if the change is identified as "yours," they may not be so enthusiastic. This may be especially important for administrators who are concerned about maintaining their leadership image.

The Change Agent's Guide
to Innovation in Education

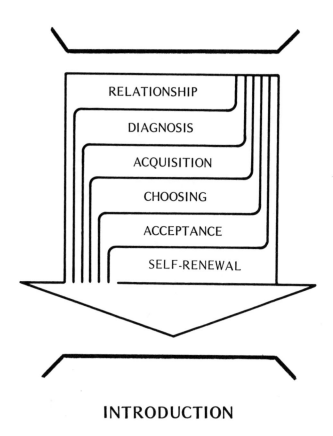

INTRODUCTION

This is a guide to the *process* of innovation. It is written for the many educators who are working for reform at all levels, helping school systems, schools, and individual teachers learn about new developments in administration, classroom management, curriculum, and teaching methods. These people are the CHANGE AGENTS OF EDUCATION. This book is designed for them. It does not tell *what* changes should be made nor does it recommend specific innovations, but it does provide a good deal of information on *how* successful innovation takes place and *how* change agents can organize their work so that successful innovation *will* take place. It is intended to be an easy reference in the planning and day-to-day management of change.

WHY USE THIS BOOK?

No one book can be a complete "guide" to a process as complex as "innovation," but this one is designed to be helpful in a number of ways:

- It provides a CONCEPTUAL ORIENTATION, a way to organize your thinking and planning about specific activities.
- It gives you ideas on WHAT THINGS TO LOOK FOR (including THINGS TO AVOID) in yourselves, in your clients, in your procedures.
- It serves as a CHECKLIST-REMINDER on important aspects of the process which you might have forgotten or missed.
- It directs you to important LITERATURE AND RESOURCE PERSONS AND

ORGANIZATIONS who have something to say about specific issues you are dealing with today or will have to deal with tomorrow.

- It provides guidelines for MEASUREMENT, EVALUATION, and DIAGNOSIS of the problems which confront you and your clients.
- And, it provides you with ideas about TACTICS and STRATEGIES that have been used successfully by others.

However, it does *not* give you all you need to know about planned change. Most of all it will not replace experience and the detailed understanding of the process which comes from years of experience with many clients in many situations.

It also *does not give special advice* to change agents in special roles facing special circumstances, such as the superintendent who wants to set up a planning office or the principal who wants his teachers to use more teamwork. These are serious change agent problems, which are in some ways general and in some ways unique. This *Guide* gives some of the general principles, leaving to the reader much of the task of adaptation and interpretation in the light of his unique circumstances. The case studies of Part One may help make the process more "real" for some readers, but ultimately each will need to formulate his own case in his own terms. The *Guide* should help by providing a framework and some guideposts.

HOW WAS IT MADE?

This manual combines the experience of researchers and practicing change agents on how innovation comes about. It is based on an analysis of over 1,000 studies of innovation and knowledge utilization in education and other fields.* In addition, it has been reviewed in draft form by 115 educators who identified themselves as change agents. Subsequent revisions have been guided by their comments. Although these reviewers represented different organizational levels, diverse subject matter areas, and diverse functions, nearly all of them (over 90%) saw the *Guide* as a highly relevant and useful source book on the process of change.

DEFINITIONS

Although we have tried to make the writing informal and non-technical, there are a few terms which probably should be defined at the outset, because they mean different things to different people.

Change: Any significant alteration in the status quo, but usually in the *Guide* this will mean an alteration which is intended to benefit the people involved.

Innovation: Any change which represents something new to the people being changed. For example, a kindergarten is an "innovation" to a school system which has not had one heretofore. In the *Guide* an "innovation" will also usually mean a change which benefits the people who are changed.

---

*For a thorough review and synthesis of this literature, see Havelock, Guskin, *et al.*, cited in Appendix C.

Change Process Innovation Process:	How the change or innovation comes about. The *Guide* is a book about "process."
Planned Change Planned Innovation:	Change or innovation which comes about through a deliberate process which is intended to make both acceptance by and benefit to the people who are changed more likely.
Change Agent:	A person who facilitates planned change or planned innovation. The *Guide* is intended to be a manual for the change agent.
Client:	A person, group, organization, or community which the change agent chooses to serve.
Client System:	Equivalent to "client" but indicating the fact that the "client" is usually a *group* of people who are interrelated and at least partly interdependent.
Resources:	Persons or things which can be used to improve an innovation or an innovative process. Resources may be available both inside and outside the client system.
Resource Person: (Also: "Resourcer")	A person who is a resource or who is a provider of resources. The change agent is one type of resource person.
Resource System:	An interrelated set of people and organizations capable of providing resources. For example, a state university which provides field services, extension courses, and pre-service and in-service teacher training is a resource system for the school districts of the state.
User:	Anyone who uses resources in attempting to solve his problems; equivalent to "client."
User System:	An interrelated group of users; equivalent to "client system."
Problem-Solving:	The process by which clients or users satisfy their needs. The process of planned innovation described in the *Guide* is one form of problem-solving.

WHAT IS THE PROCESS OF INNOVATION?

"Planned Innovation" is a complex subject which has been analyzed by scholars from a number of viewpoints. However, we have found that most practicing change agents organize their work and their thinking about innovation in terms of specific projects in which they are involved, projects which have a defined beginning and an end, and a sequential history. Therefore, we chose "STAGES" of planned innovation as the framework for this book.

There are two ways to look at stages of innovation. One way is to see it from the point of view of the people who are being changed, and the other is to see it from the point of view of someone who is trying to change someone else. First, consider the viewpoint of the one who is changed.

Every person, every group, and every social organization necessarily has some sort of problem-solving process in order to survive in a changing world. This does not mean that everyone is an expert problem-solver, and it does not mean that everyone finds innovative solutions when he has a problem; but everyone *does* develop some sort of procedure for coping with change. The most primitive, but sometimes the most effective, strategy for coping with change is to do *nothing*: "It will pass"; "These things come and go in cycles"; "If we ignore them, they will go away." These are not unfamiliar responses in the educational community. However, in Figure 1 we try to represent the stages that someone might follow in solving a problem when and if he does decide to act. Figure 1a shows the process in its simplest terms. A *stimulus,* internal or external, leads to a *response:* we are hungry—we eat; we are cramped—we shift positions; the teachers strike—the school board fires the teachers or surrenders to their demands; students assault teachers—the superintendent puts policemen in the classroom. A good deal of the "problem-solving" behavior in education is of this reflexive, trial-and-error variety. However, in Figure 1b, as a possible alternative, we suggest a somewhat more detailed and more rational problem-solving model. This model also starts with a disturbance, but it subdivides the responsive "activity" into four steps: (1) a decision to do something; (2) an active attempt to define what the problem is; (3) a search for potential solutions; and (4) an application of one or more potential solutions to see if it will satisfy the need. In this book we are not going to assume that everyone in education who has a problem will follow this rational model, but we will assume that he can learn to follow such a model, especially if he has some help from this man we are calling the "change agent."

This leads us to the second way to look at the stages of innovation: the perspective of the change agent.

FIGURE 1:   *Stages in Innovation from the Point of View of the People Who Are Changed (the Client System)*

a.   *Change by Simple Reflex:*

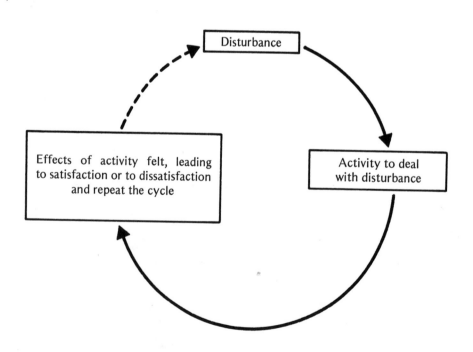

b.   Change by Rational Problem-Solving:

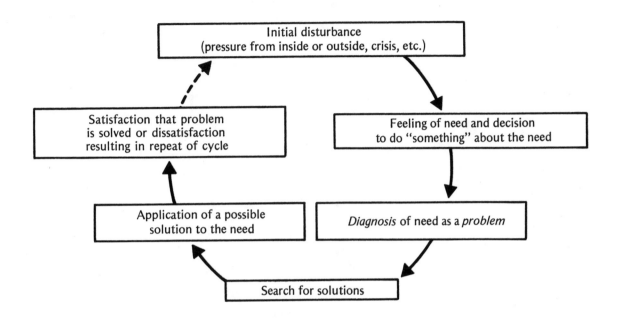

WHAT IS THE ROLE OF THE CHANGE AGENT IN THE PROCESS?

Regardless of his formal job title and his position, there are *four* primary ways in which a person can act as a change agent. He can be:

1.   A CATALYST
2.   A SOLUTION GIVER
3.   A PROCESS HELPER
4.   A RESOURCE LINKER

These four change agent roles are represented symbolically in Figure 2.

FIGURE 2: Four Ways to Be a Change Agent

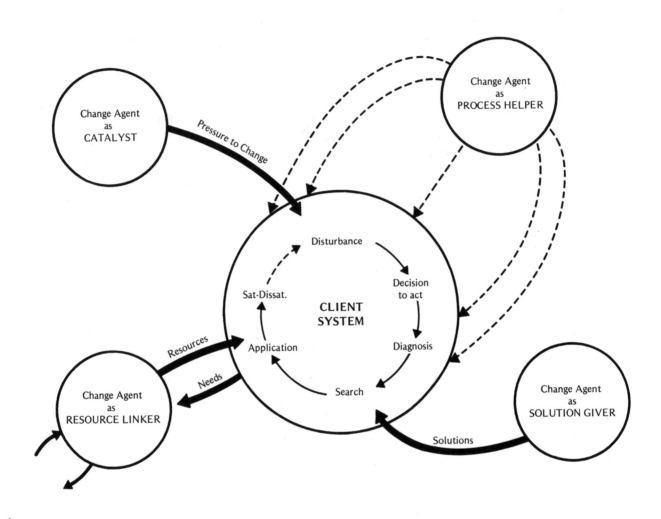

1. The Change Agent as CATALYST

Most of the time, most people do not want change; they want to keep things the way they are, even when outsiders know that change is required. For that reason some change agents are needed just to overcome this inertia, to prod and pressure the system to be less complacent and to start working on its serious problems. In education today this role is often taken by students, concerned parents, or school board members. They do not necessarily have the answers, but they are dissatisfied with things the way they are. By making their dissatisfaction known and by upsetting the "status quo," they energize the problem-solving process; they get things started.

2. *The Change Agent as SOLUTION GIVER*

Many people who want to bring about change have definite ideas about what the change should be; they have solutions and they would like to have others adopt those solutions. However, being an effective solution giver involves more than simply having a solution. You have to know when and how to offer it, and you have to know enough about it to help the client adapt it to his needs.

3. *The Change Agent as PROCESS HELPER*

A critical and often neglected role is that of helper in the processes of problem-solving and innovating. That is what this book is all about. It tells you HOW change comes about in individuals and organizations. Because most clients are not experts on the "HOW TO" of change, they can be helped greatly by people who are skilled in the various stages of problem-solving. The process helper can provide valuable assistance in:
   (a)   showing the client how to recognize and define needs
   (b)   showing the client how to diagnose problems and set objectives
   (c)   showing the client how to acquire relevant resources
   (d)   showing the client how to select or create solutions
   (e)   showing the client how to adapt and install solutions
   (f)   showing the client how to evaluate solutions to determine if they are satisfying his needs.

4. *The Change Agent as RESOURCE LINKER*

Effective problem-solving requires the bringing together of needs and resources. "Resources" can be of many kinds: financial backing, knowledge of solutions, knowledge and skills in diagnosing problems, formulating and adopting solutions, and expertise on the process of change itself. Resources may also consist of *people* with time, energy, and motivation to help. A very special and underrated change role is that of the "linker," i.e., the person who brings people together, who helps clients find and make the best use of resources inside and outside their own system.

DEFINING YOUR OWN ROLE

Persons with any of a number of job titles may find that they fit one of these four role definitions. In *italics* below, we suggest some of the typical educator assignments where some concept of "change agent" is highly relevant.

**Some Examples of People Who Might Act as
Change Agents in Education**

Curriculum Coordinators
Directors or Coordinators of Federal Programs
State Department Curriculum Consultants

Regional Laboratory Dissemination Staff
County and Intermediate School District Consultants
Supplementary Center Staff (e.g., those supported by Title
*   III of ESEA: see our case example of "Henry")*
Continuing Education and Extension Instructors
Professors in Schools of Education Who Do Field Consult-
*   ing*
Salesmen of Educational Products and Publications
Superintendents and Other Administrators (at least part of
*   the time: see our case example of "Steve")*
Teachers (at least part of the time: see our case example of
*   "Mike")*
Counselors (at least part of the time)
Board of Education Members (at least part of the time)
Students (at least some of them some of the time: see our
*   case example of "Linda")*
Concerned parents and other citizens

In defining *your own role*, keep in mind these points:

The four primary change agent roles are not mutually exclusive. Some change agents can be catalysts, solution givers, process helpers, and linkers all at the same time. Furthermore, knowing how to be effective in one role will help you to be effective in the others.

You can be an effective change agent either as an insider or an outsider. Sometimes outsiders see things more objectively and they are usually more free to work in a variety of ways with different members of the client system. But insiders are effective, too, in different ways. As an insider you are more familiar with the system and you feel its problems more deeply; you are also a familiar face and a "known quantity." Sometimes change agents have to be insiders.

You can be "line" or "staff." Sometimes it helps to be in a formal position of authority as leader or supervisor to bring about change in a group. Most research studies show that the administrator is the most important gatekeeper to change. He sets the tone, opens the doors, and provides the support (psychological and material) even when he is not the change agent in a formal sense. The more he knows about the process of change, the better. On the other hand, a "staff" man can be equally effective and sometimes can provide the kind of help-without-threat that is difficult to get from a superior.

Lastly, *you can be an effective change agent working from above or below.* It is much harder to work from below and to bring about change when you do not have formal power, but it can be done (see for example our case of "Linda" in Part One). The first step is, once again, understanding the process, the points of leverage, the most efficient channels, the best times, places, and circumstances.

Understanding that all four change agent roles are important and partly interrelated, we will focus our concern in the *Guide* on the process helper. Figure 3 illustrates a six-stage model which we will use throughout this book in describing his activities.

FIGURE 3:   Change Agent as Process Helper: How the Guide Is Organized

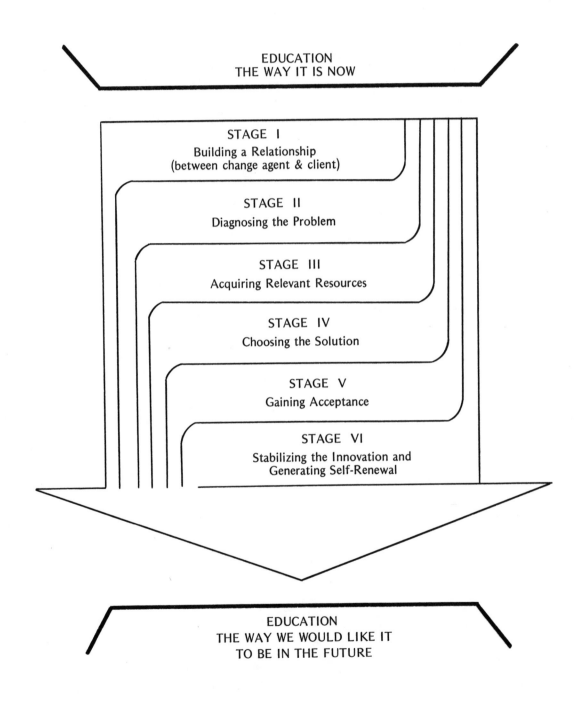

EDUCATION
THE WAY IT IS NOW

STAGE I
Building a Relationship
(between change agent & client)

STAGE II
Diagnosing the Problem

STAGE III
Acquiring Relevant Resources

STAGE IV
Choosing the Solution

STAGE V
Gaining Acceptance

STAGE VI
Stabilizing the Innovation and
Generating Self-Renewal

EDUCATION
THE WAY WE WOULD LIKE IT
TO BE IN THE FUTURE

The first task of the change agent is to establish contact and build a relationship with the people he wants to help. (We will frequently refer to these people individually and collectively as "the user," "the client," "the user system," and the "client system.") Once he has established this relationship he can begin working with them collaboratively in a step-by-step problem-solving process. However, the end of this process for the change agent is not the solution itself, but the development in the client system of an ability to solve its own problems effectively on a continuing basis. We call this "self-renewal." Each chapter* corresponds broadly to a significant stage in the overall planning and installation of innovation.

We also believe that the focus of innovation planning has to be the USER himself: *his* needs and *his* problems must be the primary concern of educational reform. Therefore, our orientation is PROBLEM-SOLVING BY AND FOR THE USER THROUGH EFFECTIVE USE OF RESOURCES.

Not every one of these stages is necessarily a part of every innovative process, however, nor will they always occur in this particular order. The different "stages" often occur simultaneously and the final objective may be achieved by a process which does not follow a clear-cut developmental sequence. The vertical corridors in the figure are intended to suggest the interrelationship among stages and the fact that each function deserves some consideration at every temporal phase of a project.

*Henceforth, the word "stage" will be used to designate each of the six main sections of the text interchangeably with the word "chapter."

HOW THE CHANGE AGENT WORKS: A CHAPTER OUTLINE

AN IDEAL EXAMPLE:

Stage I: RELATIONSHIP

The first thing the successful change agent needs to develop is a viable relationship with the client system or a solid base within it. A secure and reasonably well-delineated helping role is an essential place from which to start. Some readers may be able to take this for granted because they already have a good client relationship, but others will find important points to consider from a reading of our first chapter.

Sam Davis is the newly appointed director of in-service training and special projects for the Highland Hills school district. Early in his tenure he learns that the McKinley school is notorious for teacher turnover, and, for this reason, he decides to work in that school as his first project. He attends several of the coffee hour/evaluation sessions in the school, where he chats with small groups of teachers and begins to become aware of their needs and interests; wherever he can he tries to develop their confidence in his ability to help them.

Stage II: DIAGNOSIS

Once established in the client system, the change agent must turn to the problem at hand. He must find out if the client is aware of his own needs and if the client has been able to articulate his needs as problem statements. The second chapter discusses this topic from several angles.

From interviewing and observing the classroom techniques of McKinley teachers, Sam suspects that the team teaching method in use throughout his school system has been ineffective in this particular building. He finds evidence of a lack of cooperation within the teaching teams. Because many of these teachers were previously in self-contained classrooms, they have had a difficult time adjusting to this new method and, consequently, many feelings of anxiety and mistrust have arisen.

Stage III: ACQUIRING RELEVANT RESOURCES

With a well-defined problem, the client system needs to be able to identify and obtain resources relevant to solutions. The third chapter should give some good leads on how this information seeking can be carried out successfully.

In order to help his teachers, Sam finds it necessary to learn more about the adjustment from the self-contained classroom to the teaching teams. He turns first to a colleague who has had longer experience with team teaching. This friend tells Sam about some articles that might be helpful and suggests an agency that he may contact for assistance in training teachers for group interaction.

Stage IV: CHOOSING THE SOLUTION

With a defined problem and a lot of relevant information, the client needs to be able to derive implications, generate a range of alternatives, and settle upon a potential solution. Even a good solution needs adaptation and needs to be reshaped to fit the special characteristics of the client. The fourth chapter discusses both the choosing and the adaptation process.

From his retrieval of information, Sam learns that the unsuccessful attempts in team teaching are often a result of misconceptions about the need for cooperation. He organizes a committee of teachers to discuss the research findings and the diagnosis. Together they decide that the teachers require an educational program in the methods, goals, and values involved in team teaching. After considering the different ways in which this "innovation," the proposed educational program, can be introduced to other teachers, Sam and his committee decide that a "workshop" plan would be most efficient. This plan can be designed to interfere very little with regular classroom teaching time and, in the long run, its advantages would offset the cost of its operation.

Stage V: GAINING ACCEPTANCE

After a solution has been developed and adopted, it needs to be moved toward acceptance and adoption by the widest possible number in the client system. By describing, discussing, and demonstrating, the change team helps the client to gain awareness, develop interest, evaluate, try out, and finally adopt the innovation. In doing so they rely on many channels and make maximum use of natural leadership and informal communication. In the fifth chapter, we consider how initial acceptance of innovations can be generated and how the client may be able to develop attitudes and behavior supportive of the innovation.

Sam and his committee now have a well-conceived solution but they still need to persuade the other teachers and administrators of the school to go along. They approach the principal and lay before him what they have in mind, tracing the process by which they arrived at their conclusion. The principal then calls a meeting of the staff to discuss the plan. Various teachers raise objections based on "time pressures" and express doubts that a program developed elsewhere is "relevant." Sam listens and later arranges for substitute teachers to reduce the load of the regular staff while they are participating in the workshop. He also makes sure that they get personal recognition and credit for their innovativeness.

Stage VI: STABILIZATION AND SELF-RENEWAL

Finally, the client needs to develop an internal capability to maintain the innova-

Using this experience as a model, Sam shows the teachers how they can be their

tion and to continue appropriate use without outside help. The change agent encourages members of the client system to be their own change agents and to begin to work on other problems in a similar way. As this self-renewal capacity begins to build, it allows the gradual termination of the relationship so that the change agent can move on to other projects, other problems, and other clients.

own change agents by building an internal capacity for diagnosis, retrieval, and problem-solving. When the teachers commit themselves to try this approach with another issue which has come up, Sam leaves them alone to work on it, but comes to the school as a consultant when they ask him. Gradually he moves on to other projects in other parts of the system, knowing that a self-renewal capacity has begun to emerge in McKinley school.

Individuals rarely become catalysts by deliberate strategy but rather because they have come to feel deeply on a particular issue. Either they personally feel injured, exploited, oppressed, or ignored, or they are deeply committed and identified with some subgroup which they feel is in such a state. Hence, they become advocates of the poor, the blacks, the "kids," the gifted student, the slow learner, etc. Specific solutions are often advocated, e.g., black studies, community control, special classes, the abolition of special classes, and so forth. However, the essential point that the catalyst change agent stresses is the *need* for change and for special recognition of the interests of the disadvantaged group.

Nevertheless, catalysts can plan their activities to maximize their effectiveness. Basically, this means being sensitive to the points and issues about "process" raised in these pages. However much they care or feel about the oppressed and the oppressors, they should think reasonably about the steps that need to be followed to win support for their cause and to reduce resistance to the changes they wish to see come about.

Probably the hardest task for the catalyst is to see these situations from the point of view of the existing system leadership (sometimes referred to as "the establishment"). To understand a point of view is not to accept it, but such understanding helps the catalyst to know when and how he can be an effective influencer. He needs to know this because sooner or later he will be required to confront the leadership and either overcome their resistance or win their support.

Another special skill which the catalyst must cultivate is developing indigenous leadership for change among the people he is serving. Disadvantaged minorities are disadvantaged partly because they are disorganized, isolated, and powerless. Often they do not even recognize a common cause. The catalyst change agent therefore needs to be an organizer and a promoter of togetherness, one who can infuse a feeling of common identity and purpose.

A catalyst must also be sensitive to the fact that he alone does not have the full range of skills to bring change about. One of his problems as a change agent is that he may be seen by many in the client system as a trouble maker and deliberate disrupter. He may be able to undo this image but in any case he should be forming alliances with others who can take on different types of change roles such as process helper and linker. Teamwork, collaboration, and utilization of both inside and outside resources remain important aspects of change planning even for the catalyst.

Finally, a catalyst must cultivate a sense of timing. He must be willing to wait for and must be able to judge the most opportune moments for change. Several factors are involved in good timing. One is judging the likelihood of widespread support or sympathy either within the educational system or within the community; if an issue is not "hot" or if it tends to run counter to other current trends, it may fall on deaf ears, however worthy the cause may be. Another factor is general stability; if the "establishment" is secure, there are few symptoms of unrest, and no voices of protest but your own, you are not likely to have much of an impact (see the case study of Linda below). Systems in a state of stable equilibrium are unlikely to be shifted by the acts of single individuals. On the other hand, systems undergoing crisis and struggling to "hold on" in the face of a number of disturbing or disrupting elements are more likely to be unfrozen and more susceptible to organized change efforts.

HOW TO BE A GOOD SOLUTION GIVER

By far the most common form of change agent is the "solution giver." Most of us at one time or another feel that we have the best answer to someone else's problem *and a lot of the time we are probably right!* We also often think that we know how to get our solution communicated to the client and on that we are almost always wrong. Clients can be notoriously obstinate, especially when they think someone is trying to sell them something.

Some of the things would-be solution givers need to know they can probably get from advertising executives and other experts in the art of selling, but there are some other things that this *Guide* would like to get across to the solution giver. Among them are the following.

(a) Don't ignore the real needs of the client, and make a sincere effort to find out what his needs are *before* you decide he needs what you've got (see Stage II).

(b) Do what you can to *adapt* innovations so that they are maximally relevant and beneficial for particular clients (see Stage IV).

(c) Have more than one solution to offer and think flexibly and diversely about the number of ways you might be helpful as a "resourcer" (again see Stage IV).

(d) Try to provide help for a client beyond the point of "adoption" so that he can use and continue to use the innovation to best advantage (see Stage VI).

(e) Help a client to be a good judge of innovations, yours included, so that he can evaluate and decide for himself when one should be adopted and another discarded. In the short run this may work to your disadvantage as a salesman but in the long run it will build trust between you and the client so that he will listen when you have a good solution (see Stages I and VI).

(f) Try to build an open and authentic relationship with your would-be client. Without encounter, dialogue, and knowledge-sharing neither you nor your client can know your actual helping potential for each other.

(g) Finally, try to make yourself more than a solution giver by becoming a resource linker.

HOW TO BE A RESOURCE LINKER

A large part of successful change is *ex*change. Each of us has needs and problems and each of us also has knowledge resources which can be useful to both ourselves and others in solving problems. Hence problem-solving is in large part a matter of matching resources in one person or group with needs in another.

Yet most of us have difficulty in asking for help and in giving help. This is why persons with special skills in communicating and relationship building are important change agents.

FIGURE 4:

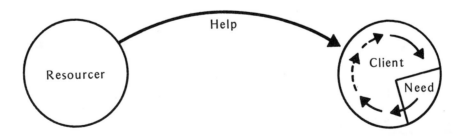

How does resource linking work? Consider the simplest case of a person, the client, who needs some sort of help, and another person we will call the "resourcer," who has knowledge, skill, products, or materials which could be useful to the "client." As we noted earlier, every client will have his own customary processes of problem-solving. Without help from any outsider he will find some sort of solution, however inadequate (dotted arrows in Figure 4). On the other hand there may be someone somewhere who has a better solution (or can make a better *diagnosis* or can *adapt* and *apply* solutions more effectively). If this person exists and if he can intervene in the right way at the right time, the client will be "helped."

We sometimes forget, however, that the resourcer has his own way of formulating the problem and defining appropriate solutions. Can he, in his effort to be "helpful," successfully match the client's need and provide the right kind of resource at the right time in the right way? Unless he is either a mind-reading expert or an extremely lucky gambler, the resourcer will not be able to provide meaningful "help" without first listening to what the client has to say about his problem and what he has done so far in trying to solve it (Figure 5).

FIGURE 5:

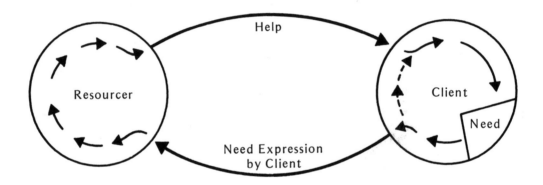

In other words, some sort of *two-way communication* between resourcers and clients has to take place before "helping" can really be relevant and effective.

At the beginning two-way communications are clumsy and difficult, but over time, with the experience of repeated contacts, trial expressions of need, and trial efforts at helping, a truly effective helping relationship is built up.

FIGURE 6:

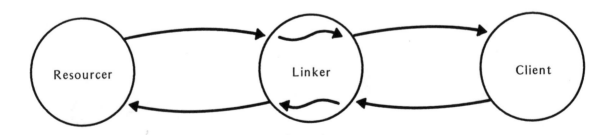

Because these human resource linkages are difficult to build, there is a special need for the "linker," someone who knows about resources, knows about people's needs, and knows how to bring clients and resourcers together. Like the process helper, the primary mission of the linker is to put himself out of a job by helping clients to become effective resource linkers for themselves. Resource linkers should also be able to show clients the resources they have *within* themselves and among their own group. Linking therefore is important not only for client-to-resourcer but also for client-to-client. Ultimately the client is best served by a *network* of two-way contacts with other clients and with a variety of resource persons, groups, and institutions, as depicted in Figure 7. Effective problem-solving and self-renewal over time requires multiple exchanges with inside and outside resourcers, each representing special knowledge, skill, or service relevant to different needs at different times. The linker therefore is not simply a one-time joiner but a network builder. His efforts at one point in time on one problem may seem trivial but each link established adds to a growing client capacity for reaching out and pulling in relevant others to work collaboratively on his problems.

FIGURE 7:

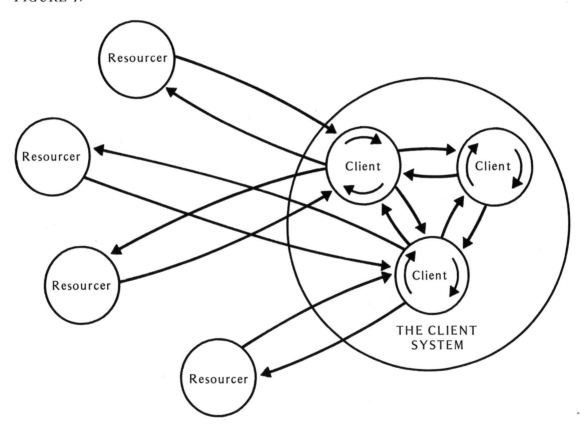

The skills of the resource linker have never been adequately specified in the literature of planned change, but certain parts of this book are especially relevant. In particular Stage I on "Building a Relationship," Stage III on "Acquiring Relevant Resources," and Stage VI on "Self-Renewal" should have much to say to anyone choosing to build a role on this model.*

*In early drafts the *Guide* was entitled *The Knowledge Linker's Handbook*.

ORGANIZATION OF THE TEXT

Part One: *Case Studies of Change Agents in Action.* Examples of actual innovation projects in school settings. These cases help illustrate the "do's" and "do not's" of the process.

Part Two: *The Stages of Planned Change.* The major text of the manual, with quotes from prominent authors and references to the case examples of Part One.

Part Three: *Supplementary Resource Information.*
          Appendix A: Common change strategies and tactics.
          Appendix B: Major information sources in education.
          Appendix C: A guide to the literature on planning of change in education.

PART ONE:
CASE STUDIES OF CHANGE AGENTS IN ACTION

This first section of the handbook is devoted to the stories of four change agents and the innovations they introduced. These change agents represent a wide range of educational roles: *student, teacher, administrator,* and *outside consultant.* Each has a unique perspective on innovation and on the client system with whom he is working. Nevertheless, the experiences of these four people and their clients will probably sound familiar to most readers.

Because these case studies are drawn from life, they illustrate the process of change at its best and at its worst. Change agents are *not* always successful, and sometimes they are successful in ways that they did not intend. None of these change agents had the benefit of a handbook on the change process, and their analysis of what they did and why they did it is retrospective. Most of them did not follow a deliberate step-by-step strategy which included all the stages we will describe in the *Guide*. Nevertheless, it is possible to see most of these steps illustrated in one or another of their stories. These cases are included in the hope that they will be helpful in relating the concepts of the *Guide* to real-life situations.

STEVE

CASE EXAMPLE: SYSTEMWIDE CHANGE INSTIGATED BY
A CENTRAL OFFICE ADMINISTRATOR

The following example relates the experience of Steve, a forty-two-year-old central office administrator, as he and other members of his school system tried to institute an in-service training program in human relations. It highlights many of the issues and pressures which impinge on the local school administrator who takes on the role of change agent in his own system, but it also contains elements common to all change attempts regardless of who their initiator is. It was rated as a "typical" or "very typical" case by 82 per cent of our reviewer-change agents.

"Several years ago my school district had an opportunity to develop and try out a program that we hoped would help us build the quality of 'innovativeness' into our system. In this program, which was funded as a project under Title III of E.S.E.A.,* we tried to set up training workshops in human relations skills for school personnel and other relevant people from the community. These workshops were operated with the collaborative effort of trained staff from our system and personnel from our state's affiliate of the National Training Laboratories.**

"Let me begin by telling you what our formal goals were for the project. Then I'll fill you in on the background leading to this project and some of the things that happened when we got into it.

"Our primary goal was to develop a strategy that would provide continued support for educational innovations. Hopefully, this strategy would enhance pupil motivation to learn; it would improve relations within each group in the school system (teachers, students, staff, etc.); and it would provide a generally congenial atmosphere for both working and learning. We also wanted to build linkages between various groups, individuals, and resources both inside and outside the school system. We were concerned with the skills of problem-solving and with the technique of collaboration with *all* members of a system, from administrators to students and custodians. We also wanted to institute a method by which system members could get evaluative feedback and self-criticism for self-improvement. In short, what we really wanted was to have our staff become involved in HOW they were performing their assigned duties.

Stage II: Diagnosis
"When I came to this school system four years ago as Director of Adult Education, I saw what appeared to be a lot of inbreeding in the faculty. The roots of tradition seemed to be very deep, and there was little effort being made to bring about the changes that would make for a better learning situation for the kids.

Stages I and IV: Building Relationships
and Choosing a Solution
"When Title III became available, our system decided that we would like to take advantage of

---

*This section of the Elementary and Secondary Education Act of 1965 provided for the establishment of "innovative" programs and projects at the local district level.

**The NTL Institute for Applied Behavioral Science, associated with the National Education Association, provides training in human relations skills for individuals and groups in all professions and fields.

its funds to develop an in-service training program for our staff. I was convinced that the way to go was through sensitivity training because I had seen how helpful it could be. After participating in only one sensitivity training lab, I felt I profited greatly, and it seemed to me that this would also be a very relevant kind of training for this school system.

"We set up a committee to draft a proposal for an in-service training project. This Title III committee actually contained public school, parochial school, and community representatives. Because of conflicting work schedules, we found it necessary to meet in the evenings and on Saturdays rather than during the day. Although we tried very diligently to get more teachers involved in the committee, these time slots were evidently inconvenient. I guess the teachers were reluctant to use their own free time for the meetings.

"We also had some difficulty in trying to get involvement from the people we would need to advance the training program. The superintendent was kept apprised of our plans as they developed, and he made some suggestions along the way. He was the kind of man who would hire leaders and let them lead, but I feel there might have been more he could have done to gain support for the program, particularly since there were differences of opinion about it within the school district. Moreover, he had a heart attack at about the time that our planning phase was completed, and so the support we probably could have counted on during the actual implementation was lost.

"It is a common practice in our school system to have administrators chair the various committees that are organized and, I guess, because of my experience and interest I had been designated chairman of this Title III committee. Although the other committee members contributed to the development of the proposal during our meetings, the bulk of the actual writing was done by me, a school psychologist, and a third fellow—who eventually became the coordinator of the training program.

"We came up with a three-year program of nine lab-learning sessions for groups made up of administrators, teachers, secondary school students, parents, school custodians and secretaries. These participants were organized into teams by school building and department. At the first—and what turned out to be the only—set of labs, we planned to devote our time to developing the interpersonal and communication skills of our participants by using problem-solving techniques. Then when they returned to their own school building and department, they were to try these same techniques on the real problems existing there.

Stage III: Acquiring Relevant Resources

"Part of our plan was to train our own people, and we proposed to achieve this with three levels of participation: The largest group would be trained in the use of the problem-solving process. A second group would receive further training so that they could serve as consultants in the problem-solving process. Finally, we wanted a couple of our own people to be able to be trainers for the sensitivity groups we would use in the project. In order to become sensitivity group trainers, the three of us who had written the proposal went to the National Training Laboratory at Bethel, Maine, during the following summer. At Bethel, we all took part in six-week sensitivity training laboratories designed for school administrators. There was a tremendous display of materials related to the project that we were concerned with, so we purchased quite a number of books on the change process to establish a small library on the subject for our system back home.

Stage V: Gaining Acceptance (Gaining Rejection)

"While we were away that summer a minor crisis in our schools came to a head. Although this didn't have anything to do with our in-service training project, it did create a generally bad atmosphere for us. The previous spring three attempts at a tax millage increase for schools had been defeated at the polls. It was thought that the schools would be unable to operate the following year without it. While we were at Bethel it was discovered that the alleged shortage was due to a mistake in the audit; there was, in fact, no shortage. Unfortunately, as it turned out, the amounts of the mistake and of the millage requests were precisely the same as we had acquired in Title III funds to operate our project. There had been plenty of adverse publicity in the local newspaper about the federal government throwing away money on 'frills' while the school system went into the red. Top this off with the taxpayers' loss of faith in the budgeting ability of our school administration and you can get an idea of the antagonism that had built up by the end of that summer.

"This was the situation that the three of us walked into when we returned from Bethel for the new school year. With the enthusiasm of the summer's experience we immediately began organizing the first set of training labs, confident that the community antagonism could be overcome.

"We were able to handle a group of 90 for a week's session at a local community camp. In those training labs we had some marvelous assistance from our State Training Lab, NTL, and several other expert resource people in the state. We were planning to utilize some data on our school system that a university research team had collected in a questionnaire survey about that time. We hoped that this data would help us identify *real* problems in our system for our 'building' and 'departmental' teams to work on. However, because the data processing took so long, this information was not available for our in-service training project.

"Well, needless to say, we had several problems with the lab. As luck would have it, we managed to select for our sensitivity training some people who were in need of psychiatric help. I realize now that our selection process was probably not the best: we had delegated the task of selecting participants to the building principals. I don't think that the principals realized the impact that they had on some staff members by merely suggesting, 'I'd like to have you take part in this program.' We had a few teachers who took part because they felt that they *had* to participate, and we had problems with three of these people who had really bad hang-ups. They did need psychiatric help when they returned from the training labs. Because of their experience we were criticized by a local psychiatrist who wrote a newspaper report on our program. His primary concern was about the use of non-verbal exercises in the sensitivity training portion of the program, and although he said 90 per cent of this program was tremendous and excellent, he suggested that we needed to do something about this 10 per cent. We could agree with his criticism, but the publicity he got—and the public furor that was aroused—distorted the whole issue. The local newspaper had never viewed our efforts too kindly in their editorials, and after this article, things only got worse. Not only were the press accounts distorted, but rumors really began to fly throughout the town. Also, I think that it was at about this point that the extreme right-wing group in our community became mobilized. After waging some remarkably effective campaigns against open housing and sex education in the schools, they then turned their attention to the evils of sensitivity training labs.

"I really believe that most of the criticism that our program received was a result of the organized efforts of this right-wing group. They distributed a lot of propaganda and they had considerable influence with community power sources and with the media. The frustrating thing is that most of their membership is from the rural areas surrounding our town; they are not local taxpayers and their kids do not even attend our schools. All the mail that I got—all the distorted versions of what sensitivity training is—was postmarked from some small village out in the country. The phone calls that the school board members received were, for the most part, from outside of the community as well. We were attacked rather vigorously. Both the coordinator of the program and I were called 'Communists.'

"I have a feeling, too, that there are people in high places within the city who belong to this conservative organization, who support it financially and in other ways, but who do not want it to be known that they are actually members. There are plenty of others who are willing to sign letters . . . It always seems difficult to get people who are in favor of a program to write letters, but extremely easy to get those who are opposed to write.

"A citizen's committee was set up to review the program. Inadvertently, the board of education appointed as chairman of this committee a man who did not even live in the school district. In addition, it turned out that the fellow was a member of the organization which was leading the campaign against our program. Of course, when these facts were discovered the chairman was immediately replaced, but by that time his anti-sensitivity training propaganda had done its damage and eventually the program was phased out.

"I can see now some mistakes we made and some things I'd want to do differently if we had another chance, but there were also some unavoidable problems like the millage issue and the organized resistance in the community. Maybe the goals of the project were too grand. Maybe it wasn't humanly possible, considering the staff time and energy we had available, to handle all the exigencies of this kind of change. We thought about terminating the program, but once you're involved in a change effort how can you pull out? . . . And, anyway, despite the fact that the program was not carried through to completion, I feel it had considerable positive impact on most of those individuals who participated in our training labs.

"When you're being innovative, you're never quite sure of your end result, simply because what you are doing has never been done before. It's like setting out on a trip and not being sure where you're going to go, but hoping that you'll end up in the right place."

Editorial on the Case of Steve

Was Steve a hapless victim of circumstances beyond his control? We do not think so, not completely. Steve believed that members of the system needed problem-solving skills but he did not appear to follow a problem-solving process in his own approach. Because he had one solution in mind (sensitivity training) and was convinced very early that it was the way to go, he was more of a **solution giver** *than a process helper. He spent very little time working in a genuinely collaborative way with key members of the system to define what their problems were (* **diagnosis** *) and how they might* **choose** *appropriate solutions. Having chosen the solution, the Title III group proceeded to implementation without gaining widespread support for what they were going to do and apparently without anticipating the type and degree of resistance that could be aroused. Because they had not laid the groundwork for* **acceptance** *, the roof fell in when other events triggered legitimate community concern with the project. Key members of the community were apparently not behind the project and not adequately informed about it early in the game. Hence it became a vulnerable target to right-wing pressure.*

Steve's goal was installation of a **self-renewal** *process in his system. We think the goal is laudable, but it is a long-term goal and for a conservative community a very tough one. Perhaps if Steve had moved a little more slowly with more planning and more widespread community collaboration in diagnosing, choosing, and implementing, he might have weathered the storm and given his community the beginnings of a truly self-renewing school system. When Steve talked to us, he was emphatic about one thing: if he had had something like the* **Guide** *to work from, he would have done a lot of things differently.*

MIKE

CASE EXAMPLE: TEACHER-GENERATED CHANGE IN A SCHOOL SYSTEM

Mike's case is an illustration of change that originated from within the teaching staff of a school system and, thus, it serves to illuminate the unique characteristics of such "grass roots" innovations. Coincidentally, it happens to be the story of the introduction of sex education into the schools' curriculum. As such, Mike's story also has many of the ingredients typical of the nationwide controversy over this particular innovation. It is worth noting that Mike is not only a teacher but an articulate spokesman for educational reform in his community, being president of the local NEA chapter at the age of 30. His story was rated as "typical" or "very typical" by 77 per cent of our reviewer-change agents.

Stages I and II: Building a Relationship and Diagnosis

"Six years ago I became a junior high school physical science teacher in a city of about 100,000. I found the students there very rewarding to work with, but I also found that many of them were coming to me with what were, to them, tremendous problems. I was able to identify these problems for them at times, and yet I could see a need for something with a little more depth and a little more structure. At the regular weekly meetings of the science teachers in the school with the science consultant for our district, I began to bring up the need for some kind of course, or some innovation within established courses, that would allow these young people to talk about their personal lives.

"The science consultant was sympathetic, and together we reviewed the courses currently available to see if any provided an opportunity for students to express and try to solve their problems. We found that a summer school enrichment program which had recently been introduced into the high school included a course in psychology where there was opportunity for some discussion of personal issues. In the regular school curriculum, however, the only courses which could be considered to be in this area were the eighth and ninth grade health classes where human sexuality was considered, but which segregated the boys from the girls.

"Many of the teachers felt that these few courses fell far short of offering the students an opportunity to discuss in the classroom the kind of problems which were concerning them. We were convinced that a need for a new course existed, and we started to explore the issue with the other members of the school system. The science consultant obtained permission from the superintendent of the school district to get started on a project which would lead eventually to the introduction of some kind of 'human sexuality' course into all the junior high schools of the district.

Stages III & IV: Acquiring Relevant Resources and Choosing a Solution

"The science consultant organized a team of teachers and administrators from all the schools in the district to work on this stage of the project. After preliminary discussions among the team members, people from SIECUS (Sex Information and Education Council of the United States) were called in to discuss with us how we should go about setting up such a class. In addition, we contacted people from other communities which had adopted similar courses and they helped us outline a realistic program that involved teachers and enlisted community support. They also told us where we could go for information in planning the content of the proposed course.

"After about six months of such discussions and information gathering, all the team members had a good general idea of what would be involved in setting up our course. What we felt we needed at this point, however, was someone working directly with us who had had personal experience in running a course of this type. We discussed the possibility of hiring an experienced teacher of sex education to work with us on the team and to set up a pilot course in our schools. In the end we decided against this, partly because we felt that we wanted to work out the course content ourselves. But in addition to this, we felt that the hiring of someone specifically for this purpose might cause a stir in the community and a lot of questions would be raised before we were ready to answer them.

Stages IV and V: Further Work on Choosing and
Adapting the Solution and Gaining Acceptance

"We decided, therefore, that we would gain the necessary first-hand experience by having one of our team members run a pilot project in one of the existing courses. By so doing we not only expected to gain some experience, but we also anticipated being able to sample the opinions of the students and their parents. We felt that if such a project were a success, this would be a valuable start in enlisting community support since we could present the citizens with the example of a course run by one of their own teachers in their own school system.

"I volunteered to conduct the pilot project since I felt there would be no problem working it into the science courses which I was teaching at that time. My objective was to aid the students in developing their ability to use logical reasoning to make responsible value judgments about social issues which affect them personally. Thus, I planned to investigate not just sexuality, but also other topics related to both the social area and science; e.g., the use of drugs and alcohol. I planned my pilot project with members of the social science department of the state university, and with their help I dug up information from the city library, our state department of education, the U.S. Office of Education, and SIECUS.

"I must say that teaching the pilot course was the most rewarding experience I've ever had in my life. We started with *The Naked Ape,* and we went on from there. Everything just fell into place; it was lovely. The students were hungry for all the background materials I had prepared, and we all became tremendously involved. With my goal in mind of helping the students become able to make responsible value judgments, I included two special sessions in the course. In the first one, I had a teacher come to the class one morning and tell the kids the problems of homosexuality. He had spent 14 years in our state prison as an inmate, and he could talk about the problem of homosexuality from his own experiences. In the second special session, I had my pregnant wife and our one-year-old baby come in. We sat the class in a circle and put the baby in the center and talked about the natural sex life in the family. I still meet the kids from these classes on the street today and there is a relationship between us that I have never seen elsewhere between a student and teacher.

"In order to get some comparative data on the effectiveness of this pilot project, I matched my three science classes, which would receive the new course material, against three 'control' classes which were being taught by other teachers. I administered an attitude test before and after the 9-week unit to all six classes—my three sections and the three control classes. There were significant differences between the experimental and control groups, but on some of the concepts the results were a little different than we had anticipated. The results showed that, as a result of the course, students had become more permissive in their thinking on the issues of sex and drugs and that their value judgments had a more humanistic foundation.

"When I reported the experience and findings from the pilot course to the project team, the project really got under way. The pilot project confirmed our observation that the students would welcome such programs. Although I did not make a formal survey of parents' reactions, I tried to feel them out when I talked to them at PTA meetings and in individual conferences. I was elated to find that all their comments were favorable.

"We felt that the course we were planning should not be introduced solely at the junior high school level, but rather that it would be important to have courses at all levels, K through 12. Approval for this expanded plan was obtained from the superintendent, and our project team was increased to include teachers from the elementary and high schools in the district, in addition to the junior high teachers who were already on the team.

"My pilot project also demonstrated one other important point, that those who would actually be involved in teaching these classes would have to be well prepared. I had found the students able to handle a large amount and variety of materials, and as a result of this experience, our project team decided to send at least one teacher from every school building to a workshop at the university in order to develop pilot courses.

"Looking back, I can now see that one real problem which we had within the school system was the method of selecting the teachers who headed the program for each school: the principals appointed teachers who seemed to be working in this general area. That is, they tended to appoint home economics, biology, or health teachers, irrespective of the teachers' ability to establish good relationships with the kids. Despite this problem, I still give these teachers credit for being highly involved in the project. Everything continued to go smoothly within the school system.

"Our efforts to build community support also seemed to be going well. We prepared slide shows to illustrate the materials that would be used in the course; we gave talks to PTA groups; and we held a series of community meetings to discuss the program. All of this continued over a period of a year. The feedback we were getting by the end of that period indicated that the vast majority of our citizenry was interested in the program and was very complimentary about any work that had already gone into it.

"However, we should have been forewarned by the experiences with community antagonism which had been related to us by school personnel in districts which had established similar programs. If we had, we would have been prepared for what happened during the last part of the year in which we discussed the program with the community. At one meeting questions were raised about how we were going to teach Judeo-Christian ethics. Our spokesman stated that 'We can't teach morals,' and BOOM! the lid flew off. I think that had we clarified our goal of teaching the young people how to make 'responsible value judgments,' this would have helped. This was still our goal, and we felt it was a reasonable one to strive for in a program which would cover the grades K through 12. However, because of the rather puzzling findings which I had obtained in my pilot project (that attitudes toward marijuana, etc., became more favorable), we had been intentionally sliding over this issue in our discussions with the public.

"Nevertheless, it was the statement that 'we would not teach morals' that was picked up. Various extremist groups got hold of it. A paper was published by some of these people which was rather inflammatory in its attack on the program we were proposing. About six people started coming to our community meetings and expressing very hostile attitudes. They seemed terribly adept at twisting everything we said to make the whole program sound immoral; they asked questions and made insinuations which planted doubts in the minds of other citizens. From these six people the opposition to the program began to spread. Most of the opposition came from rural areas around our city and about 90 per cent of the opposition was not even in our school district, but they did have control over some media, and they could get their word out and spread it. They put enough doubts in the minds of others so that it became clear to us that we could not go ahead on schedule and introduce the pilot courses in the schools.

"Having the program suspended right at the moment that it was to be introduced was quite a letdown to those involved in planning it, but fortunately the program was not blocked entirely. We reassessed the situation and settled on two methods of handling the opposition. First, we were very fortunate in having developed over a period of time the support of a diverse group of people from churches, government, schools, and various civic organizations in the community. These people have now formed a committee to get public support. It will be a tremendous relief to us because we got to the point where we were using up all our time and energy trying to sell the program to the public. More important though, I think these people will have a greater influence with the citizens than we have had. This gives us a chance to proceed with the other aspect of our plan for overcoming public opposition. We have decided to work out the curriculum for all the course units for every classroom period in all the grades, K through 12. Then we will go back to the community with the full program on paper, and then they can take a shot at it. If they do not like something, we can change it; but we must have their support.

"If we could start all over again on this project, one thing I would change would be the time to bring the project to the community. We waited over a year before introducing the program, and this did not give us time to explain the plan and to overcome the resistance. We should have started community meetings sooner. On the other hand, I think there might also have been a problem if we had approached the community very early in the process. We were in a strong position and knew what we were talking about when we began to talk. I had run my pilot course and the parents of the kids involved could already see that their youngsters had benefitted. We felt we had succeeded in convincing many people in the community that our program would be a good one; and when the last opposition is overcome and the community approves our class materials, I know we're going to have a strong and exciting program."

Postscript on Mike's Case

One year later we contacted Mike again. As he had indicated, the newly organized citizen group paved the way for community acceptance. They organized widespread support for the program in newspaper ads and public meetings, and made an effective presentation to the school board which resulted in authorization of a phased program. In the 1969-70 school year, the K-6 curriculum was pilot tested with selected teachers. In the spring of 1970 the program was then approved for all schools and pilot testing for 7-12 was also authorized. By design, each phase is conditional on evaluation and approval by the community. Complete acceptance and incorporation of a K-12 program seems assured by the 1971-72 school year. Meanwhile, vocal opposition from extreme groups has virtually disappeared.

Editorial on Mike's Case

*Why did Mike and his colleagues succeed where Steve and his colleagues had failed? Was his program less controversial? Hardly; as one of our reviewers put it, ". . . involvement with SIECUS is about like holding a lighted firecracker!" As with Steve's program there were unexpected slip-ups and chance happenings which stalled the effort and seemed at times to make it look hopeless. Likewise there was a militant, organized, and antagonistic minority who seemed to operate in an almost identical manner in the two situations. Therefore, what made the difference? In general, it seemed that Mike's program was more thoroughly planned and more thoroughly checked out with all concerned parties (teachers, administrators, students, and parents) at each stage of development. Secondly, there was a very thorough effort to **acquire relevant resources**, not just from SIECUS but* *also from the university, other school districts, and many other sources. Thirdly, there was a very public process of **choosing the innovation**, which involved a great deal of local adaptation and reformulation so that teachers and the community could feel it was their own. Finally, there was the successful (though belated) mobilization of community opinion leaders to build widespread **acceptance** and to quell the irrational doubts and fears which the extremist groups had been able to exploit. In short, Mike and his colleagues followed a sequence of problem-solving steps not unlike those proposed in the **Guide**.*

HENRY

CASE EXAMPLE: SYSTEMATIC CHANGE INITIATED BY A CHANGE AGENCY

*Henry's example comes from a new type of educational organization: a "change agency." Such an organization as the one described here is unique in that it has been established for the exclusive purpose of facilitating innovation on the **practice** level . . . this one apparently had the resources to initiate major change projects. Organizations like Henry's are becoming increasingly common throughout the United States. Intermediate school districts, supplementary centers, and a large number of local and regional centers supported by state and federal funds are being organized and reorganized as "change agencies." Henry's case was rated as "typical" or "very typical" by 60 per cent of our reviewers.*

"I have been associated with this agency almost since its inception three-and-a-half years ago. At that time I was involved in experimentation on some new instructional techniques at the university where I taught. The proposed 'change agency' seemed like an exciting venture—and just the kind of 'change' I needed after spending so much of my professional life under the sheltering wing of academia!

"I'd like to explain a little of how our change agency operates before getting into the details of the particular curriculum innovation that we implemented.

"Our organization is designed to help school systems in our part of the state try out new practices and programs. Our *role* has actually been that of an agent of change. We visualize our working environment in this way: our 'client,' the school district with all its component parts—students, teachers, administrators—is on one side. All the information resources are on the other. We see ourselves operating from that never-never land between the two as we try to 'bring them together':

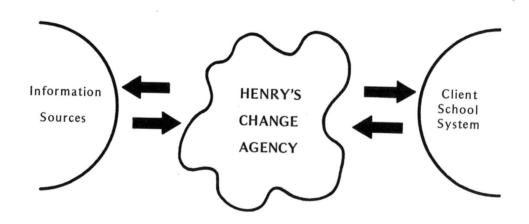

"Because we must move in both directions, i.e., deal with both resources and clients as we try to facilitate innovation, we divide our tasks among three 'functional' teams: (1) The responsibility of the 'research team' is to establish contacts with the information sources and to obtain from them the scientific information needed by the clients we are trying to help. In most cases the research team also adapts or translates the information they get into a more useful form. (2) The 'implementation team' is that part of our staff which interacts directly with the client school system. They are the people who do the actual helping and consulting. (3) The 'planning team' is our 'link within a link.' It works to ensure that there is adequate coordination and communication between the other two teams. It has final responsibility for the design and administration of our projects.

Stage I: Building a Relationship
(and Resource System Identification)
"In building a relationship with *potential clients,* we try to ensure their commitment by requiring that the superintendent of every school district which wants to participate be on our board of directors. This group meets four times a year as the policy-making arm of our organization. These board members all have a voice in the decisions about our work with their own schools. Also, when our organization was first beginning I conducted a series of meetings with administrators and lay people from a few school districts in the area. Our purpose in the discussions was to have these people identify for themselves how they felt their respective communities *should* function. These discussions served to open them up to ideas about the need for change and the types of new things that could be tried.

"In building a relationship with *information sources* we have used both formal and informal means. We have an executive advisory committee that meets nine times a year and a college advisory committee that meets monthly; people in both of these groups have the expertise relevant to our work. We also stress the importance of developing personal contacts in centers of research and innovation: the colleges, the Title IV centers, ERIC, SRIS, Phi Delta Kappa, etc. We deliberately build close ties with colleges both inside and outside our area by incorporating some of their faculty members as special consultants to our organization. I would say that all these things were intentionally designed for the purpose of 'building a relationship.'

Stage II: Diagnosis (and Continuation of
Relationship-Building)
"I guess you could say that we had a backwards approach to the step you call 'diagnosing the problem in the client system.' There are a total of 240,000 students and 16,000 teachers in our area, all of whom were potential 'clients' for our organization. In order to keep our operations manageable, especially at the beginning, we limited the types of innovations with which we could offer assistance. At first we defined our probable foci as (1) language arts, (2) social sciences, (3) behavioral change, and (4) in-service training. We then went to the school systems in our area to find out which, if any, had interests or needs in these areas. We found that a number of districts shared our interest in developing new approaches to a social science curriculum. From these systems we chose only those which could afford and were willing to commit time, staff, etc., to a project with us.

"After limiting our potential clients in this way, we sent our 'implementation team' to collect information about the chosen school systems. They interviewed staff and administrators and reviewed school records to find out about practices and textbooks being used, strategies they were trying, and the kind of community in which they were working. The purpose of this step was two-fold: to collect diagnostic information and to do more 'relationship building.' The members of our 'implementation team' had previously worked as teachers, counselors, and administrators in the school systems that were now our clients and, with their interviews, they were accomplishing the important task of gaining the trust of their former associates for our new organization.

Stages III and IV: Acquiring Relevant Resources
and Choosing a Solution

"We turned our 'research team' loose on the subject of 'social studies curricula.' By means of bibliographies and search services such as those of ERIC, they tracked down 326 programs around the country that were somehow related to the field of social sciences. Of course, not all of their discoveries were practicable. Many of the programs were not yet more than vague pipe dreams. However, with the data collected by our implementation team, we were able to identify some programs and materials that were relevant to our particular clients' needs. Looking back, we probably could have gone to 'Project Social Studies' and approached several other experts in the field in order to narrow the list of 326 programs much more quickly. However, as this was our first experience, we went the total route. We could do the next one a little more easily. The nice thing about the work we did with these 326 innovations is that we had gathered enough information to disseminate material about them to all the school districts in our area. Even districts that were not directly involved in any of our projects could use our information as a ready reference for their own efforts. A good number of them wanted to use it, so we published and sent out a descriptive list of the full 326.

"In the end, however, we did find four innovative projects for the elementary level that were far enough developed at this time to be useful to our clients. These were projects originally developed by Hilda Taba, the University of Minnesota, Science Research Associates, and the Greater Cleveland Educational Research Council. However, each was geared to a different grade level and proceeded in a different direction.

Stage V: Gaining Acceptance

"Then, our 'planning team' got to work designing strategies for the introduction of the four projects into our client schools. ... And, we made sure before we started moving with the projects that our *specific objectives* for each one *were written in behavioral terms;* that is, that we could state precisely what new behavior we were trying to elicit by using these social studies curricula. It was very difficult to translate some of the concepts into behavioral terms, but we got as close as we could. In some cases we had to be satisfied with stating the 'general conditions which we are trying to establish.'

"With these behavioral objectives in hand, our 'implementation team' went out to the schools again to assist them with the introduction of the new programs. Our team members conducted demonstrations and in-service training sessions and consulted individually with teachers who were trying out the new social studies programs.

"At this time the 'planning team' also set up a research study to determine to what extent we achieved our 'specific objectives.' We developed a series of pre-tests and post-tests that we gave to the students participating in the projects and to control groups of students. What we hope to have when we're through is a research report that we can send to anyone in the country to tell them what they can get; what they cannot get; what they'll lose; what they'll gain; and what they'll spend if they use any of the same projects!

"We have continually tried to use dissemination strategies to keep our clients up to date on the progress of the innovation in their own schools. We have had newsletters, meetings, reports to superintendents, training workshops, microfilm and videotape replays—actually a whole strategy, a 'synergistic multi-media approach.' We even sent one of our people to a university-sponsored training program in these kinds of strategies.

Stage VI: Stabilization and Self-Renewal

"In order to ensure the continuity of the innovation, we installed in the client system (1) a specialist in change, (2) a research person, and (3) a field person whom we call a 'curriculum specialist.' However, we're not really sure that *stabilizing* the innovation is our ball game. Part of the reason that we're not interested in stabilizing is that we think that change must be a continuous process, particularly in the area of curriculum. As new approaches are discovered we find much better ways of developing a program. For example, right now we are talking about 'Taba' social studies, but we are finding some real weaknesses in 'Taba.' What I'd like to do is combine 'Taba' with 'Minnesota,' using the structures and content of 'Minnesota' and the teaching strategies of 'Taba.'

"There are some major weaknesses in our organization that I have observed in our first couple of years of operation. However, I need to have more information before I can deal with them:

"First, I need to know a lot more about what happens to a person involved in trying to bring about innovation—about the side effects of innovating. Also, I have observed that people who have been successful as professors, department chairmen, or curriculum specialists find it necessary to function in entirely new ways as they experience for themselves the total process of change when they work with our nebulous kind of organization. We need some kind of description of what happens to the change agent when he is placed in an environment where he *must* learn and is forced to change. He experiences many changes that he never really anticipated. This needs a special study of its own."

Editorial on Henry's Case

Henry speaks from a different vantage point than either Mike or Steve; he is an **outside** *change agent and as such he has more freedom of choice in the clients he serves and in the resources he can mobilize. This has been an unusual model in education to date, but it may represent the wave of the future in many areas of educational reform. The question we should ask ourselves is whether all these advantages were adequately exploited in the case example described. We need to know more about how* **relationships** *were built, how the* **diagnosis** *was made, and how they encountered the dynamics of change and resistance to gain* **acceptance** *by each of the target schools. We are also surprised at the large number of programs that had to be identified. Was this "overkill" in* **resource acquisition** *fully necessary? Henry indicates that a more efficient strategy might have been developed.*

What is especially important on the positive side in this case is the care taken to build adequate institutional arrangements. Advisory and executive committees representing both resource and user systems were set up, and commitments were obtained at the highest level before proceeding with change projects. Also noteworthy is the care taken to **structure** *the agency internally into interrelated functional teams with an appropriate division of skills and experience. Likewise, individual projects were carefully planned, evaluated, and documented. This kind of planning and structuring of the change organization and its activities are important ingredients of success.*

LINDA

CASE EXAMPLE: CURRICULUM CHANGE STIMULATED BY A STUDENT

Not so long ago the idea of a high school student as a "change agent" would have been absurd to most people, but change even strikes the world of change agentry. Linda's story is an example of a change (specifically, the addition of "black studies" to a high school curriculum) in which student demand apparently played an influential, though informal, role. This case study also raises questions which have been all too common to innovations which are initiated in response to client demand, i.e., the lack of an adequate means of incorporating the clients' specific requests in the actual decision-making for implementation. The story of this innovation, narrated by the change agent's mother, was rated as "typical" or "very typical" by 47 per cent of our reviewers. It was more controversial than the other cases, being seen as highly illuminating and real by some and totally inappropriate and suspect by others.

Stages II and IV: Diagnosis and Choosing the Solution

"My daughter, Linda, who is in the ninth grade, might be called a 'flaming radical' in our community. About a year ago she came up with the idea that the kids who really *need* to learn about black history were not necessarily the blacks, but rather the white kids who live in the suburban neighborhoods. She figured out that the blacks were going to force that change for themselves, but who was going to initiate 'black studies' in the schools of a middle-class white suburb? As a student she wanted to take such a course in high school, so she decided to take it upon herself to try to get it into the curriculum in our system.

"Let me begin by telling you a little about the situation in our community when she began to attempt this change. We live in a very conservative state. Some areas have integrated their schools only within the past two years. Our particular area has a fairly cosmopolitan population, although a number of residents have recently come from the South; a number of people work on the factory assembly line; and many expressed extremely conservative political views in a recent election. Our community is multi-racial though I would not say that we are actually 'integrated': only one black family lives in the area served by Linda's junior high school. Of the three junior high and two senior high schools in our district, more than a token number of black students are found in only one of the junior highs and one of the senior highs. There has been a significant amount of tension and several racial incidents in that one high school, so our superintendent felt that some sort of action was needed in response to the black students' problems. Initially this response took the form of restrictions on student extra-curricular programs.

"Because the new regulations concern a very salient aspect of the students' lives, much of their activism recently has focussed on effecting a 'change' in these rules. I don't think that even the black students have ever pushed for the introduction of a black history course. There was a rumor that one of the high school teachers voluntarily started teaching a black studies class and the other teachers managed to have him resign. There was no such course at the time Linda started to become involved.

"When Linda first began her campaign she had a lot of questions: Was there any course in the present high school curriculum which in any way resembled 'black studies'? What kind of black studies should she push for? . . . 'Negro history in the United States'? . . . 'African studies'? . . . a section in the 'world civilization' course? The answers she found to these questions seem to me to relate a most interesting tale.

Stage III: Acquiring Relevant Resources

"I introduced Linda to a black fellow who was a student at the university in our town. He talked with her about some of the needs for a course in black studies. He helped her get an appointment with a sociology professor who was interested in the subject and he also told her of an education professor who might help. She made an appointment to see that professor herself. Throughout all of this I was amazed at the marvelous cooperation these people gave and the interest they took in helping a thirteen-year-old. . . . And they *were* very helpful. Through her discussions with them, she came to feel that the most relevant kind of course would be one that emphasized the cultural development of the blacks, from their African origins through the varied American experience. The education professor even offered his services—contingent upon my daughter's success in selling the course to her school system—to develop and conduct the in-service teacher training sessions needed for adding black studies to the curriculum.

"They identified for her several books and articles that would be appropriate for a high school level study of black history. She found only one of these catalogued in the university library, which confirmed her fears about the paucity of written material available locally. The professors assured her that it would not be difficult to obtain other good materials, but they did express concern over getting school officials to authorize their use, for these books were not the traditional genre of classroom reading material.

Stages I, III, and IV: Establishing Relationships, Acquiring More Resources, and Learning More About the Appropriate Solution to Choose

"Her information-seeking discussions with administrators of the school system were just as revealing but not as productive. She talked first with the principal and guidance counselor of her junior high school. They didn't know whether such a course existed or where one might go to find out, perhaps because they were not *directly* involved in the high school curriculum. However, after three months of her badgering them, they finally located an official copy of the course descriptions for the schools' curricula so that Linda could read for herself whether or not black studies were covered in the existing program.

"Linda felt there was a potential opportunity for black studies in the 'world civilization' course since 'sub-Sahara Africa' was listed as one of the topics. She contacted a 'world civilization' teacher in the high school that she will be attending to find out how much emphasis was currently being given to studying sub-Sahara Africa and if the unit could be developed into a 'black history' section. The response she got was hardly encouraging: 'The world is too big and we've got to cover the ancient Egyptians and the . . . '—you know.

Stage V: Gaining Acceptance

"Because she seemed to be getting nowhere with the school administration, Linda then tried to rally her fellow students to bring pressure on the system. I must admit she was not very successful. She and several other ninth graders took petitions to the two high schools and tried to conduct organizational meetings, but only 20 students showed up. It was at this point that Linda and the rest of the small group of her friends really gave up the battle. They didn't seem to be making any headway in selling their 'clients' on this innovation. Perhaps I am making excuses for them, but it did seem that they had an impossible task; they were also trying to keep up with full study schedules.

"What happened next was a rather surprising turn of events. The school system has a curriculum development committee that consults regularly with the university staff. The education professor with whom Linda had spoken had apparently been putting a bee in the bonnet of a colleague who was one of these consultants. At this man's urging, the curriculum committee had become a proponent of 'black studies.' Also, the time finally seemed ripe: several further confrontations had occurred between black and white high school students; and a new, more progressive superintendent of schools had recently taken office.

"With the superintendent's blessing, the curriculum development committee set about to design the course: 'The Study of the American Negro.' During the first year, classes will be limited to eleventh and twelfth graders, and one third to one half of the course will be spent on current events. Also, the course is to be an 'elective' that students can take after fulfilling their American history requirements, if they have the appropriate time slot free. The administration has stated that the black studies program will be extended to K through 12 'as soon as other qualified teachers are found or trained.'

"My daughter and her cohorts were happy that at least something had been done about a black studies program. However, the specific program that was set up was not exactly what the kids had in mind. Linda had hoped that the course would be given equal status with all other history courses and that it would be available to all students at any grade level. For the time being, their zeal for further change has been quieted by the administration's compromise offering. Nevertheless, they are already excitedly planning what they'd like to have in the course when they become eligible to take it in a year or two. I only hope that the program will then be flexible enough to rise to the needs of these kids."

Editorial on the Case of Linda

*It is very difficult to be an effective change agent when you start from a low-status position within the system, but Linda's case suggests that it is possible. With some valuable advice from her mother she was especially aggressive in acquiring **resources** (professors, course plans, etc.) and in establishing contacts with people at all levels in the system (principals, counselors, teachers, professors, **and** students). Linda was, above all, a **catalyst** for change. She stimulated, inspired, cajoled, and nagged other people into action. Some of our reviewers rightly asked, "Was Linda really responsible for getting the program established?" Probably not, in any complete sense, but she seems to have been one of the key people who got things going.*

*Linda probably would have been more effective than she was, however, if she had been more sophisticated about the change **process**. It is very hard to trace the six steps of problem-solving in her strategy. She did not spend much time thinking about how to build **relationships**. She did not try to **work collaboratively** with teachers and administrators, and she approached students only belatedly. She apparently spent very little concerted effort on developing a collaborative **diagnostic** strategy or solution-**choosing** strategy. **Acceptance** seems to have been brought about by persistent pressure without regard to human relations or the psychology of resistance. For example, did an image of being a "flaming radical" stand in her way with this conservative community?*

*Because Linda, like all students, is only a temporary member of her system, we wonder what provision can be made to make this type of innovating a permanent part of the behavior of permanent members such as teachers and administrators. Will the system continue to depend on the necessarily sporadic efforts of concerned and energetic individuals like Linda? How does one generate **self-renewal** processes which allow a continuous contribution from students to the decision-making process?*

PART TWO:
THE STAGES OF PLANNED CHANGE

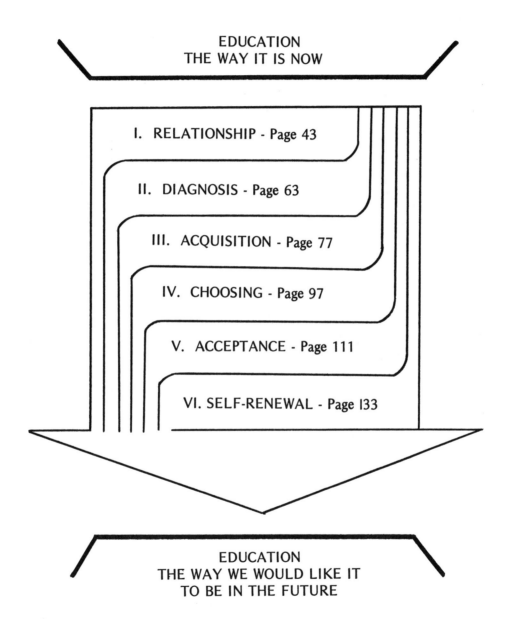

EDUCATION
THE WAY IT IS NOW

I. RELATIONSHIP - Page 43

II. DIAGNOSIS - Page 63

III. ACQUISITION - Page 77

IV. CHOOSING - Page 97

V. ACCEPTANCE - Page 111

VI. SELF-RENEWAL - Page 133

EDUCATION
THE WAY WE WOULD LIKE IT
TO BE IN THE FUTURE

The six "stages" which follow should also be seen as *functions* which are important at every phase of a change project.

A NOTE ON FORMAT:

The right-hand column of each page is devoted to case references (in dark capital letters) and quotes and other comments (in italics). There is also a considerable amount of blank space which you may find useful for jotting down your own notes. A number of our reviewers commented that the format was distracting but a large number were pleased with it and we stuck with the majority in preparing this edition. If you do find it distracting, we suggest that you ignore the right-hand column entirely on first reading, at least. It is not integral to the text and should not be essential to the flow of thought.

Stage I:

BUILDING A RELATIONSHIP

Build a good relationship with the people you are trying to help.

This is where any innovation or change effort should begin. A strong, creative relationship can carry a change program through the most difficult obstacles. While innovation is generally difficult it can become impossible if there is a bad relationship between the change agent and his client. Your relationship with a prospective client system must be carefully planned and thought through if you are going to succeed with a project. This first chapter provides some specific criteria to help you—the change agent—assess your relationship with a client system. If you know where you stand with a client and if you know how he sees you, you will be in a better position to adapt and enhance this relationship as the change effort progresses.

A. WHO IS THE CLIENT?

Throughout this manual we will use the term "client" to refer to the people whom the change agent is trying to help. This "client" might be an individual or a group of any size from a classroom to a community. Sometimes we will refer to this group of people as a "system" if they seem to have common goals and are trying to work together to achieve those goals. Sometimes it will not be entirely clear just who the client is. We often find that we cannot work effectively with one group unless, at the same time, we are working with others to whom they are related. This network of relations can get pretty complicated and unmanageable. Therefore, it is important, at the outset, to define who the client is. This boils down to two basic questions:

What group are you going to work with *directly?*

What are the *other groups* to whom your direct client is related?

"Agents who have worked with communities point out that the change agent in this setting has especially difficult problems of deciding which groups he should begin to work with. He may work with a group which consists of representatives from the various subparts of the community, he may form a new group with a special interest in community welfare and improvement, or he may choose to start with one of the official or semi-official elements of the community, such as a community council. In any case, though the change agent hopes to work toward a broader involvement of community subparts as the change project moves along, he usually cannot expect a very broad base of contact or very formal contact with the community in the beginning. Usually he must develop his relationship with the community from small beginnings."

Lippitt, Watson and Westley[1]

1. Relating to the Client System

What Are the Norms of the Client System?

Boundaries of various kinds define the client system because they separate people who are members from those who are "outside." Some boundaries are physical and obvious—like the wall and the barbed wire fence—but most boundaries are less visible. For example, the members of any social group share a number of common beliefs, values, and rules of behavior. These shared "norms" describe what it means to be "us" instead of "them." A change agent should make himself familiar with these features of his client system. He should know how sharply they are defined and how strictly they are adhered to by all members.

Although these shared beliefs and behaviors are seldom unique, they may be viewed as unique by the members. Most social systems maintain their group identity partly through the mechanism of local pride which identifies what "we" have as special, as high status, as most important and most relevant. This belief that "we are unique" can be a major stumbling block to any program for change: it may hinder both the awareness of a need for change and the acceptance of innovations from "outside."

Who Are the Leaders?

In attempting to establish a satisfactory relationship, an understanding of the formal leadership structure is also important. Some systems are only loosely and vaguely structured while others have a strict chain of command. The more clearly defined and structured the leadership pattern, the more critical it is for us to establish solid relationships with the leaders.

Who Are the Influentials?

In addition to the formal chains of command, there are many *informal channels and leadership structures.* It is most important that the change agent know the informal leaders. You should know the "influentials," those key people to whom others turn for new ideas. Most social systems contain such "opinion leaders," respected friends and colleagues who set the standard for the group even though they may not have formal status as "leaders" or "supervisors."

Who Are the Gatekeepers?

The change agent may also find certain individuals who hold key strategic positions with respect to the flow of new

"Norms in social systems correspond to habits in individuals. They are customary and expected ways of behaving. Members of the organization demand of themselves and of other members conformity to the institutional norms."

Watson[2]

TEACHERS IN STEVE'S SYSTEM HAD A "NORM" OF NOT WORKING EVENINGS AND SATURDAYS. BECAUSE HIS PROJECT VIOLATED THAT NORM HE WAS UNABLE TO GET THEIR COMPLETE INVOLVEMENT IN HIS PROGRAM.

ALL FOUR CASE STUDIES ILLUSTRATE THE IMPORTANCE OF THE CHAIN OF COMMAND IN EDUCATION. FOR STEVE, THE SUPERINTENDENT WAS THE KEY MAN WHO WAS NOT THERE WHEN HE NEEDED HIM. HENRY'S AGENCY ESTABLISHED FORMAL COMMITMENTS FROM THE SUPERINTENDENT BEFORE DOING ANYTHING WITH A SCHOOL DISTRICT. STUDIES OF INNOVATION IN EDUCATION POINT TO THE CRITICAL ROLE OF THE FORMAL LEADERSHIP STRUCTURE OF THE SCHOOL SYSTEM AND THE PERSONALITIES OF THE LEADERS.

MIKE WAS AN "INFLUENTIAL" IN HIS SYSTEM.

ideas and information. Such *gatekeepers* play a critical role in innovation and they may be distinct from both the formal leadership and the opinion leadership discussed above. The librarian, the guidance counselor, or the assistant principal may hold little formal power or informal influence, but they may still be in key positions because they control channels of information on certain topics. The "boss's secretary" is probably the most famous example of the gatekeeper in this sense.

With Whom Should You Choose to Work?

Most change agents find themselves in the position of having to select from the entire client system only a few members with whom they will be able to work *directly* throughout the change effort. Successful change agents have found it wise to try to include people who represent the following system characteristics:

- opinion leadership
- formal authority
- representative of major factions or vested interests
- public relations ability
- credibility and respectability.

By keeping in mind these major characteristics you can identify *direct* clients who will be very effective in aiding change efforts. With such people working on your side, you will have a good chance of influencing the entire client system. In choosing this "change team," however, you should not forget a sixth criterion which in some ways is more important than all the others. This is *compatibility with you.* If you cannot work together effectively as friends and colleagues your project will be in trouble.

2. **Relating to the Larger Social Environment**

What Are the Norms in the Community?

No group of human beings is completely isolated from the influence of "outsiders." All systems and organizations exist within a context of other systems of which they are a part and upon which they are dependent. Therefore, the change agent must not only consider the characteristics of the particular client he is serving, but he must also consider the nature of the community, the larger social system of which his client is a part.

THE NEWSPAPER EDITOR IN STEVE'S COMMUNITY ACTED AS ONE KIND OF GATEKEEPER TO POPULAR INFORMATION ABOUT HIS PROJECT.

HOW DID STEVE'S THREE-MAN PROJECT TEAM (P. 24) MEASURE UP ON THESE CRITERIA?

". . . a change in teacher-pupil relationships is likely to have repercussions on teacher-principal contacts, on pressure groups operating on the superintendent, on Board members' chances for reelection, and perhaps on the relationship of the local system to state or Federal agencies. Any estimate of resistance which takes account only of the persons primarily and centrally concerned will be inadequate."

Watson[3]

45

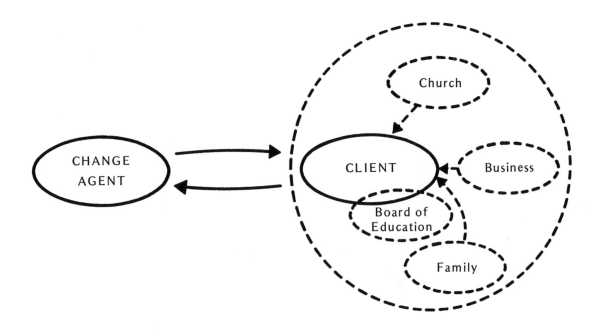

At this initial point in the relationship, there are three questions about this larger system that you should be able to answer:

Who are the most powerful and influential people in the community?

How do these people usually react to innovation in the community? (Are they conservative or progressive?)

How can these people be approached and influenced to endorse the change effort?

Who Are the Influentials
in the Community?

If you are able to review the history of the community, you will usually be struck by the prominence of certain groups—pressure groups, key individuals, and key institutions—which have had a very strong influence over what has gone on in the client system. For example, in studying a school in a particular community you may find that the

STEVE AND LINDA'S MOTHER BOTH THOUGHT THAT THEIR COMMUNITIES' LEADERSHIP WAS CONSERVATIVE AND THEY CITED THIS FACT AS AN IMPORTANT CONDITIONER OF RESPONSE TO THE INNOVATION. HOWEVER, NEITHER STEVE NOR LINDA APPROACHED THESE LEADERS DIRECTLY.

"Public schools are structured in such a way that the chief administrator can be kept responsive to external demands: the superintendent serves in a contractual relationship to a lay board of education. Parents' and other citizens'

46

school board has a great deal of power, that the superintendent or one of his assistants is particularly important, or, perhaps, that certain progressive or conservative pressure groups have major influence in either fostering innovation or in inhibiting or disrupting it. Outside pressure can lead to increased conflict within the client system; it can create an atmosphere of rigidity and complacency. You must be sensitive to the likely effects of these different "outside" pressures on your clients, for you will need to be able to make a quick assessment of the relative potency of various forces while you are in the process of developing the relationship.

What Is the Community Leadership Like?

Certainly, the change agent will want to take a good look at the leadership structure in this social environment, remembering that the environment, like the client itself, is a system. It would be useful to know to what extent the leadership of the social environment is cohesive. Does it work as a harmonious system? Is it factional and strife-ridden? Or is it merely diffuse and weak? Also, as a change agent, it is important to know how the leadership may be approached. Can an outside change agent safely make contact directly or should he use inside representatives as emissaries? If the leadership is factional, are all factions approachable? Furthermore, are there specific kinds of conventions and rituals that must be observed when dealing with the leaders?

What Percentage of Your Efforts Should Be Devoted to These Outside Forces?

The effort you expend in identifying and dealing with these outside social forces will vary greatly from case to case. Sometimes, it may only be necessary to make a casual accounting of these external forces. Nevertheless, the testimony of countless change agents suggests that these outside forces are almost invariably underrated in the early stages of a project.

B. *WHAT IS YOUR RELATIONSHIP AT THE VERY BEGINNING?*

A new change project seldom represents a completely new beginning. Here, as in most of the affairs of life, past is prologue. The success of a client's past encounters with change and with change agents will color greatly the success of future relations with you. When you are starting out on a new project you are likely to be in one of four situations: (1) no prior relationship with the client; (2) reestablishing a

groups in most communities do not exert a direct influence on the adoption of new types of instructional programs, probably because they do not know enough about educational methodology to favor or to oppose specific innovations. Their influence is ordinarily limited to creating a climate of interest—or the lack of it—in better results. However, if for some reason the public develops a lively interest in a new type of program— foreign languages in the elementary school, for example— that program is likely to appear in the local classrooms."

Brickell[4]

THE EFFORTS OF STEVE TO INTRODUCE A HUMAN RELATIONS PROGRAM AND OF MIKE TO INTRODUCE A "HUMAN SEXUALITY" PILOT DISCUSSION COURSE WERE BOTH THWARTED BY OPPOSITION FROM ORGANIZED CITIZEN GROUPS.

FOR STEVE AND FOR MIKE OUTSIDE COMMUNITY FORCES WERE OF CRUCIAL IMPORTANCE.

formerly positive relationship; (3) reestablishing an ambiguous relationship; and (4) redefining an on-going relationship. Each of these situations has special advantages and disadvantages which we will discuss below.

1.   The Blank Slate

A good relationship is a complex and delicate bridge, very difficult and expensive to build and very important to maintain. One can only really appreciate this fact when starting completely new. In a new relationship, nothing can be taken for granted. You must be acutely aware of norms and values, leadership, influence patterns, and so forth, while at the same time you are maintaining an image of complete trust and serene confidence. The number of concerns which will tax your energy and absorb your attention is greatly multiplied.

A completely new relationship is beset by a host of uncertainties and unknown quantities. The change agent is faced with the task of acquiring information from every available source, while at the same time he is making crucial decisions about the project. Such decisions will inevitably be based on partial and distorted knowledge which may make or break the project. Needless to say, it is a delicate task.

Nevertheless, there are many benefits in the brand new relationship. First of all, the new change agent is not initially identified with any special internal faction. Thus he may have a chance to become and to remain an objective observer as well as a friend. Secondly, he may derive special benefits from his initial "guest" status. For a complete newcomer, even potential enemies will be polite and will not try to shout him down or shove him out without a fair hearing; he may be granted a kind of honeymoon period during which he is relatively free from critical scrutiny and harsh judgments. If you sense that most members of your client system start out with this open-minded attitude, you should take full advantage of the opportunity to assure all factions of your own open-mindedness and eagerness to be a friend and helper to all. A new face may suggest to the clients that new things are truly possible, whereas an old face with new ideas may merely be seen as an old face with old ideas.

THE EXAMPLE OF HENRY'S "CHANGE AGENCY" ILLUSTRATES THIS KIND OF START-UP SITUATION: BECAUSE THE AGENCY WAS NEW IT HAD A "BLANK SLATE" WITH ALL POTENTIAL CLIENTS. HOWEVER, IT ALLEVIATED SOME OF THE PROBLEMS OF BECOMING ACQUAINTED WITH NEW CLIENTS BY RECRUITING STAFF FROM CLIENT SCHOOL SYSTEMS TO WORK FOR THE NEW AGENCY AND BY INCLUDING KEY DECISION-MAKERS ON ITS GOVERNING BOARD.

2.   Reestablishing a Good Relationship

If the client already knows you and values your past service, you have a very strong base from which to begin a new change project. Such an advantageous starting point should not be taken for granted, however. The cautious change agent might ask himself the following questions in preparing for a new project with an old client:

> Does the client still view the former relationship as having been positive?
> Are there any aspects of this relationship which could stand even further improvement?
> Have there been any intervening events which could have muddied the waters?
> Could the nature of the prior relationship lead the client system to any erroneous expectations about this forthcoming change activity?

By preparing in advance to deal with such potential snags, the change agent can ensure continued growth from a solid base.

3.   Reestablishing an Uncertain Relationship

It is difficult, but not impossible, to make a fresh start with a client with whom the prior relationship was not fully adequate. In such a situation it is advisable, however, to have substantial assurance that the prospects for success are now, indeed, better. The change agent can evaluate his probabilities for succeeding by answering the following questions:

> Have you made an adequate diagnosis of the problems in the prior relationship? Has anything been done in the interim to correct any of these?
> Have you attempted to build a new image of yourself as a change agent, and to instill new expectations among your clients?
> What, if anything, has happened to the client in the interim that would alter the prospects of success— either positively or negatively?

If the previous encounter was, in fact, a failure, it would be unwise to begin all over again before the problems in that relationship are patched up and new expectations are instilled. Even then there should be some dramatic evidence that a new start would be successful (e.g., a major change in the leadership of the client system).

4.   Redefining an Existing Relationship

Very frequently, in assuming the role of change agent, a person is moving out of a previously held role with which the client system has him firmly identified. This is almost always true of the change agent who emerges from the client system itself, as the teacher or administrator who becomes director of a new federally funded project. Modifying or redefining an existing relationship may require a good deal of skill and sensitivity to human relations. Some of the major pitfalls are indicated below:

> Has the client been adequately informed that you have assumed a new and different role?
>
> Does he show concrete signs of recognition that his relationship to you as a change agent is new, and that he accepts this fact happily? (E.g., is he willing to bring you problems that he would not formerly have discussed with you? Are you referred to in informal conversation and in writing by your new role?)
>
> Are you sufficiently comfortable in performing this new change agent role so that you will not slip back into "old role" behavior patterns if, for example, your associates start making demands of you to perform in your old role?

The need for training and practice in the skills of relating to clients is nowhere more apparent than in the situation which requires you to modify an existing relationship.

C. INSIDE OR OUTSIDE?

Although such distinctions are not always clear, change agents have long debated the relative advantages of beginning as an *insider* or as an *outsider*. When all the pros and cons are tallied, however, neither position seems to be clearly superior. A recounting of the major advantages and disadvantages of each may be helpful.

1. The *Inside* Change Agent

The Insider Has These Advantages:

He knows the system: he knows where the power lies, where the strategic leverage points are; he is better able to identify the gatekeepers, the opinion leaders, and the innovators than a newcomer.

He speaks the language, literally and figuratively; he knows the special ways in which members discuss things

LINDA WAS A STUDENT, MIKE WAS A TEACHER, AND STEVE WAS AN ADMINISTRATOR. EACH WAS ATTEMPTING TO SERVE AS A CHANGE AGENT WITHIN HIS OR HER OWN SCHOOL SYSTEM. FOR LINDA IT WAS PROBABLY ESPECIALLY DIFFICULT TO BE SEEN AS A LEGITIMATE CHANGE AGENT RATHER THAN "JUST ANOTHER RADICAL STUDENT."

MEMBERS OF HENRY'S "IMPLEMENTATION TEAM" HAD PREVIOUSLY HAD STAFF ROLES IN THE SCHOOLS THEY WERE NOW SERVING. THIS FACT WAS FACILITATING IN SOME WAYS, AS HENRY NOTES, BUT IT PROBABLY CREATED A LOT OF CONFUSION AND ROLE CONFLICT AS WELL.

"Whoever provides the leadership for change—inside man or one from the outside—should be aware of the complex forces working for and against change."

Watson and Glaser[5]

and refer to things; he has the accent, the tone, and the style.

He understands the norms (the commonly held beliefs, attitudes, behaviors) and, at least in part, he probably follows them and believes them himself.

He identifies with the system's needs and aspirations. Because he is a member, the system's need is also *his* pain. Thus, he has a personal incentive for helping.

He is a familiar figure, a known quantity. Most of what he does is understandable and predictable as "member" behavior; therefore he doesn't pose the threat of "the new" and "the unfamiliar."

The Insider Also Has These Disadvantages:

He may lack perspective. He may not be able to see the client system as a "whole" because of the particular place from which he views it and from which he has always viewed it.

He may not have the special knowledge or skill relevant to the innovation. He may not have had enough outside training or experience to be a true expert.

He may not have an adequate power base (unless he is at the top of his system). His plans may be confronted by superiors or competing peers.

He may have to live down his past failures or the hostility generated in some by his past successes.

He may not have the independence of movement so often required to be an effective change agent. The obligations of membership may severely limit the time and energy that he can invest in his new role.

The inside change agent usually faces the difficult task of redefining his on-going relationships with the other members of the system. In assuming the new role of change agent he must be able to change the expectations that his associates have about how he will behave and how they will relate to him. As noted in the previous section, this is sometimes difficult.

"When a top management man takes the lead in making changes, he . . . runs risks. He depends on others in his organization to keep him informed—before, during, and after the change process. But he may only get the kind of feedback his subordinates think he wants to hear, for no one wants to be the bearer of ill tidings to his boss. If the manager is brashly eager to make a name for himself as the result of the change, he may get only tepid cooperation. If he is too impatient with reluctance on the part of others to understand or support the changes he desires, he may incur resistance or even sabotage."

Watson and Glaser[6]

THE FACT THAT LINDA, MIKE, AND TO SOME EXTENT STEVE WERE ALL CHANGE AGENTS IN THEIR SPARE TIME MADE THEIR WORK MUCH MORE DIFFICULT.

HENRY'S "IMPLEMENTATION TEAM" MEMBERS WERE OUTSIDERS WITH SOME INSIDER CHARACTERISTICS.

2. **The *Outside* Change Agent**

The Outsider Has These Advantages:

He starts fresh in many cases and is not burdened by negative stereotypes.

He is in a position to have perspective; he can look at the client system objectively. Thus, he may be able to see problems that the insider would not see and he may be able to identify needs and opportunities which insiders would be unable to perceive. Moreover, insiders often have a special axe to grind. They tend to see this or that problem as most pressing because it is the problem which impinges upon them most directly. The outsider, on the other hand, can look at the problems of all members collectively and, thus, make a more objective diagnosis. (Outsiders are not always so objective, of course. Often, indeed, they are heavily invested in the "sowing" of particular innovations and, consequently, the stressing of certain needs. Nevertheless, the outsider is in the *position* to be objective about diagnosis.)

He is independent of the power structure in the client system. He always has the option of pulling out if and when he deems it necessary. He is not compelled to identify with any particular faction and he is not forever threatened and inhibited by superior authorities.

He is in a position to bring in something genuinely new. As an outsider he is more likely to have had the opportunity to gain expertise beyond that which the client system already possesses.

The Outsider Also Has These Disadvantages:

He is a stranger. Therefore, he represents a potential threat. What he will do is unknown and unpredictable; it might cause discomfort, conflict, or some sort of disturbance to the natural order of things.

The outsider may lack the knowledge of the insider; he may *not* understand the system, its language, norms, or values.

He may not "care enough." He may not be able to identify adequately with the needs of the client. The

"The outside advisor may be variously viewed as a troublemaker, as a knowledgeable specialist, or as a helpful friend. In any case, he needs more than courtesy from the rank-and-file personnel if he is to be fully effective: he needs their trust. Whether he gets this or not depends, in large measure, on how he sees himself, how sensitive he is to others, and how competent he is in his specialty. The way in which he is perceived depends, too, on the context in which he meets the members of the organization—on how his presence is explained and used by the power figures in the organization. Do the rank-and-file understand why the outside advisor is there? How his being there may affect them? What they might gain from his mission?"

Watson and Glaser[7]

". . . Learning about the supporting and conflicting relationship between subgroups is a crucial task, and success in getting these facts will determine to a great degree whether the consultant is able to develop the necessary and appropriate relationship to the total group and to its various subparts. One of the most frequent forms of resistance to change in group clients is the perception by certain subgroups that the consultant is more closely related to other subgroups and is 'on their side' in any conflict of interests."

Lippitt[8]

pain is not his pain, so he may be relatively indifferent to the needs which the client feels most acutely.

3. The Inside-Outside Team

In order to capitalize on the advantages and avoid the problems of both insider and outsider, many experienced change agents have suggested that the best solution is a "change agent team" in which both insiders and outsiders work together. Hence, the insider who is initiating a change effort would do well to enlist someone from the outside to work with him. Such an outside person could provide an "expert" legitimacy for the insider's efforts, in addition to contributing some real expertise. He could provide an objective perspective on the world in which the inside change agent is working. And the outside expert could give moral support to the insider whose efforts to do what is "right" for his system are being received by his colleagues with something less than enthusiasm.

Conversely, the outsider who initiates change would do well to enlist the inside support of some member who both understands the client system and is familiar with the change process. Preferably, this insider would be someone with reasonable security and status within the system, either as a leader, an influential, or a gatekeeper. Any selection of members for the inside-outside team should try to maximize the strengths of both positions in the service of innovation.

D. *MANAGING INITIAL ENCOUNTERS*

A relationship builds on the first encounter. What happens in the initial contacts between you and the client, how he sees you and how he feels about you initially, will determine whether or not you will be able to proceed into any other stage of problem-solving. In a sense you are a package which the client is going to buy. Most clients want to look the package over and read the label first. The first contacts are used by the client and by you to size up each other and take a quick first reading. Therefore, you must plan and prepare for these encounters with special care. Four considerations are paramount: friendliness, familiarity, rewardingness, and responsiveness.

1. *Friendliness:* A change agent is an intruder, and as for any intruder the client must ask himself, "Does he mean us well or ill?" The question may seem absurd to the change agent; after all, he knows he's a nice guy. To the client, however, there is nothing

"He must gather data as he enters, and he must face the possibility that the need is not seen by the most powerful member; that there is no place for the consultant role in the correct perception of the role, resource, and reward allocation; and that the typical emotional reaction to the prospect of the consultant role is one of hostility or fear or both. The entering consultant can assume that, in spite of manifest pleas for help, within the informal channels for communication in the client system, many members are committed—each to a different diagnosis, doctor, and treatment plan. Considering the amount of resistance that consultants regularly encounter, the fact that a consultant will enter in the dark is either a compliment to his courage, a comment on his conceit, or a manifestation of his masochism—or all three."

Glidewell[9]

MIKE AND THE SCIENCE CONSULTANT AND LINDA AND HER MOTHER ARE BOTH EXAMPLES OF INSIDE-OUTSIDE TEAMS.

"Some large change projects have . . . a special place for a consultant within the change-agent team. In a counseling center, for example, the counselors may meet each week with a psychiatrist to discuss their work—that is, to raise troublesome questions which they cannot answer by themselves. The questions may concern a client, the agent himself, or the relationship between them. Whatever the problem, a discussion with a competent advisor can help to reduce anxiety and restore

obvious about this unless he starts with a high trust for strangers. On the other hand, initial criteria of friendliness are usually not hard to meet: a smile, a firm handshake, a straight look in the eye, a warm greeting (making a firm mental note of the name of the person we are greeting and using the first name whenever we can). It also helps to make some positive and sincere comment of recognition such as some special attribute or accomplishment of the school, the place, or preferably the person himself. Most of this probably falls in the category of "etiquette" but it is not trivial in the first encounter.

2. *Familiarity:* As a person who has deliberately chosen to make himself an agent of change, you are *different.* Yet effective change agents are usually *similar* to their clients in most respects or are seen so by the client. Therefore a change agent should try to be a familiar object to the client in ways that are not important to his mission. In most cases this means at least in dress, outward appearance, speech, and bearing. It also may help to identify some common interests which are far removed from any change project, such as sports, entertainments, or politics (that is, if you are both likely to be on the same side of an issue). Jokes or humorous comments which are likely to be shared are especially effective in draining out some of the tension that will inevitably be in the situation. In any case, small talk, even about the weather, helps to make you a familiar object in initial encounters.

3. *Rewardingness:* The change agent should find the earliest opportunity to do *something* for the client that will be perceived as helpful or useful. The point of such an act is not the help itself, but the idea that is planted that "this person can be helpful." Usually this token reward can be merely in the form of a useful piece of knowledge relevant to a problem that the client is concerned about. It might be a book or a pamphlet or perhaps a useful lead to a person or a technique which the client has not thought of.

4. *Responsiveness:* The change agent should always be a good listener but this is especially true at the beginning of a relationship. Most importantly he should *show* the client he is a good listener by nodding if he understands, by asking for clarifica-

self-confidence. The same effect can be achieved in a workshop or in any other setting where a group of individual agents is working with different client systems. The opportunity to raise and discuss disturbing questions with fellow change agents or with an expert consultant can provide both reassurance and direct help, and the resulting gain in the change agent's security and self-confidence can give both stability and a sharper focus to the change process."

Lippitt[10]

"If I were organizing in an Orthodox Jewish community I would not walk in there eating a ham sandwich unless I wanted to be rejected so I could have an excuse to cop out."

Alinsky[11]

tions when he doesn't, and by indicating verbally and non-verbally that he is interested and cares about what the client is saying, shares his feeling, and wants to be helpful in whatever way he can.

One specific way in which the change agent can indicate responsiveness without commitment to solutions is by repeating back to the client what he has said in different words. This gives the client a chance to hear his own thoughts from another and to correct misunderstandings. In any case it shows the client that the change agent is *trying to listen.*

These first steps in relating to a client might fit in the category of "good politics" or "good public relations." They should not be taken as the substance of change agentry but only as preliminary and sometimes nonessential preliminary niceties. As soon as possible you should start moving toward a serious dialogue on problems. This dialogue might be seen as a series of cycles of problem-solving starting with something small and manageable which the client sees as manifestly urgent. Successful problem-solving at this micro level cements the relationship and builds the trust necessary to move to issues that are more serious, systemic, and controversial.

E. *THE IDEAL RELATIONSHIP*

Good relationships have no formula and each has its own unique dimensions, but the best seem to have several properties in common. We have identified nine characteristics of a change agent-client relationship that comprise an ideal base from which to launch the innovation process. These nine points do not cover everything and they are not completely independent of one another, but they may give us a yardstick against which we can measure our own circumstances.

1. *Reciprocity:* The relationship should be one in which both parties are able to give and take. To the extent that there is transfer of information, there should be transfer both ways, from agent to client and client to agent. This reciprocity increases the mutual appreciation of the problem and makes the diagnosis more accurate. One-way relationships tend to breed dependency and inhibit the initiative of the client to help himself.

2. *Openness:* Openness to new ideas is the *sine qua non* for innovation. Both the client and the change

"Most consultants seem to try to strike a balance between an assaultive consultation in conflict and a pedestrian consultation in comfort."

Glidewell[12]

MIKE'S GROUP DID A LOT OF SHARING WITH STUDENTS, TEACHERS, PARENTS, AND COMMUNITY LEADERS ON HOW THEIR PROGRAM WAS BEING DEVELOPED.

agent should be willing and ready to receive new inputs from each other. There are several dimensions to openness that should be considered, e.g.: (a) openness to receive new ideas; (b) active eagerness to seek out new ideas; (c) active desire for self-renewal; (d) willingness to share new ideas with others; (e) openness to listen to the problems of others; and (f) openness to give authentic feedback to each other.

3. *Realistic Expectations:* All too often the client will entertain the belief that the change agent is some sort of miracle worker, and sometimes the change agent will not discourage this view. The client may imagine that enormous benefits will come from the innovation. At later stages of the change process these unrealistic expectations may return to haunt the project, giving undue disillusionment and discouragement to the client and change agent alike. An important rule of change agentry is, therefore, to set reasonably realistic expectations from the outset. Do not oversell yourself or the innovation.

4. *Expectations of Reward:* The change agent should not, on the other hand, set expectations too low, because it is equally important to give the client some reason for optimism,* an idea of how much better things would be if the innovation were to be successful. The change agent must be seen as providing a valuable resource which will solve problems and provide the client with a significantly improved state of affairs.

Sometimes it may be necessary to start out the relationship by providing some token to the client of a future reward. Demonstrations or pilot programs sometimes serve this purpose because they show the client what can be done without committing him to major involvement in time and expense. The client needs some tangible evidence that you are a helpful person. If you can provide him with even the smallest bit of such evidence, you will be nurturing the belief that the relationship will be rewarding in the long run as well as the short run.

---

*i.e., not false optimism but rather a faith that change is possible and worthwhile.

"*...Above all, the client must not be allowed to fall into the trap of believing that his case will be solved more quickly or easily than it can be. Most change agents assume, for instance, that even though they may begin with the client system's definition of the problem, further diagnostic explorations will reveal more fundamental difficulties, more complex underlying problems. These must be solved if there is to be an effective change. Hence the client's original ideas about his difficulties and the length of time it will take to remedy them may be totally upset, with the result that the client becomes disheartened and inclined to give up.*"

Lippitt, Watson and Westley[13]

THE SUCCESS OF MIKE'S PILOT COURSE HELPED TO BUILD A BETTER RELATIONSHIP WITH THE COMMUNITY AS HE COULD TELL BY THE POSITIVE COMMENTS OF STUDENTS AND PARENTS. IT ALSO HELPED TO MOTIVATE MIKE HIMSELF.

"*The change agent must try to find a creative compromise between discouraging the client system and leaving it without any clear concept of what will be expected. If the client is too discouraged by the work prospect, he will abandon the*

5. *Structure:* Successful relationships need to have some structural basis, some definition of roles, working procedures, and expected outcomes. Although under most circumstances it may not be wise to lay out the structure too rigidly or specifically, there should nevertheless be some designation of expected goals and procedures and a meaningful distribution of labor and reward.

    The formalization of structure in the shape of a contract is often advisable, particularly when the change agent sees certain aspects of the relationship as problematic; as, for example, when he has serious cause to doubt the commitment of the leadership of the client system. In any case, such contracts should probably be open-ended on a reciprocal basis. That is, they should specify a sequence of points in the process at which the project could be terminated by mutual consent.*

6. *Equal Power:* It is difficult to build a successful relationship between parties of grossly unequal power. This is perhaps the overriding consideration in including an outside agent in a change agent team. When the power of the two parties is equivalent, power itself no longer plays the significant role in bringing about change. Where there is an unequal distribution of power the *appearance* of change may be brought about by the compliance of the weaker partner without the commitment necessary for lasting effectiveness. Under most circumstances, neither the change agent nor the client should have the power to compel the other to do anything.

7. *Minimum Threat:* The very idea of change is threatening to most of us, particularly when presented to us by an outsider who bills himself as a "change agent."† In most respects most of us like our own world pretty much the way it is, and we look upon changes first as potential *disturbances* before we see them as potential *benefits*. It is, therefore, most important that the change agent do

change project before it starts; if, on the other hand, he is allowed to form his own conceptions of the work to be done, he is likely to create a falsely optimistic view, in which case his discouragement is only temporarily delayed. Where the compromise will fall in any particular case cannot be predetermined, of course. Everything depends on the change agent's ability to judge each of the factors of personality and capacity which are presented to him in the specific circumstances of his work."

Lippitt, Watson and Westley[14]

HENRY'S AGENCY LAID OUT THE STRUCTURE OF THEIR PROJECTS VERY CLEARLY AND WORKED ON A CONTRACTUAL BASIS. STEVE'S GROUP ALSO WORKED WITHIN THE FRAMEWORK OF A FORMAL CONTRACT (THE TITLE III PROJECT) BUT COMMITMENT OF THE SCHOOL SYSTEM WAS APPARENTLY NOT ADEQUATELY INCORPORATED.

"Often the client system seems to be seeking assurance that the potential change agent is different enough from the client system to be a real expert and yet enough like it to be thoroughly understandable and approachable."

Lippitt, Watson and Westley[15]

---

*In the following section we will discuss a number of situations in which withdrawal and termination may be desirable.

†The expression "change agent" is used in the *Guide* because it is descriptive of a certain functional role in education, but the words themselves may not be the best ones to use in explaining your role to clients.

all he can to minimize the perception of threat by his client.

8. *Confrontation of Differences:* The change agent and the client should have the ability to talk out their differences. They need to be able to be frank with one another on critical matters which disturb them about their relationship. Suspicion of hidden motives should be frankly discussed and fears of exploitation brought out in the open. A relationship which tolerates the honest confrontation of differences may be a stormy one at times, but it will also be a healthy one and a strong one when the going gets tough.

9. *Involvement of All Relevant Parties:* As noted earlier, the change agent must relate not only to the client but also to those others in the community who are most directly influential in the client system. In school settings this usually means the school board and perhaps the local chamber of commerce, the newspapers, and the churches. It is most important that these other relevant parties be involved to a degree, but it is not so easy to decide what degree is appropriate. It seems fair to say, however, that those "others" you have initially identified as highly potent should at least know *that* you are there, know *why* you are there, and *approve* to some degree of your being there.

RELEVANT PRESSURE GROUPS IN MIKE'S AND STEVE'S COMMUNITIES OBVIOUSLY DID **NOT** APPROVE OF THEIR WORK. COULD THEY HAVE BEEN INVOLVED?

There are probably very few change agent-client relationships which will live up to all of these nine criteria. One must usually settle for less than the ideal. Nevertheless, it is well to keep these nine points in mind in making the best of what you have. Be aware of where you are weak and how you can change if the opportunity arises.

F. *DANGER SIGNALS*

At best the change relationship can be an exciting and rewarding experience, but there can be times when it degenerates into a stagnant and meaningless exercise which produces only frustration and disappointment. Sometimes, you may feel that you have to go ahead with a project regardless of an unpromising relationship. However, there are other times when it is really important for you to question whether to start at all. Below, we have listed a few circumstances which should tip you off to the existence of a bad relationship and a probable failure of your change effort.

1. *A Long History of Unresponsiveness to Change:* If the client is persistently indifferent, showing no interest either in changing himself or in accepting innovations of any sort, then there is probably little point in expending much energy trying to help him. "Interest," of course, is sometimes hard to measure and you should not assume that the first try will be greeted with enthusiasm. Nevertheless, even though the change agent may view his talents as unique and his ability to bring about change as impressive, he would do well to study the past history of his prospective client in dealing with similar change efforts. If the system has persistently responded to change efforts with indifference or rejection, it is probably a signal that the system is a poor bet for future efforts.

2. *The Client Wants to Use You as a Pawn:* Sometimes a client will be eager to seek outside agents only to serve his special purposes in an internal power struggle. The change agent should be very wary of this common type of exploitation.*

3. *The Client Is Already Committed to a Particular Position:* Sometimes a client will be eager to enlist the support of a change agent only to help him prove a point or to affirm a position to which he is already committed. Under such circumstances there is little opportunity for genuine reciprocity and genuine innovation in the client system.

4. *The Client Is Powerless in His Own House:* Sometimes a client will be eager to invite a change agent into the system and will be open to his ideas and wholeheartedly committed to cooperation, even though he has no real power to effect change in his own situation. Some client systems, for example, will be completely dominated by a remote and inaccessible leadership which is fundamentally hostile to change, though it may allow a certain degree of latitude to the membership to "play games." This pattern is frequently found in bureaucratic business organizations controlled by

"... An eagerness by one subgroup to change may not be a clue to readiness for change of other subgroups or of the total group or organization ..."

Lippitt[16]

Do not let

---

*In rare instances, on the other hand, if he is an opportunist and has his eyes wide open, he may be able to exploit such a situation to his own advantage.

conservative boards of directors or school districts controlled ultimately by conservative school boards.

5. *The Client Shows Many Signs of Pathology or Major Incapacity:* Change agents should learn to recognize certain signs of pathology in a client system which will make a continuing relationship difficult or impossible. Among such signs might be excessive rigidity or obsessive concern with particular kinds of issues, an excessive tendency to externalize conflicts and to see issues in rigidly black-and-white terms. The system may also suffer from some sort of incapacity, such as an inability to effectively assemble resources when needed, to communicate clearly, to assemble key members for important meetings, and to provide financial and administrative backup for inside members of the change team. Regrettably such signs of incapacity may only reveal themselves long after the project is underway. However, if such signs do appear *in large number* in very early stages, it may signal to the change agent that his efforts will be wasted. On the other hand, no single one of these signs would necessarily indicate a "no-go" situation. Indeed, various signs of pathology and incapacity may be singled out by the change agent as targets for change effort.

6. *The Client Makes a Negative Response to a Well-Managed Initial Encounter Effort:* The initial encounter is partly a test of the client as well as the change agent. If the change agent feels he has done everything right in presenting himself as "friendly," "familiar," "rewarding," and "responsive" but is then greeted with hostility or indifference, this may bode ill for the future. On the other hand, the change agent should be very cautious in drawing such a conclusion. Sometimes a tough exterior is simply one of the client's norms in dealing with initial encounters. It is important to assess the *true* feelings of the client, which may be at variance with outward appearances.

G. *HOW TO SIZE UP YOUR RELATIONSHIP*

In this chapter we have tried to identify the major facts that should be considered by the change agent in establishing a good relationship with his client. We recognize, however, that most of the readers of this manual will already be committed to various types of relationships which exhibit varying degrees of stability. For such readers to make maximum use of the material presented here, they might ask themselves five questions which would help them size up their present circumstances and give cues as to how they might improve them.

1. *Have you managed to build an inside-outside team?* This is perhaps the most important single building block of effective linking to the client system.

2. *Have you worked out a strategy for initial encounters?* Does it include friendliness, familiarity, reward, and responsiveness?

3. *Can you identify in your situation the nine features we have listed as dimensions of the ideal relationship?* Can you rate where you stand on each of these nine dimensions?

4. *Do you suspect that you have any of the danger signals which have been listed above?* If you suspect that they are present, can you mitigate their effects? Alternatively can you exit gracefully if the necessity arises?

5. If you are in the midst of an on-going relationship *are you doing all that you can to protect and maintain that relationship?* Maintenance is far easier and far less expensive than rebuilding.

Unquestionably the successful relationship is the key to successful planned change. We hope that this chapter has provided a useful introduction to the essential features which make up such a successful relationship. We recognize, however, that the chapter cannot stand alone. A good relationship continues to build as it goes along. It will be strengthened by a successful collaborative effort in diagnosis and resource acquisition, and in selecting and installing the innovation. It will also be heavily dependent upon the personality and the skill of the change agent himself and upon how clearly and adequately he has defined his own role.

"Change agents . . . have usually developed a considerable investment in their plans and are often far more committed to defending them than to attempting to understand objections to them. They are not prepared to repeat with newcomers the long process of planning which finally led them to their conclusion. And they are hardly in the most favorable position to entertain consideration of new social data or of alternative actions which might be recommended on the basis of new information. The result often is that the ultimate clients sense that their reactions will not materially influence the outcome in any way short of defeating the plan in open conflict."

Klein[17]

DIAGNOSIS

Stage II:

DIAGNOSIS: FROM PAINS TO
PROBLEMS TO OBJECTIVES

The relationship between you and your client is based on an assumption of need. You both believe that something is wrong with the status quo and you both are ready to work for something better. All too often, however, we accept this assumption of need without much further thought because we are eager to move on to "solutions." If you do not take the time to study and understand the current state of the system, your change efforts are likely to be misdirected—and disappointing in the long run. For this reason you and your client should pause, at the beginning of your relationship, and take a careful look at the system around you. This is what we mean by "diagnosis."

Diagnosis is a systematic attempt to understand the present situation. A good diagnosis is a description of the client's problem which includes the essential details of symptoms, history, and possible causes. You will probably begin this diagnostic stage with the client's "pain"—his feeling of need—as the most obvious fact. As you begin to work on diagnosis, however, you help the client to _articulate that need_: to describe the type of pain, to pinpoint its location, and to recall its origin. When diagnosis is complete, that original need should have been transformed into a _defined problem_ stated in such a way that both you and your client can work rationally on its solution.

Good diagnostic skills are not acquired easily or automatically. The change agent has to learn what questions to ask and he needs to know how to order the facts once he has them so that he can identify patterns and potential underlying causes.* This chapter will not give you these skills, but it may help you to identify the more important questions and to avoid some of the pitfalls.

The chapter has two major sections. The first describes _how_ to make a good diagnosis: it notes the principal questions that should be asked, it suggests how an inventory

STEVE AND LINDA HAD AN AWARENESS THAT THERE WAS A SERIOUS PROBLEM IN THEIR RESPECTIVE SYSTEMS BUT THEY ARRIVED AT A SOLUTION BEFORE THEY HAD DONE VERY MUCH TO FIND OUT WHAT THE **REAL** PROBLEM WAS.

"Often the client system holds well-established, not to say hidebound, views of itself; these views are hard to change, yet they must be changed if any lasting improvement is to occur. Thus much of the change process may consist of interaction between the change agent and the client-system, directed toward a questioning of the client's self-image and an acceptance of some of the diagnostic insights offered by the change agent."

Lippitt, Watson and Westley[1]

---

*He also needs to know procedures for acquiring diagnostic information. Such procedures will be discussed in STAGE III, Section B-l.

of the client system could be taken so that a balanced picture will emerge, and it stresses the need for collaboration with the client. The second section suggests some of the important *how nots,* identifying five common pitfalls encountered by change agents who have tried to work through this stage.

A. *HOW DO YOU MAKE A GOOD DIAGNOSIS?*

There are three ways to approach a diagnosis. One way is to identify the *problems,* the things that are wrong. A second way is to identify the *opportunities,* the areas of strength and maximum potential. Yet a third way is to look at the client as a *system,* a set of elements that are supposed to work together to achieve some common goal. Each approach is perfectly valid and can serve as an adequate framework for diagnosis, but the best diagnostician probably asks questions in all three categories. He starts with the pain, the need as the client feels it, but he goes on to identify what is right with the client as well as what is wrong, and finally he puts these elements together to make a coherent picture of a total system which has goals and is striving to achieve those goals.

1.   Identifying the Problems

Perhaps the most important thing to remember about diagnosis is to beware of the obvious. At the beginning the most obvious "problem" will be the pain or the need that the client says he feels. However, most problems have several layers. The topmost layer is what the physician calls the "patient's complaint." It is the initial concern which led the client to seek help. The change agent may choose to work only at this level. He may feel that the client's initial definition of what is bothering him is a valid and sufficient expression of the *real* problem. Usually, however, this will not be quite enough, and most change agents would do well to make a brief *survey of the surface symptoms.* You should therefore ask what other things are wrong: Are there any other indications that the client system has not been functioning the way it should? If the original stated problem was "low achievement test scores in this school," you may want to ask if there is also evidence of poverty, racial conflict among students, high teacher turnover, and so forth. These different problems should be listed and looked at together to see if they show any common pattern.

When you have assembled these surface symptoms you may want to probe further to get at some of the less obvious factors that lie beneath them. Here you might look for

"If the system is currently in pain or trouble, this in itself may generate defensive obstacles to accurate self-diagnosis. The pain may be so great that attention is riveted upon symptoms; the client's only clear thought is that the symptoms must be removed. At the same time, both individuals and groups may be afflicted by a motivated inability to see their own responsibility for their pain: it is hard to admit one's own shortcomings, whether they be simple disabilities or complex expressions of hostility and destructiveness. Moreover, the factors which permitted the system to get into trouble in the first place are still working to sustain the trouble and block alternative courses of action."

Lippitt, Watson and Westley[2]

64

certain attitudes and beliefs on the part of students, parents, teachers, or administrators which led to the outbreak of those symptoms. You may also find that there are features of the learning climate or the structure which breed such surface symptoms. These various *second-level elements* should be identified and weighed.

At a still deeper level, you may wish to *interpret* the evidence and infer *underlying causes.* You might conclude from a thorough analysis of surface symptoms, such as low achievement scores, the second-layer features, such as low classroom involvement and parent indifference. You might go beyond these symptoms to infer that the school is not culturally relevant, that it is not adapted, for example, to the "culture of poverty." Some might go even further to infer that the existing school system is only a manifestation of "white racism," on the one hand, or "genetic inferiority" on the other. Such "depth" interpretations may be valid and valuable in some circumstances, but a change agent should always judge them on two criteria:

> Does the interpretation stem from an honest and objective analysis of the available evidence?
> Is it useful in helping us understand what sort of *solution* we should be looking for?

Sometimes an analysis of underlying causes may suggest solutions that would never be apparent at a more superficial level. On the other hand, deep causal interpretations are sometimes quite irrelevant to the search for solutions and can delay constructive work.

As a practicing change agent you may choose to work on any level of problem definition, but you should be aware that there are other levels and that successful problem-solving can proceed from these levels also. Regardless of which level he chooses, the change agent should be sensitive to his client's self-perceptions as well as his willingness and his ability to define the problem on the *same* level.

2. Identifying the Opportunities

The change agent should avoid an exclusive focus on what is wrong with the client. He should spend some time identifying areas of strength and areas of greatest *potential* for change. There are sound practical and psychological reasons for adopting this posture. Psychologically, an accent on the positive makes the client feel less defensive and more hopeful that change can be beneficial. Moreover, from a practical point of view, the overall diagnostic picture is made much clearer when the strong points are noted. It shows the

MIKE SENSED A NEED FROM THE PERSONAL PROBLEMS THAT HIS STUDENTS WERE BRINGING TO HIM.

....

LINDA SENSED A NEED FROM THE STORMS THAT WERE BREWING OUTSIDE HER COMMUNITY AND THE NATIONAL CALL FROM LIBERAL GROUPS TO DO SOMETHING ABOUT WHITE RACISM.

WHEN STEVE SAID THE TEACHERS OF HIS SYSTEM HAD A PROBLEM OF INBREEDING AND DEEPLY ROOTED TRADITIONAL IDEAS, HE WAS MAKING AN INTERPRETATION OF SURFACE SYMPTOMS (WHICH ARE NOT DESCRIBED IN THE CASE REPORT). HOWEVER HE PROBABLY NEEDED TO DO MORE WORK ON COLLABORATIVE DIAGNOSIS WITH THE TEACHERS SO THAT **THEY** WOULD BE ABLE TO MAKE THE **SAME** INTERPRETATION.

HENRY'S AGENCY PURPOSELY SOUGHT OUT DISTRICTS WHICH HAD STRENGTH, INTERNAL RESOURCES, AND MOTIVATION TO WORK ON SOCIAL SCIENCE CURRICULUM CHANGE.

client that he can begin his change effort by using his strongest capacities and capitalizing on his areas of greatest potential.

Strengths as well as weaknesses may be identified at various levels and some things that appear to be "problems" on the surface may, in reality, indicate an underlying strength. For example, students from some cultures may resist competition in the classroom (a surface problem) because they are holding fast to cultural norms of group solidarity (a potential underlying strength). Likewise the "resistance" of students to classroom teachers of different races (a surface problem) may signify growing racial pride and a desire for independence and self-initiative (potential underlying strengths).

The change agent should take special note of the history of the client system in coping with problems. Sometimes a school or a community which seems hopelessly disorganized and strife-torn will reveal surprising resiliency and competence in coping with difficulties in certain areas at certain times. These areas and times should be noted and recorded in the diagnosis.

Internal analysis is not the only way to define opportunities for change. Sometimes the comparison to other systems gives the client ideas about what he needs and what he can do. For example, the awareness of an innovation which has been successful elsewhere will often induce an awareness of need and create the motivation for change. Outside innovations are sometimes suggestive of inside opportunities and in this sense they *create* needs. Furthermore, outside systems which appear to be successful and innovative also provide a comparative yardstick against which the client may measure his own performance.

IN MIKE'S STORY, THE SIECUS MATERIALS AND THE ADVICE ELICITED FROM EDUCATORS IN OTHER SYSTEMS WHICH HAD INSTALLED SEX EDUCATION PROGRAMS DID HELP TO MOBILIZE THE INITIATIVE OF SOME CONCERNED EDUCATORS IN HIS OWN SYSTEM. THEIR AWARENESS OF THESE OUTSIDE RESOURCES MAY HAVE SUGGESTED TO THEM WHAT THEIR OWN NEEDS WERE IN THIS AREA. HENCE THEY MAY HAVE INFLUENCED THE DIAGNOSIS.

3. Understanding the Client as a System

A long listing of problems and opportunities is not enough to give us a clear picture of the whole man or the whole organization. That is why we use the word "system" in describing the client. The change agent should try to see the client as a number of people and groups who are interrelated and at least partly interdependent, trying to work together to achieve some common goals. Usually in education these goals are not very clearly spelled out, but they are there, nevertheless, and when members of the client system sit down together to talk about their goals, they are usually able to arrive at a consensus on what their major goals are. This is a useful exercise and can be used by the change agent as a first step in getting clients to think clearly and diagnostically about their problems.

"It is useful to visualize a system by drawing a large circle. We place elements, parts, variables, inside the circle as components, and draw lines among the components. The lines may be thought of as rubber bands or springs, which stretch or contract as the forces increase or decrease. Outside the circle is the environment, where we place all other factors which impinge upon the system."

Chin[3]

66

With the goals clearly in mind the change agent and the client can begin to define the kinds of activities which have to be included and coordinated to achieve those goals. They can start by looking at their "system" as it exists today, and ask themselves if this "system" really achieves these goals. Let us illustrate this by a very simple diagram of a system.

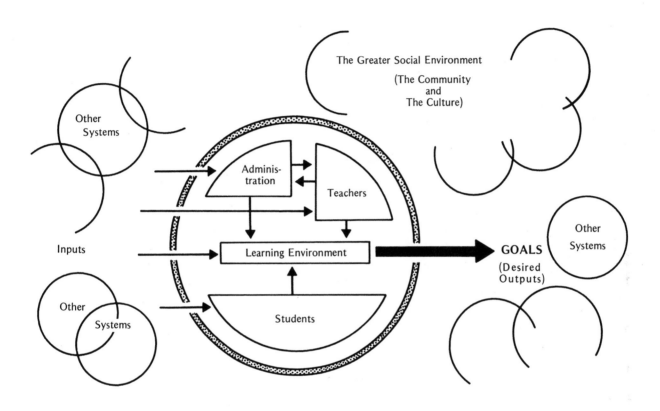

Although the diagram is greatly oversimplified, it does show the major elements that should be considered in a systematic diagnosis. First of all, it shows the goals as desired "outputs," or products which are generated by the system and dispensed to the greater community. The prime output of an educational system is an educated citizen, a graduate.

Secondly, it shows us a process through which the goals are achieved, namely a "learning environment." This learning environment, in turn, is created and sustained by people and resources within the system in addition to some from outside. Three social groups work together to keep this system going: the administration, the teachers, and the students.

Thirdly, the diagram shows the system being supplied with a continuous flow of new "inputs" from the greater environment: new ideas, new teachers, new students, and

"The classroom teacher is not an independent professional, much inspirational literature to the contrary notwithstanding. He is instead one member of the staff of a stable institution. His behavior reflects his position."

Brickell[4]

new materials. These inputs are the fuel which allows the system to keep functioning.

With the help of the diagram we can begin to spell out the critical diagnostic questions which emerge from a view of the client as a system. At the broadest level we can ask if this diagram accurately represents the major *existing elements* (e.g., have we forgotten to include the counselors as a separate element on the staff side, or the black students as a separate subculture among students?). Then we can ask if these elements are sufficient for making a system which will achieve the client's stated *goals*.

Are additional elements needed? Are there some elements that are incomplete? . . . under-supplied? . . . overloaded?

Another set of questions could be addressed to the *inputs*:

Are there enough inputs?
Are the inputs provided in the right proportions?
Do the inputs come in a form in which they can be used?

A third set of questions may be addressed to the *internal dynamics* of the system:

Are the three major subsystems really working together?
Are the student, teachers, and administrators adequately coordinated?
Do they have a clear idea of what their respective roles and functions are?
Are they able to communicate freely with one another?
Do they trust one another?

Finally, this system view suggests a fourth set of diagnostic questions pertaining to the *boundaries* of the system. As noted by the shaded area in the diagram, a system needs to be separated from the greater culture; it needs to be protected from continuous interruption and interference from outsiders so that it can fulfill its objectives smoothly and regularly. These boundaries or barriers must be partly closed but partly open. They should be designed to prevent some kinds of inputs from interfering with the system, but they must also allow responsiveness to valid needs of the greater culture. Barriers must also be designed to let in needed inputs in sufficient quantity to keep the internal system fully supplied.

"Given the intersystem nature of the school, long-lasting innovations may require . . . not only system-wide involvement in the change process, but also careful work on linkages among the system, other socialization agencies, and other key community groups."

Miles[5]

Therefore, our diagnostic inquiry should include full consideration of these barriers.

Is the system adequately protected?

Can it defend itself against attack or exploitation?*

Conversely, does it get enough stimulation from outside?

Does the school get resupplied by skilled and well-trained teachers?

Does it have a continuous influx of motivated students?

Is it able to acquire enough new materials and new ideas?

This discussion of the client as a system is not a sufficient basis for a full systemic diagnosis, but hopefully it has given you the idea of what we mean by "system." Most change agents will have their own favorite way to describe the functioning of their client and, as we have noted previously, several different approaches are probably valid and useful. The important thing is to look at the client as a totality, a functioning organism whose parts have a definable and meaningful relationship to one another.

4. Making a Diagnostic Inventory

In this chapter we have been talking about the kinds of questions that go into a good diagnosis. In this section we would like to get a little more concrete in suggesting how you might build an *inventory* of the salient diagnostic facts about your client. This should help you to be as systematic and specific as you can be in your diagnostic strategy.

At a minimum there are five questions that should always be asked and answered as part of a good diagnostic inventory:

a. WHAT ARE THE SYSTEM'S *GOALS*?

b. IS THERE AN ADEQUATE *STRUCTURE* FOR ACHIEVING THESE GOALS?

c. IS THERE *OPENNESS* IN COMMUNICATIONS?

d. DOES THE SYSTEM HAVE THE *CAPACITIES* NECESSARY TO ACHIEVE ITS STATED GOALS?

e. DOES THE SYSTEM *REWARD* ITS MEMBERS FOR WORKING TOWARDS ITS STATED GOALS?

*Many observers have commented on the extreme vulnerability of school systems to community pressures.

"The practitioner must open his eyes to the possibility that the nature of the power system with which he is dealing is not like some popular textbooks have described it. He can describe the system for himself by active observation of decision making in the system and by seeking the observations of others about the system. What have been the significant political, economic, and social decisions within recent years? What decisions currently being made seem to have the greatest importance in the system? Who are the persons in the system who have had and are presently exerting the greatest influence in these decisions? How do these influentials and other leaders work together or in competition? What are the major formal and informal subsystems in the system? What is the level of citizen participation (that is, broad, narrow, etc.) in these decisions and how is this participation manifest? Are the beliefs of the influentials and other leaders and citizens characteristically liberal, moderate, conservative? What are the critical norms in the system concerning how a leader should use his power to influence the system? What are the latent sources of power (such as, executives and workers of absentee owned corporations, teachers) that could become active in the structure? Leaders in different sectors of community living in the system have tried to answer these questions. Some of them will share this information if the school leaders will seek it."

Kimbrough[6]

These five questions can form the core of an inventory. Each question might be written at the top of a sheet of paper and underneath could be listed the related *problems* and *opportunities* which are emerging in the client system you are working with. Each question defines an area of diagnostic inquiry within which several additional questions should be investigated. Below, we consider each in more detail.

Question A: What are the **goals***?*

(1) Are the goals *clear* to both the leaders and members?

(2) Is there *consensus* on goals?

(3) Are members fully satisfied that the stated goals are *adequate*?

(4) Have leaders and members sat down to discuss what their goals are and what their goals should be?

(5) Are the goals *flexible*? Are they able to change with changing times and circumstances?

Question B: Is there an adequate **structure** *for achieving these goals?*

(1) . Is there an adequate *division of labor*?

(2) Do members have a *clear understanding* of what they are supposed to be doing in the system? (Job clarity and role clarity.)

(3) Do the different jobs and roles *fit together* as elements of a system for achieving goals?

(4) Are some of the elements necessary to make the client work as a system *missing*?

(5) Are there *weak* elements? (i.e., are some *overloaded* and others *underused*?)

(6) Are existing elements adequately *coordinated*?

(7) Is the structure *flexible*? Can it be changed to meet new conditions?

Question C: Is there **openness** *in communication?*

(1) Are major subgroups within the system (teachers, administrators, students) able to talk to one another? Can they express their *feelings* and exchange *ideas* freely back and forth?

"Communication is defined as the sum total of information about feelings, attitudes, and wishes, transmitted directly and indirectly, consciously and unconsciously. Whenever social equilibrium is upset, communication occurs. It is

70

(2) Are members of the system open to *new ideas from within*? Do they actively seek such ideas?

(3) Are they open to *new ideas from outside* (e.g., universities, consultants, other systems)? Do they actively seek these outside sources?

Question D: Do they have the necessary **capacities**?

(1) Does the system have (or can it muster) the needed *resources* in:
> people?
> time?
> money?
> materials?
> facilities?

(2) Does the staff have the necessary *skills*:
> Can the system train the people they have?
> Can the system recruit the type of people they need?

Question E: Does the system **reward** *its members for working toward its stated goals?*

(1) Are the *students* rewarded:
> for learning?
> for contributing to the learning process?

(2) Are the *teachers* rewarded:
> for innovating?
> for learning?
> for contributing to the learning process?
> for working collaboratively with students and administrators to keep the system going and to improve the system?

(3) Are the *administrators* rewarded:
> for innovating?
> for learning?
> for being open to students and teachers?

(4) Are the rewards that people get *reliable* and *predictable*?

(5) Do the rewards that people get *come soon enough* to be associated with their behavior?

(6) Are the rewards required by individuals and subgroups compatible with and *supportive of the overall goals* of the system?

the means, therefore, by which a system takes corrective action in the presence of difficulty; obviously, communication is essential if the source of difficulty is to be diagnosed. In a hierarchical structure, communication must proceed both ways, up and down. Upward communication can be effective only when the bottom and middle are free from any sense of intimidation and when the top accepts and even seeks communication from below."

Lippitt, Watson and Westley[7]

TEACHERS IN STEVE'S SYSTEM SHOULD HAVE BEEN REWARDED WITH RELEASE TIME DURING WORKING HOURS RATHER THAN BEING ASKED TO GIVE UP EVENINGS AND SATURDAYS.

UNDERSTANDABLY, LINDA WANTED INNOVATION "NOW" SO SHE COULD BENEFIT FROM IT WHILE STILL A STUDENT. THE IMPATIENCE OF STUDENTS WITH THE SPEED OF REFORM IN SCHOOLS AND UNIVERSITIES MAY BE TRACEABLE TO THIS CONCERN FOR PERSONAL BENEFIT.

71

With a list of questions such as those enumerated above, you can make a diagnostic inventory that should be of help to you and your client throughout the change process. It is not important that your list include all these questions, but it is important that you make some effort to identify and record what seem to be salient facts in each of these five general areas so that you can have a profile of the system as a whole in addition to a list of specific "problems." It is only when you have such a profile that you will be able to start making judgments about priorities for change effort. Later this inventory should also serve you and your client as a base line against which progress can be measured.

5. Collaborating on Diagnosis

The change agent should not assume the task of diagnosis as his own personal responsibility. Much of what has been said in the previous section points to the importance of involving the client in the diagnosis of his own problems. Having the client's participation in the decision-making and planning of the change process from this stage onward is an important prerequisite for his later adoption of the innovation. At the very least, you should work collaboratively so that your perceptions of problems and needs are shared by the client. At best, you should provide guidance while the client makes his own diagnosis so that the findings are acceptable by virtue of being his *own* conclusions.

B. *HOW NOT TO MAKE A DIAGNOSIS: SOME PITFALLS*

If you do decide to undertake a diagnosis before going further in suggesting and making changes, you should be aware of some of the special problems which you can get into. Although diagnosis is an important and worthwhile step in the change process, it can be a trap for the change agent if it is not handled properly. In this section, we have identified five patterns which the change agent should be careful to avoid. They are:

1. TOO MUCH DIAGNOSIS.
2. DIAGNOSIS AS A PATTERN OF AVOIDANCE.
3. USING DIAGNOSIS FOR DESTRUCTIVE CONFRONTATION.
4. IMPOSING YOUR OWN FAVORITE DIAGNOSIS.
5. FIRE FIGHTING.

We will devote a brief paragraph to each of these points.

"Change agents differ greatly in the extent to which they try to share their diagnostic orientations with the client system. Some agents believe that the client's work toward change in some cases can be best sustained by a policy which withholds some of the agent's information and analysis. At the opposite extreme, other agents think that clients should always participate fully in the fact-finding processes and that their diagnostic understanding should emerge spontaneously from their own analysis of the facts as they are revealed. These agents emphasize the client's emotional commitment to change goals which the client himself has formulated."

Lippitt, Watson and Westley[8]

1. Too Much Diagnosis

Sometimes the change agent may get stuck on diagnosis, using up most of his time and energy just in the process of defining the problem. This is not only wasteful, but may have very negative side effects. For example, the client may begin to feel so overwhelmed by the number of problems coming to light that he cannot take constructive action. On the one hand, he may be overcome by the hopelessness of his situation and on the other he may become unduly defensive. In the preceding section we suggested a systematic and comprehensive approach to diagnosis, but this does not mean you must be *exhaustive*. On most questions you will have to be satisfied with sketchy and partial answers; your diagnosis may not get you an "A" in survey research but that is not your purpose. The diagnosis should merely be adequate for giving you a good general picture of the client's situation.

2. Diagnosis as a Pattern of Avoidance

Diagnostic studies can be used by a client as a way of stalling or putting off needed changes. The call for "further study" is a familiar form of brush-off. Change-minded members of the client system may therefore be understandably restless and suspicious of prolonged diagnostic activity by the change agent. The change agent should not only get to it, he should also get *through* it and move on to the other steps in the change process.

3. Using Diagnosis for Destructive Confrontation

His perception of serious defects and urgent problems may impel the change agent to speak to his client in very blunt terms. He may do this as a deliberate attempt to unfreeze the client, to shock him into awareness of his needs and the necessity of change. If you pursue such a strategy, you should realize what the consequences could be. You should, above all, have a good estimate of *how much your client can take.* The biggest danger is that such a confrontation will destroy the relationship which you have with your client. If the client rejects you completely because he cannot accept your drastic diagnosis, then all your labors may be lost.

Even when the change agent does not intend a confrontation he should be aware of the negative power of the information he is gathering. It may make the client feel stupid, childish, naive, or incompetent. Such self-images will

"The change agent must become a 'probability expert.' He should be a gambling man, who eschews 'sure bets' and 'long shots' simultaneously. But, like a professional gambler, he should seek the bets that give him a probability edge over chance. This is the best he can do in the immediately confronting problem."

Bennis, Benne and Chin[9]

73

not give him the motivation to change. Therefore, the form and timing of diagnostic presentations is critical. Too much bad news too suddenly is a circumstance to be avoided. As noted earlier, diagnostic analysis should include positive information as well as negative and should be cast in a constructive form which makes it amenable to solutions and encourages the belief that solutions are possible.

On the other hand, if the client *can* accept confrontation, he may come to respect your honesty and may be moved to work more actively with you to bring about change. The use or avoidance of a strategy of confrontation is a difficult matter to resolve; it is a dilemma which illustrates the importance of assessing the basic *strengths* of your client as well as his weaknesses.

4. Imposing Your Own Favorite Diagnosis

It is very difficult for an expert in one particular area to be truly objective in his diagnostic approach. Most of us tend to see our own specialty as *the* important area. If our skills are in the area of human relations training, for example, we will be more inclined to see a client's problems as human relations problems; if our skills are in the area of systems engineering we are likely to see the client's problems mostly in terms of planning; if we are curriculum specialists we will see problems primarily in terms of course content. We all have these professional blinders and it is natural and inevitable that we do. However, the change agent specialist, even if he sees his role as that of a solution giver rather than a process helper (see pages 8 and 9), should be aware of his limited perspective and should consciously make an effort to avoid imposing his favorite diagnosis on the client.

5. Fire Fighting

Finally, the change agent should avoid falling into the opposite trap of attending only to those problems which the client sees as immediate and important. Meaningful and lasting changes are more likely to come about if they are based on careful planning from a well-rounded and reasonably comprehensive diagnosis. Many clients, however, may not appreciate this fact initially; they may see their problems as fires that have to be put out *now* before anything else is done, and they may want to cast you in the role of fireman. Sometimes you may have to accept such a role briefly if only to prove that you are somebody who is useful, but it is a potential trap. In the long run, fire fighting is a waste of your

*"The **diagnostic orientation** of the change agent is in many ways a self-fulfilling prediction. If he looks for difficulties in communication, for instance, he will find them; and if his help is directed toward improving communication patterns, success will demonstrate to the client system that a solution of communication problems necessarily results in a more satisfactory state of affairs ... The orientation of the change agent is a primary factor in determining the 'facts' which the client system will discover to be true about its own situation."*

Lippitt, Watson and Westley[10]

STEVE WAS ASSUMING THAT THE IN-SERVICE TRAINING NEEDS OF HIS SYSTEM'S PERSONNEL WERE RELATED TO THEIR PERCEPTIONS OF SELF AND OF OTHERS IN HIS CONVICTION THAT "THE WAY TO GO WAS THROUGH SENSITIVITY TRAINING." WAS STEVE IMPOSING HIS OWN FAVORITE DIAGNOSIS?

FROM LINDA'S POINT OF VIEW THE BLACK STUDIES PROGRAM THAT WAS ADOPTED WAS A RESULT OF SUCH "FIRE FIGHTING." THE ADMINISTRA-

energy and your client's resources, for it rarely precipitates real and lasting change.*

SUMMARY

In STAGE II we have tried to spell out the major considerations that should help in formulating a diagnosis. The key points are these:

(1) Above all, make some kind of diagnosis. Try to find out what the client needs before you charge in with "solutions."

(2) Identify and list the obvious symptoms as stated or presented by the client.

(3) Look for second-level symptoms which may underlie the obvious ones.

(4) Infer underlying causes when you see patterns of symptoms but do not assume them when you lack sufficient evidence.

(5) Identify opportunities and strengths as well as problems and weaknesses.

(6) Look at your client group as a "system" and construct a diagnostic inventory from a systemic viewpoint.

(7) Work with your client to establish meaningful, obtainable, and measurable objectives.

(8) Try to get maximum participation from members of the client system in the diagnostic process.

And finally

(9) Always consider the impact of diagnostic information on your relationship with the client. Even if you must confront the client with unpleasant facts about himself, try to do it constructively, not destructively, stressing the benefits of changing rather than the horrors of his present state, and using specifics, not general and sweeping indictments.

TORS WHO IMPLEMENTED THE COURSE DID NOT CONSIDER THE NEEDS OR DESIRES OF THE STUDENTS AND SO THE PROGRAM WAS NOT GIVEN EQUAL STATUS WITH OTHER AMERICAN HISTORY COURSES AND IT DID NOT INCLUDE "AFRICAN ORIGINS."

SYSTEMS WHICH ARE BUSY FIGHTING FIRES WILL HAVE LITTLE PATIENCE WITH COMPLEX INNOVATIONS WITH LONG-TERM OBJECTIVES, AS STEVE DISCOVERED IN THE AFTERMATH OF THE SCHOOL TAX CRISIS.

*In reading this section a few of our reviewers thought that a case could be made for fire fighting as a means of building relationships with clients and testing out innovations in new areas. Conservative communities like Steve's may not be open to comprehensive innovations until they can see the change agent as a successful fire fighter.

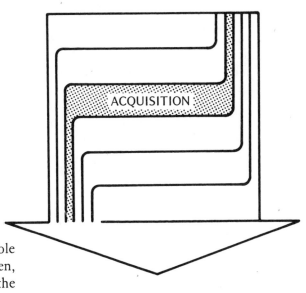

ACQUISITION

Stage III:

ACQUIRING RELEVANT RESOURCES

Resources come in many forms: they may be available as print materials, people, or products. Knowing when, where, and how to acquire them are essential skills for the change agent to have and to pass on to his clients. Before you can make intelligent decisions and choices about what changes should be made and how to make them, you and your client should have an adequate understanding of what has occurred, what is available, and what is potentially relevant and useful. The task of information retrieval can be handled competently and with a minimum of effort if the searcher thinks about what he needs before he starts and plans an acquisition strategy which makes sense in terms of his needs. This chapter should help you acquire the information you need.

The chapter has three sections. Section A lists the major purpose which information serves in each of the stages of a change project. These purposes, summarized in the acronym "DAETEIM," provide a context for thinking about resources and planning how to acquire them. Section B describes three distinct resource acquisition problems: (1) how to acquire *diagnostic* information; (2) how to build and maintain *awareness* of potential resources; and (3) how to *home in* on specific solutions. In Section C we consider how to build and maintain a permanent resource acquisition capability.

This chapter should be used in conjunction with two sections at the back of the *Guide*:

Appendix B: "Major Information Sources in Education" and
Appendix C: "Major Works on Change in Education: An Annotated Bibliography."

Appendix B lists some important and current information sources and services for education; it is especially relevant to the "homing in" process which will be described in this chapter. Appendix C is a bibliography for the change agent who wants to know more about the process of change

On June 1, 1965, Robert Manry set out from Falmouth, Massachusetts, in a 13-foot sailboat to cross the Atlantic to Falmouth, England. Manry was confident that he could make it, not because he was foolhardy or exceptionally brave, but because he had done a very thorough and systematic job of resource retrieval. He had read the accounts of past voyages; he knew the weather patterns, the currents, and the shipping traffic. He knew what food, navigational gear, emergency equipment, and clothing to provide for himself, and above all he knew his boat. He knew what it could take and how it would behave in various conditions. Manry made a successful crossing largely because he had done such a complete job of resource acquisition.

than he can learn from this *Guide*. For the change agent, acquiring knowledge about the process of change may be the most important type of resource acquisition. As you read through STAGE III keep in mind that we are only discussing resource *acquisition,* not resource *evaluation* or *utilization;* these will be the topics of subsequent chapters. Here we are concerned with "how to get it," not "what to do with it once you have it." The latter question will be taken up in STAGE IV.

A. *SEVEN MAJOR PURPOSES FOR RESOURCE ACQUISITION: D-A-E-T-E-I-M*

Resource acquisition is appropriate at any point in the change process when the change agent and his clients find that they need additional facts, ideas, materials, or equipment to help them make a decision or understand their situation more fully. These general purposes for resource acquisition are summed up in seven concepts: Diagnosis; Awareness; Evaluation-Before-Trial; Trial; Evaluation-After-Trial; Installation; and Maintenance.

1. For Diagnosis

resources which help us to understand the client system and its needs and problems.

2. For Awareness

information we get from scanning the field of education, showing the range of alternative possibilities for change: "awareness" is general knowledge of what is "new" and what is available; it provides images of solutions but not details.

3. For Evaluation-Before-Trial

information which allows us to judge and compare alternative solutions; information about "validity," "reliability," and "effectiveness" of the innovation as demonstrated in other settings.

4. For Trial

resources which allow us to demonstrate the

DISCUSSIONS BETWEEN LINDA AND HER GUIDANCE COUNSELOR AND PRINCIPAL AND HER READING OF THE SCHOOL'S OFFICIAL COURSE LISTINGS YIELDED INFORMATION FOR **DIAGNOSIS.**

STEVE HAD PLANNED TO USE **DIAGNOSTIC** DATA ON HIS SCHOOL SYSTEM COLLECTED BY A UNIVERSITY RESEARCH TEAM.

THE 326 PROGRAMS CATALOGUED BY HENRY'S "RESEARCH TEAM" WERE DISTRIBUTED TO THE SCHOOLS OF HIS REGION SO THAT THEY COULD BECOME **AWARE** OF THE RANGE OF MATERIALS THAT WERE AVAILABLE IN SOCIAL STUDIES.

INFORMATION ACQUIRED FOR **EVALUATION-BEFORE-TRIAL** IS REPRESENTED IN TALKS BETWEEN LINDA AND THE BLACK UNIVERSITY STUDENTS AND THE PROFESSORS; CONVERSATIONS BETWEEN REPRESENTATIVES OF MIKE'S SCHOOL SYSTEM AND PEOPLE FROM **SIECUS** AND FROM SYSTEMS THAT HAD TRIED TO ADOPT SEX EDUCATION PROGRAMS ARE ALSO IN THIS CATEGORY. MIKE'S GROUP UNDERRATED

78

innovation in our own setting; information which explains in detail how to try out an innovation on an experimental basis; a sample; a home demonstration.

5. For Evaluation-After-Trial

information which helps us to evaluate the success of the trial and helps us determine if the innovation solves *our* problems and meets *our* needs. Such information must be generated within the client system itself. It cannot be acquired from outside sources.

6. For Installation

resources which provide detailed information on start-up costs and requirements for new staff, training, and readjustments so that we can plan for systemwide adoption of an innovation.

7. For Maintenance

information on long-term costs and problems of upkeep; what we need to know to evaluate and to assist in maintaining the innovation on a continuing basis after installation.

The formula, "DAETEIM," corresponds roughly to the process of planned change as it is experienced by the client system. However, two points should be kept in mind in reviewing this list. First, because different client systems experience the change process differently, the sequence in which information is acquired rarely follows the order in which we have presented these purposes; for example, the clients' "awareness" of change possibilities may *precede* their "diagnosis" of a need for change in their system. Second, it is likely that resources relevant to several purposes will often be acquired simultaneously.

The following examples illustrate how certain resources can serve these DAETEIM purposes:

Example A:

If a change agent and his clients want to learn more about how their system operates and what the sources of some of their problems may be (Diagnosis), they may find

INFORMATION FROM THE LATTER ON COMMUNITY RESISTANCE AND AS A CONSEQUENCE THEIR PROJECT ALMOST FAILED.

A PREGNANT MOTHER AND CHILD AND AN EX-PRISONER WERE SOME OF THE RESOURCES USED BY MIKE IN HIS PILOT COURSE.

DATA FROM PRE- AND POST-TRIAL TESTS ADMINISTERED TO STUDENTS BY HENRY'S AGENCY AND BY MIKE IN HIS PILOT COURSE ILLUSTRATE INFORMATION FOR EVALUATION-AFTER-TRIAL.

THE OFFER OF ASSISTANCE IN STAFF TRAINING GIVEN LINDA BY ONE UNIVERSITY PROFESSOR IS ONE EXAMPLE OF AN INSTALLATION RESOURCE. MIKE'S TALKS WITH OTHER SCHOOLS THAT HAD IMPLEMENTED A SEX EDUCATION PROGRAM ALLOWED HIM TO ACQUIRE VALUABLE INFORMATION ABOUT INSTALLATION PROBLEMS.

VALUABLE MAINTENANCE INFORMATION WAS GENERATED BY HENRY'S AGENCY IN STUDYING THE SUCCESS, COST, DEMANDS, ETC. OF THE PROGRAMS IT WAS IMPLEMENTING. HENRY'S AGENCY ITSELF, BECAUSE IT WAS A PERMANENT SYSTEM WITHIN THE REGION, WAS A RESOURCE AVAILABLE FOR CONTINUING MAINTENANCE OF THE PROGRAMS ADOPTED.

help in books and articles on organization theory or systems analysis. Such information will provide them with a general understanding (Awareness) of the nature of systems and of human interaction and will familiarize them with concepts such as "role," "influence," "communication networks," etc. If they wish to explore the operation of their own system further, they might get information on procedures and instruments for diagnosis from other people's research (e.g., see opposite). They might even call in a specialist in diagnosis.

Example B:

Quite different resources might be tapped by members of a system whose purpose in resource acquisition is to *install* an innovation which they have tried, evaluated, and decided to adopt. They need facts and figures on installation costs, necessary space, training, etc. They also may want to show all members of their system how effective the pilot model has been, and so they may choose to find out how to conduct a successful demonstration. They will want to involve their own people who participated in the pilot project in the demonstration and training aspects of the installation. They may also call on outsiders who have had experience with the innovation to get advice on time, cost, and special requirements of installation. A film or other promotional material from developers or manufacturers may also be very useful at this stage.

B.   AN ACQUISITION STRATEGY

Each user has habitual methods of searching for and tracking down needed resources. Often these methods are efficient and reliable; at times they are not; but however effective they may be, they are probably going to be hard to change. The "rational" strategy which is described below should be seen in this light. It should be viewed as a model which some change agents will find compatible and others will not. However, many of the ideas about acquisition contained herein should be adoptable in part even if they are not adoptable in whole.

Problem-solving calls for three kinds of acquisition processes which parallel the purposes described earlier. The first of these is *acquisition for diagnosis*. The change agent should have a set of procedures for acquiring information about the client system so that an analysis of needs can be made, problems formulated, and objectives set along the lines described in STAGE II.

Rensis Likert, in his book **The Human Organization,** *lists several dimensions of organizational functioning based on analysis of standard questions administered in a large number of organizations. A change agent or his client might want to use the same or similar questionnaire items to get a reading on the same dimensions in his own organization.*

The results of these diagnostic activities in turn must be matched with relevant information from the environment which has potential for contributing to solutions. However, the environment presents the client with a bewildering universe of "potential" resources; therefore it is essential to limit the task of retrieval, and to settle on a sequence of steps which permits *homing in* on sources which have the highest probability of payoff. This "homing in" strategy is the second acquisition process that is required for problem-solving.

However, "homing in" assumes general knowledge of these "high probability payoff" sources. Therefore successful problem-solving also requires a general *awareness* of the potential resource universe. The key to success in matching problems with solutions is *awareness* of the resource universe. A user with a broad span of resource awareness is rarely stopped by a problem because he knows where to go to start homing in on solutions. When he hears a problem stated he says to himself: "I remember reading (or hearing or seeing) something that pertains to that problem." Once that mental connection has been made he can start "homing in" on solutions, contacting the relevant people and organizations, retrieving the relevant research, acquiring the relevant materials, etc. Figure 8 may help to illustrate the three processes.

1. How to Acquire Diagnostic Information

To make an adequate diagnosis the change agent must acquire information about the client system and about the specific problem under consideration. This information should be acquired in a systematic manner and in a form which allows quantitative comparison so that we know the dimension and importance of the problem relative to other problems in the same system and the same problem in other systems. In STAGE II we offered a number of conceptual models and suggested a number of dimensions which could be applied in making a systematic diagnosis, but we said little about the actual mechanisms that could be used for acquiring information to put in these categories. Below are listed nine such mechanisms in increasing order of complexity and difficulty.

a. *Using the Problem Vocalizer as Informant*

If the change agent enters the client system by invitation of some individual in the system, that person is usually the one individual who has the most concern or the most acute sense of the problem. This person is necessarily your initial source for diagnostic information. Keeping in mind that he may not have the clearest, most perceptive, or most objective view of the total situation, you may still use him as an informant to obtain most of what you need to know. Above all, it is important that you make face-to-face contact with this individual, preferably at his location. It is also important that you have a chance for extended contact so that you can get to know each other (see STAGE I) and so that he can really share his perceptions of the problem with you in an honest and straightforward manner.

Chronologically, Figure 8 starts at the far left with the client's situation at the time the change agent enters the picture. Moving right, we see the diagnostic information retrieval from the client's situation leading to identification of some specific problems and perhaps the statement of objectives in behavioral terms (as was attempted by Henry's agency). These pinpointed problems feed into the awareness net of the change agent, and hopefully they trigger connections in his mind with various resources (print, people, and products). With such resources in mind, he can begin to home in, acquiring a range of solution-relevant items which can be used in choosing the solution alternatives (discussed in STAGE IV).

FIGURE 8:   *Resource Acquisition Is a Three-Part Problem*

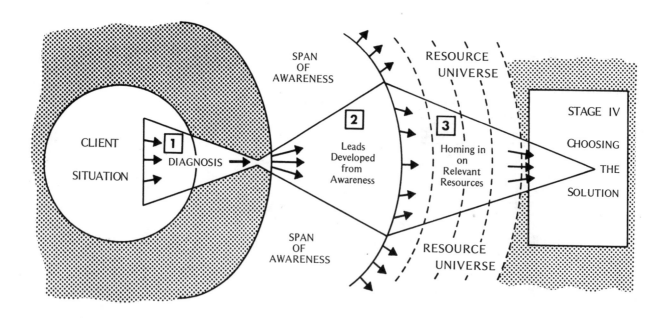

To get the most out of your informant you should follow a three-step strategy of (1) listening, (2) reflecting, and (3) inquiring.

(1) You should begin by *listening,* allowing your informant to tell as much as he wants to tell and as much as he thinks you need to know. If he is very experienced and adept at using consultative help, he may give you all you need to know without any active inquiry from you.

(2) Once he has stated the situation to his satisfaction you should *tell him what you heard,* restating as accurately and concisely as you can what you thought he was saying. When you are done, ask him if that is what he said. If you are really communicating with each other, he will agree with your *reflection* of his statement; however, there may be points of misunderstanding or unclarity. Repeating the same statement-and-reflection process again and again, the two of you will gradually move toward consensus.

(3) Finally, when you have consensus on his story you may want to make some more systematic *inquiry* or probing, especially to fill in gaps to complete a systematic diagnostic inventory such as we presented earlier.

Reflection is also a good way to build a relationship or to resolve a conflict. The end product is "trust," in the literal sense of knowing where the other man stands.

Recording diagnostic information received from human sources (vocalizers, key informants, groups, etc.) can be a tricky problem. Most interviewers prefer not to take extensive notes while the interview is in progress because this interferes with their ability to listen, reflect, observe, and respond. If accuracy and comprehensiveness of the data are very important, there is no substitute for the tape recorder, but if only highlights and overall impressions are needed, the simplest procedure is to record your summary of what was said *immediately after* the interview either on paper or into a tape recorder. An open-ended form such as might be generated from pages 69-72 would be very useful for this purpose. Do not record more than you need unless systematic *research* on the client system is what you are trying for.

b. *Using Key Informants Within the System*

It is usually important to acquire diagnostic information from more than one source and, in a complex client system, from more than one level and more than one faction. The same general rules apply to the use of key informants as apply to the problem vocalizer described above, with one *significant exception:* you cannot assume that key informants will be eager to tell you their views of the problem because it is *you, not they,* who are initiating the contact. You need to establish your legitimacy and sincerity as a diagnostician and a consultant (see again STAGE I). You may have to start by telling them why you are in the system in the first place and why you are asking them questions. For this purpose face-to-face contact is vital. Once you have established yourself with them as a trustworthy individual who is sincerely trying to help, you can proceed through the listening-reflecting-inquiring sequence.

c. *Group Interviewing*

When time is short and it is essential to get a variety of perspectives, the change agent may ask the spokesman from the client system to bring together a representative group (e.g., principal, assistant principal, older and younger teachers, white and black student leaders, etc.). With the assembled group he can proceed through the same listening-reflecting-inquiring sequence, but there are important differences from individual interviewing: e.g., he should observe how the members of the group are relating to each other, the extent to which they defer to authority, and their reticence about disagreeing or speaking up to add to or to correct the story. The interviewer should be able to test the group's willingness to open up on what the real issues are. In order to do this, he needs to have a good understanding of group dynamics and preferably some experience in human relations training. With such a background, he will be able to derive much valuable diagnostic information not only from *listening* to what members of the group say, but also from *observing* how they react to one another.

d. *Observation*

Using human resources in face-to-face interchange as described in the three techniques listed above provides *verbal* information, but there is also an important dividend: the chance to observe the people in the system, how they relate to you and to each other, how they act and react in response to a number of situations. It is also sometimes valuable to make site visits solely for the sake of observing what is going on without asking questions, provided that you have a reasonably clear idea of what you are looking for. (Understanding the points made in STAGE II should help on this.) Being a good observer, especially of anything as complex as a school or a classroom, requires training and experience, but it

LINDA HAD A NUMBER OF FACE-TO-FACE EXCHANGES WITH DIFFERENT MEMBERS OF HER SYSTEM. SHE COULD PROBABLY GET AS MUCH DIAGNOSTIC INFORMATION FROM HOW THEY REACTED TO HER AND HOW WILLING THEY WERE TO TALK TO HER AS SHE COULD GET FROM WHAT THEY ACTUALLY SAID.

is the kind of training and experience that all change agents should develop.

An alternative or supplementary source of observational information is *other outsiders* who have known the client system for a number of years. The editor of the local newspaper is one favorite source for this kind of information, but other outside consultants who have worked with the system from time to time should also be able to provide valuable insights.

e. *Observing and Measuring System Outputs (Intended and Unintended)*

Hard evidence of the attainment of meaningful educational objectives is nearly impossible to obtain from our schools today. Although there is much pressure to move toward systems which are "accountable" for attainment of measurable learning objectives, the availability of such hard data is a long way off in almost all school environments. However, there are some telltale signs that things are not going well, such as high teacher turnover, high frequency of disciplinary actions, and high dropout rates. There are probably fewer reliable signs on the positive side. College placements and national honors are likely to reflect neighborhood and parentage as much as schooling. On the other hand, high attendance rates at PTA meetings, passage of school tax millages, and even high attendance at school sporting events may indicate a healthy community concern and support. Even the printed outputs of the system—newsletters, catalogues, yearbooks, etc.—may reveal a good deal about the range of courses and activities, the degree of participation, the orientation of the curriculum, the diversity of student interests, etc. It is not possible to provide a detailed guide to these varied sources for diagnostic information but only to point out what a variety of potential sources there are. The change agent should be flexible in his search for data which can be retrieved from existing and readily available records.

f. *Organizing a Self-Diagnostic Workshop for the Client System*

Change agents with considerable skills in human relations, group work, or conference management may want to initiate a series of meetings throughout the client system where members representing all levels (perhaps including students, parents, and community leaders in addition to teachers and administrators) sit down together to make an assessment of the problems of their system. This procedure, though complex and risky, has two special advantages: first, it allows genuine confrontation of problems and involvement

STEVE MIGHT HAVE BENEFIT-TED IN A NUMBER OF WAYS FROM AN INTERVIEW WITH THE EDITOR OF THE LOCAL PAPER EARLY IN HIS PROJECT. THE EDITOR COULD HAVE TIPPED HIM OFF TO PROBABLE COMMUNITY REACTIONS AND AT THE SAME TIME MIGHT HAVE BEEN MORE WARMLY DISPOSED TO THE PROJECT AT LATER STAGES BECAUSE HE HAD BEEN INFORMED EARLY.

HENRY'S AGENCY WAS ABLE TO MEASURE OUTPUTS IN BE-HAVIORAL TERMS BECAUSE IT HAD THE STAFF, THE SKILLS, AND THE RESOURCES TO DO IT.

BOTH LINDA AND MIKE MEA-SURED "OUTPUTS" BY ACQUIRING AND EXAMINING COURSE CATALOGUES, BUT THEY HAD TO DO SOME DIG-GING TO GET THEM.

SOME OF THE MEETINGS IN MIKE'S CITY IN WHICH COM-MUNITY LEADERS, THE SCHOOL BOARD, ADMINISTRA-TORS, TEACHERS, AND STU-DENTS WERE DEBATING AND DISCUSSING THE MERITS OF SEX EDUCATION MAY HAVE HAD SOME OF THE QUALITIES OF A SYSTEM-WIDE SELF-DIAG-NOSIS.

in initiating change on the part of members at all levels; and, second, if done well, it provides a more detailed and more accurate accounting of the prevailing situation; in other words, the diagnosis which results may be better than it would be if fewer individuals representing fewer perspectives were taking part. We need much more research and development on techniques for successfully managing these system-wide self-diagnostic efforts.

g. *Using an Outside Diagnostic Research Team*

If the system is very large and the problem is pervasive and if there are considerable financial resources available for diagnosis, the change agent might well consider contracting with a university, a social research center, or a private consulting firm to administer survey instruments for a thorough, systematic, and scientific job of diagnosis or needs assessment. The problems and advantages of this type of strategy are well catalogued in many of the readings listed in Appendix C. However, the underlying problem will probably be *perceived relevance*. In spite of mountains of data and tests of statistical significance it may be hard to convince a client that a diagnosis arrived at by a team of outside experts is really relevant and valid unless the client system itself is involved as collaborator in the development of measures and the collection of the data.

h. *Collaborative Systematic Diagnostic Program*

Probably the most elaborate and elegant procedure for acquiring diagnostic information is a combination of (f) and (g) above, wherein an inside-outside team organizes a program for system self-diagnosis using trained outside experts as trainers and instrument developers for the members of the client system. This strategy can have many variants and many components; a number of these are identified in Appendix A: Strategies and Tactics (e.g., see "action research," "collaborative action inquiry," and "survey feedback").

i. *Continuous Quantitative Diagnostic Monitoring*

The most sophisticated type of diagnostic information is that which is carried on *by the client system for itself* on a continuous or periodic basis using objective behavioral criteria recognized as legitimate and valid by insiders (including students) and by outside experts. Such a diagnostic

STEVE'S CASE ILLUSTRATES ONE OF THE HAZARDS OF LOOSE COLLABORATION WITH A UNIVERSITY-BASED TEAM. BECAUSE THE UNIVERSITY TEAM DID NOT HAVE THE SAME TIMETABLE COMMITMENTS, THEY WERE UNABLE TO PROVIDE DIAGNOSTIC DATA AT THE TIME THEY WERE NEEDED.

....

IN CONTRAST HENRY'S AGENCY DEPENDS FOR ITS SURVIVAL ON THE RELEVANCE AND TIMELINESS OF ITS RESEARCH DATA. IF SUCH AN AGENCY HAD BEEN AVAILABLE TO STEVE IT MIGHT HAVE BEEN ABLE TO MAKE A VITAL CONTRIBUTION.

capability would be the equivalent of the "accountability" which so many outside experts are now insisting schools must develop. To design and install such a monitoring system is a major change project in itself, requiring the employment of all the skills, artistry, and know-how that a change agent could muster. However, a system which had such a capability would have moved a long way toward genuine self-renewal.

2. How to Build and Maintain Awareness of the Resource Universe

Awareness is the key to an intelligent overall acquisition strategy. The change agent is not, and cannot be, a universal expert. Rather he should be a knowledge broker, a linker to outside resources who can maintain a generalist's perspective in relation to specific innovations. He should be "a mile wide and an inch deep" when it comes to specific "facts." He should have the widest possible span of awareness of the resource universe while retaining his capacity to "zero in" on detailed sources when the diagnosis fits and the time is ripe. In this section we try to suggest some ways in which he can build and maintain this generalist's perspective.

a. *Building Awareness*

Usually if we consider ourselves as "professionals" in a given field, we have a broad span of awareness within that field. We were trained in it and carry with us from that formal background a general set of categories associated with names and books and sometimes places.

If you are new to a field, however, or if your training is outdated, you should build or rebuild that awareness memory bank by reading one or two introductory texts on the subject or, if possible, taking an introductory university course. Only in introductory courses and texts are we likely to find this kind of overview presented in an organized and comprehensive fashion.

b. *Maintaining Awareness*

For *maintaining awareness* a different set of media and mechanisms is appropriate. The most useful tools for maintaining awareness are periodicals, personal acquaintances, and a knowledge of information systems.

(1) *Periodicals and Mass Media*

The most direct and specific advice we can offer in this *Guide* is:

SUBSCRIBE TO THE PERIODICALS

and read them, or scan them as they come in.

There are several interesting periodicals which cover a broad range of educational topics very concisely. Through the periodicals you can keep yourself informed on what is new in the field, what is fully developed, and what is projected for the future. Periodicals also provide enough information to steer you to more specifics when you need them. At the beginning of Appendix B, we list several good periodicals of general educational interest with their price, frequency of issue, and address. We suggest that you check this listing.

There are other mass media besides periodicals which are important for maintaining awareness although they are usually not as reliable. Some popular publications such as the *Saturday Review* and the *National Observer* regularly carry education columns and stories. Newspapers and, to a lesser extent, television should also be scanned for relevant items but the coverage is likely to be spotty and sporadic, and there is no good way to file such items for future reference.

(2)   *A Personal Acquaintance Network*

Maintaining personal contacts with a variety of knowledgeable people is very important. Many studies have shown that the most innovative people in any field have numerous contacts and encounters with others outside their system, people who are different from themselves in background, role, perspective, skill, and knowledge. Maintaining a personal-contact network keeps the change agent aware of new developments in a variety of fields and within easy reach of people who can provide more detailed information when and if he needs it.

Activities likely to build and maintain this interpersonal network are:

- attendance at professional meetings
- visits to other locations (for whatever purpose)
- phone calls to outsiders (for whatever purpose)
- interacting with people who are in different roles and different systems whenever the opportunity arises

LINDA MADE GOOD USE OF HER MOTHER'S PERSONAL NETWORK OF CONTACTS WITH UNIVERSITY PROFESSORS AND OTHER RELEVANT RESOURCE PERSONS.

- maintaining good contacts and a habit of consulting with insiders and colleagues who work with you is also important (see quote opposite).

(3)   *The Where-When-and-How of Information Systems*

Approaching an information system is likely to be a forbidding prospect for the uninitiated, *but it should not be*! Most libraries, clearinghouses, document centers, data banks, and information services are manned by friendly, helpful people who can quickly steer new users in appropriate directions. For the change agent the critical factor is *awareness* of these sources, awareness of the types of information services and centers available for educators, where they are located, and how they can be contacted. Appendix B of the *Guide* provides a basic listing. Although this directory is not comprehensive, it is worth scanning and remembering as part of your "awareness bank." Each listing provides the essential information which allows you to start "homing in" on the details of problem or solution areas.

Because there continues to be rapid development in the information field, it is likely that Appendix B will be dated soon after publication. For this reason it is important to watch the periodicals for changes in programs and services (closings, openings, shifts in locale and emphasis, amalgamations, etc.).

3.   "Homing In" on a Specific Problem and/or Solution

As you and your client begin to focus on the problem and have some notion of possible solutions, you should develop a strategy for "homing in," acquiring the information and materials you will need for -E-T-E-I-M (Evaluation-Before-Trial, Trial, Evaluation-After-Trial, Installation, and Maintenance). There are probably as many ways to "home in" as there are change agents, but the optimum strategy proposed below may contain elements you will want to adapt to your own needs. We suggest a six-step sequence:

A Homing in Strategy

a.   overview from written source
b.   overview from knowledgeable person
c.   observe "live" examples
d.   obtain evaluative data
e.   obtain innovation on trial
f.   acquire a framework for evaluation-after-trial

89

"As you move outward from your own head, the first information sources you meet are other people—co-workers, family, friends. They may not know what you need to know, but it doesn't cost much to ask. People are 'switching mechanisms'; they provide leads to information they lack themselves."

Paisley[1]

"Thanks to an emerging national network of information centers in most fields of specialized knowledge, and thanks to a new appreciation of the role of other people in the flow of information, the strategy of moving 'from people to print and back to people again' can yield information of any needed depth."

Paisley[2]

"When people don't know the answer, the leads they provide are often to print sources. That's how we get 'from people to print.' The great encyclopedias, the specialized reference books, and the scholarly journals deserve the respect our society accords them. If a visitor from another planet were to drop in, who can doubt that the collections of the Library of Congress would weight his opinion of us more than Saturn V on its launching pad?"

Paisley[3]

a. *Acquire an Overview from a*
    Comprehensive Written Source

Even if you have a very specific plan in mind, it is good policy to become generally knowledgeable about research, development, theory, and past practice in the area on which you have chosen to focus your attention. This usually means reading or scanning a current textbook or current scholarly review article in that domain. In many areas of educational reform there are conflicting theories and competing innovations. To be on firm ground, you should have an overview of the field even if you are committed to one or another of these competing forces.

A scholarly review article, a book or an encyclopedia entry should give you a feel for: (1) the scope of the topic, (2) the work that has been done in various places at various times, (3) the level of solid *research* understanding of the topic, and (4) valuable leads to more detailed sources.

However, such general review sources probably will *not* give you information such as: (1) the range of innovations available, (2) enough information to evaluate specific innovations, (3) enough information to diagnose specific problems, or (4) practical suggestions about what to do. These drawbacks can be remedied by referral to more popular books or articles and to knowledgeable human resources.

b. *Contact at Least One Person*
    Who Has Had Direct Experience

Usually there will be others who have (successfully or unsuccessfully) done what you are contemplating doing. You should talk to at least one of them, preferably in person, as part of your homing in process. Such individuals will give valuable information for evaluation-before-trial. They will give you leads as to relevance, workability, and problems which promoters of an innovation are unlikely to divulge voluntarily. If you, as a change agent, find this contact person to be articulate and informed you should also consider him as a potential on-site consultant and a resource for your client.

c. *Observe the Innovation in a*
    Concrete or a "Live" Form

If the innovation under consideration is available in a printed or packaged form which can be borrowed or sampled, you should obtain it. In recent years complex innovations have become available in multi-media kits and packages which may give a more complete impression of how the innovation will really work when installed.

STEVE MIGHT HAVE MADE GOOD USE OF OVERVIEWS FROM COMPREHENSIVE WRITTEN SOURCES IN HOMING IN ON SENSITIVITY TRAINING. SEVERAL SUCH SOURCES ARE NOW AVAILABLE (e.g., Campbell, J.P. and Dunnette, M.D., "Effectiveness of T-Group Experiences in Managerial Training and Development," *Psychological Bulletin*, August 1968) AND MOST OF THEM SUGGEST THAT SUCH TRAINING INVOLVES HIGH RISK AND DOES NOT ALWAYS ACHIEVE DESIRABLE OUTCOMES.

MIKE AND LINDA BOTH MADE GOOD USE OF FACE-TO-FACE PERSONAL CONTACTS IN THE EARLY STAGES OF THEIR PROJECTS TO HOME IN ON PRINT, PRODUCT, AND PEOPLE RESOURCES. MIKE'S DISCUSSIONS WITH THE SCIENCE CONSULTANT AND LINDA'S INTERVIEW WITH THE BLACK COLLEGE STUDENT AND THEN THE EDUCATION PROFESSOR WERE ESPECIALLY CRITICAL.

....

HENRY NOTES THAT HIS AGENCY COULD HAVE SAVED CONSIDERABLE TIME, EFFORT, AND MONEY IF THEY HAD FIRST GONE TO EXPERTS SUCH AS THOSE INVOLVED IN "PROJECT SOCIAL STUDIES."

In addition, if the innovation is installed and operating somewhere, you should go and look at it, asking yourself three key questions:

Is it really *working* for them?
Is it really *benefitting* them?
Will it really *work for us*? (i.e., are there obvious differences between these users and our clients which might make it unfeasible in our setting? Conversely, are there positive advantages to our setting which might make the innovation more effective for us than it is for them?)

d. *Obtain Evaluative Data*

Even if you are really "turned on" by an innovation after observing it, you should still try to find scientific evaluative data to check out your impressions before you or your client actually make a commitment. Such data may or may not confirm what you have already concluded about the innovation and what its promoters claim. In looking for evaluative information, do not restrict yourself to one source if more than one is available. Too often evaluations are partisan and partial, especially when made by the innovation's author or promoter. The more disinterested the evaluation and the more the evaluator adheres to scientific rules of evidence, the more you can count on his results.

Evaluative data are often found in formal reports to the government (hence, they are available through ERIC: see Appendix B) or are reported in research journals. This means the language may be technical and the findings difficult for laymen to interpret. If you cannot understand what is written or if the implications for practitioners are not clear, it may be worth your while to call the author/evaluator on the phone and get him to chat with you informally. You will probably find that he has thought a great deal about practical implications and can offer his informed judgment in a clear and non-technical way. You will also probably gain more cooperation if you indicate that you have read his research.

If you find that no "hard" data are available to evaluate the innovative program you are considering, you should try to acquire "soft" data in the form of personal evaluations by at least two persons representing different perspectives, e.g., one man who has tried it, and one man who has critically observed someone else try it.

e. *Obtain the Innovation on Trial*

If your pre-trial evaluation data confirm your judgment to proceed, you should attempt to acquire the innovation or

MIKE'S GROUP APPARENTLY WAS AWARE THAT SEX EDUCATION CURRICULA HAD FAILED ELSEWHERE AND HAD AROUSED PUBLIC ANTAGONISM BUT THEY JUDGED THAT THEY WOULD NOT ENCOUNTER SUCH DIFFICULTIES BECAUSE OF THE WAY THEY WERE WORKING WITH THEIR COMMUNITY.

"Print sources have their shortcomings, when the needed information is very detailed or very special. Then we would rather talk to an expert, so that he could explain, exemplify, and adapt information to our needs."

Paisley[4]

the necessary materials for use in an experimental trial-and-demonstration in your client system. This will usually involve direct contact and negotiation with the developers and/or suppliers. In asking for materials or other resources on a trial basis, make sure you also inquire about the availability of written materials on *costs of installation and maintenance, performance specifications, and claims* concerning benefits (short-term and long-term), supplementary materials required and provided (e.g., manuals), limiting conditions, guarantees of quality and reliability, and *problems that might be encountered in terminating the innovation at a later date.* There probably won't be many answers to these questions, but if you feel that the supplier is being evasive and you find you are getting *none* of your questions answered, it is probably a good clue that you should search elsewhere.

WAS STEVE FORCED TO RELY TOO HEAVILY ON HIS OWN EXPERIENCE AND HIS OWN FEELING THAT SENSITIVITY TRAINING WAS "THE WAY TO GO"? ONE OF THE PROBLEMS WITH COMPLEX INNOVATIONS IN EDUCATION IS THE LACK OF SPECIFICATION OF THE CONDITIONS REQUIRED FOR TRIAL, INSTALLATION, AND MAINTENANCE.

f.   *Acquire a Framework for Evaluating the Results of the Trial*

Even before an actual trial effort takes place, the client system should be committed to a plan or procedure for evaluating the trial and making a "go—no-go" decision. This is critical because, all too often, a so-called "trial" experiment results in permanent adoption simply because the client has no plan for evaluating and, if necessary, rejecting what does not work; he accepts it because it is there and for no better reason.

In establishing a framework for evaluation, your first information need is for criteria on which to base a judgment. In STAGE IV we will discuss some of the criteria which are relevant under three headings: "potential benefit," "workability," and "diffusibility." At the trial stage, you and your client should be collecting *your own* data, judgments, and impressions about *installation* costs and problems and *maintenance* costs and problems.

The criteria used in available evaluation reports on the same innovation in other settings will also provide ideas for criteria to be applied in your setting. Of special value (and special rarity) are research evaluations which use the fulfillment of specific behavioral objectives as criteria. Because of the specificity and observability of the measures in such cases, you will have little trouble adapting them for use in your setting. There is a current trend in educational research and evaluation toward more and more specificity and behavioral statement of objectives and outcomes; hence in future years we may look to the research literature for more meaningful guidance in designing post-trial evaluations.

If an innovation is expensive, complex, or unusually risky, you may want to acquire the services of an outside

"Users tend to adopt innovations for their practical utility without benefit of a trial stage and then continue to use them as part of their practice (unless the innovations create major woes)."

Wolf [5]

HENRY'S "PLANNING TEAM" "SET UP A RESEARCH STUDY TO DETERMINE TO WHAT EXTENT WE ACHIEVED OUR SPECIFIED OBJECTIVES." (P. 34)

professional evaluator or evaluation team. As yet there are few individuals available to school systems who are really skilled in evaluation, but the numbers are growing and the need for them is recognized increasingly at all levels. Thus, a number of regional laboratories, Title III centers, and state education departments are working on training programs for evaluators and quality assurance specialists to fill this sort of function. With the help of some leads in Appendix B, a vigorous search should get you an experienced evaluator if you and your client decide that such help is necessary.

In laying out this proposed strategy for "homing in," we may have accentuated the positive intentionally in the belief that most change agents and their clients do not try hard enough to reach out for available resources. However, we also recognize that you will not always succeed in getting the information you want. This fact should not stop you, however, because there are always human resources, people with relevant experience and knowledge from which you can benefit. Moreover, as we shall explain in STAGE IV, it is also possible for the client to *invent* his own innovation to meet a specified need if he cannot find adequate outside resources.

C.   *BUILDING A PERMANENT CAPACITY FOR RESOURCE ACQUISITION*

Acquiring diagnostic information, maintaining awareness, and *homing in* are skills and procedures which all change agents should know and have, but they are also activities that client systems should learn to initiate on their own. Resource acquiring know-how is a large part of building a *self-renewal* capacity (see STAGE VI for more discussion of this concept). Above all, your client system should be encouraged to build and maintain a broad span of awareness of the outside world. This means establishing and maintaining meaningful human links with other school systems, universities, state education departments, regional laboratories, regional centers of various sorts, and the resource mechanisms set up by the professional associations, foundations, and the U.S. Office of Education. These linkages are built and maintained through developing habits of visiting, being visited, phoning, reading, and generally being curious and openminded about the larger social environment.

Extensive use of a variety of resources is not a common practice among innovating educators (see quote opposite). Frequently there is substantial resistance to resource retrieval as a result of people's negative impressions about its "helpfulness." In other words, they do not believe that there is anything in outside resource systems worth acquiring. The change agent can encourage his clients to become more

"If user apathy were a disease, there would be two major syndromes in education. The first is the 'Don't confuse me with the facts' syndrome, which all too often characterizes the attitude of the administrator or practitioner who is

familiar with the advantages of using outside resources. Below are listed several suggestions for helping clients learn more about resources and resource retrieval:

1. *Provide a supportive atmosphere* for the retrieval of resources in the system. Get official recognition and legitimation of the need for the use of resources through the provision of time, money, etc., to carry out retrieval and acquisition operations.

2. *Maintain existing interaction and search norms* (e.g., the "sharing" of teaching practices). It is always easier to get people to "add on" new behavior than to replace one kind of behavior with another. Some of the old habits of acquiring information are good habits. Your goal should be to support and supplement those good habits.

3. *Seek out and use "creative practitioners" and "in-house experts"* in the client system. They may supplant the need for more difficult acquisition outside the system. Also, overlooking their contributions could create antagonism.

4. *Generate open but realistic expectations* about the performance capabilities of the new information systems and services. They should not be oversold or undersold. Any resource should be approached with a realistic view of what it is capable of giving. The person who depends too heavily on one resource for a total solution to his problems is bound to be disappointed. The goal of this chapter has been to show how the acquisition of a variety of resources can be useful to the client system. They each have their own special purposes. When utilized in combination they can provide substantial impetus for the change process.

5. *Assess the impact of past experience with resource retrieval* on the prevailing attitudes in the client system about retrieval. Experience may have provided a greater sophistication about innovations and resources, but it also may have led to some disillusionment about the problems in *translating* information. Therefore, the change agent may have to work hard initially to turn these expectations around, by demonstrating *successful* resource acquisition and by expanding his client's awareness of both resources and resource-acquiring strategies.

afraid that if he gets information that goes counter to what he is doing, he'll be expected to change. The other syndrome in this dread disease of information apathy is the 'Please mother, I'd rather do it myself' syndrome, frequently found in the innovative educator and certainly in the educational researcher, who would much rather do an experiment or demonstration all over again than find out whether it has worked some place else."

Clemens[6]

"Libraries, like so many institutions these days, are the province of prophets. Some predict triumphs of technology: 'procognitive systems' faster than a speeding electron, more powerful than an army of librarians, able to span vast document collections at the pulse of a light pen."

Lanham[7]

94

Among other things he should show his clients how creative use of *human* resources can assist and simplify the retrieval, translation, and adaptation of *print* and *product* resources.

6. *Demonstrate* how acquiring resources can pay off by illustrations from successful cases; reinforce the message that there is useful information "out there" which can be acquired.

7. *Structure resource acquisition* and teach clients how to structure resource acquisition so that they do not get lost in stacks of irrelevant or overtechnical print. This chapter should help in that structuring.

8. *Localize resources and resource system terminals* wherever you can. The first law of information use is *proximity*. People, print, and product resources of *high quality* should be made available locally wherever possible. The phone is a very significant tool in resource acquisition since it makes almost all people resources proximate.

In this chapter we have outlined the use of resource acquisition strategies in problem-solving. The change agent and the client system must decide how much time, money, and energy they can or should devote to resource acquisition for their particular problems. This must be weighed against the goals they wish to achieve and their purposes for embarking on the process. When you are spending time, money, and energy on resource acquisition, you should always have a reasonably clear idea of why you are doing it, especially if your purpose is something other than maintaining "awareness." If you are too broad and loose in defining your needs and in defining relevance, you will be swamped with information you cannot use. On the other hand, if you define your information needs too narrowly, you may overlook some of the critical facts which are needed to make problem-solving and innovating effective and beneficial. In a knowledge universe which is expanding rapidly, change agents and their clients need to develop the capacity to *plug in* and to *home in* on the contents of this universe whenever and wherever they need help. This chapter together with Appendices B and C should help them build such a capacity.

"... You'd better have the information extremely accessible to the user. It comes through loud and clear from user studies in the information science field, that the first information source used and the most frequently used information source is the one which is closest at hand to the user—and hold on now—**even when the user does not think it is very good.** Bad information will drive out good information, if good information is inaccessible."

Clemens[8]

DID HENRY'S AGENCY HAVE AN ADEQUATE RATIONALE FOR ACQUIRING INFORMATION ON 326 PROGRAMS? THE GREAT COSTS OF SUCH EXHAUSTIVE ACQUISITION EFFORTS SHOULD ALWAYS BE WEIGHED AGAINST THE PROBABLE BENEFITS.

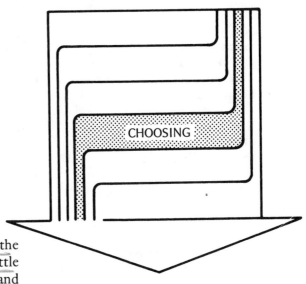

CHOOSING

Stage IV:

CHOOSING THE SOLUTION

With a problem and a lot of relevant information, the client needs to be able to derive some implications and settle upon a potential solution. This is the most creative and interesting task in the process of change, but it is a task that most change agents know little about. Some will leave the client at this point, assuming that he knows what is best for himself and knows how to pick out the best solution when he has retrieved all the "facts" and has a good diagnosis. This is not a safe assumption, however. Very few people are really skilled at generating solution ideas and choosing even when they have a clear idea of what they need. This chapter may provide a few guidelines for helping a client system generate solutions and make the right choices.

We will suggest a four-step *sequential process* that could be followed in choosing solutions, starting from diagnosis and information retrieval, and working through to the point where we are ready for implementation. The chapter is organized around these four steps:

"Our everyday experience tells us that our insight into the cause of a problem leads us spontaneously to take the right remedial actions. But the literature of change shows that this is far from being true in most efforts of social or psychodynamic change."

Lippitt, Watson and Westley[1]

STEP A: *DERIVING IMPLICATIONS FROM RE-SEARCH*
STEP B: *GENERATING A RANGE OF SOLUTION IDEAS*
STEP C: *FEASIBILITY TESTING*
STEP D: *ADAPTATION*

In proposing these four steps we are fully aware that there is going to be no one sure path to the "right" solution, and there is going to be no one solution which is "right" for a given problem. There are usually many possible solutions and many possible paths. The processes suggested below should therefore be viewed as one potential route among many. Our object in presenting this sequence is to suggest to the change agent a number of steps that *might* help his client select an innovation.

Step A, "deriving implications," is an activity which should always accompany resource acquisition, particularly when the resource information is in the form of research reports and abstract analyses. In this step we ask the question, "What does this information say about this setting and this specific problem?"

Step B, "generating solution ideas," moves you from description and analysis into the formulation of action alternatives. Some of these will be suggested by diagnosis (STAGE II), some others by implications derived from research (Step A). Still others may be generated by the client working with the change agent in brainstorming activities. Step B should leave you with a range of possible solution ideas in various stages of completeness. Having this range of possibilities puts the client in a better position to make rational and meaningful choices.

In Step C, "feasibility testing," you evaluate these alternative solution ideas according to a number of criteria. The three primary considerations in evaluation are *benefit, practicability,* and *diffusibility.* "Benefit" simply means "How much good would it do if it worked?" "Practicability" means "Will it really work, especially with this particular client system?" "Diffusibility" means "Will it be accepted by members of the client system?" By asking these questions you should be able to reduce the number of possible solutions to one or two.

Finally, in Step D, which we call "*adaptation,*" the preferred solutions are shaped to the specific needs and circumstances of the client. Hopefully your screening process will have eliminated the less developed and less relevant solutions, but some work may still need to be done to "customize" the innovation for your own particular client. Sometimes such adaptation can only take place after installation and diffusion activities have begun (i.e., in STAGE V of the overall planned change sequence).

In real life choosing a solution is not likely to follow such a clear-cut A-B-C-D sequence. For example, you may find that after *feasibility testing* you need to go back and generate some additional solution ideas, or that in *adaptation* you need to derive some more implications from research studies. This recycling applies equally to the previous stages of "diagnosis" (STAGE II) and "resource acquisition" (STAGE III). Figure 9 tries to suggest these sequences and the ways in which they relate to each other.

As illustrated in this diagram, choosing the solution cannot easily be separated from diagnosis and resource acquisition activities. At each step in the selection process you may have need for additional diagnostic information and additional resources of various kinds. You may even have to cycle back from STAGE V, i.e., when you meet unexpected resistance in the client system you may have to do more work on adaptation or you may even have to select another innovation.

FIGURE 9:   Steps in Choosing the Solution

The four steps involved in generating and choosing solutions are related to the other stages of a change project as partially illustrated in the diagram below.

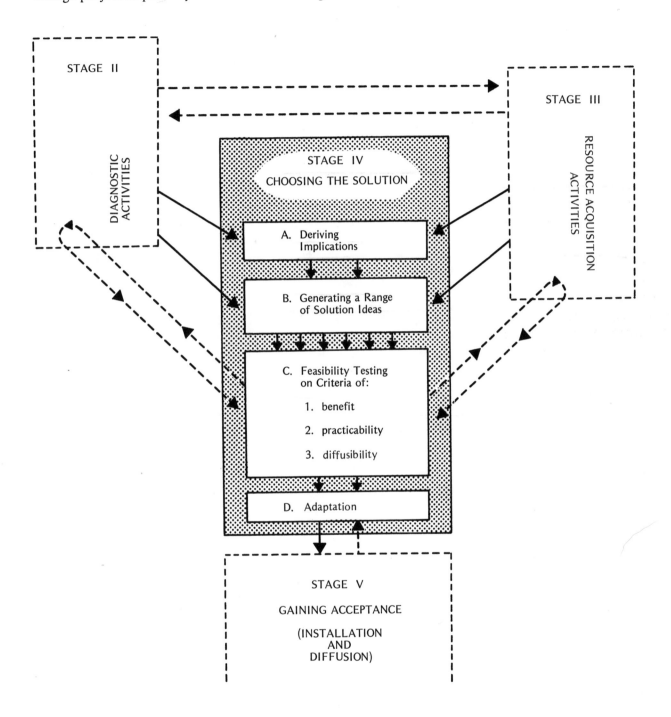

STEP A *IN SELECTING A SOLUTION: DERIVING IMPLICATIONS FROM RESEARCH*

Most of the information which comes to us from outside sources requires some translation or reformulation before it is meaningful as a basis for solving specific problems. This is especially true when the information comes from research reports. The standard research report is an efficient and appropriate medium for communication *among researchers* but it is not a good vehicle for communication from research to practice. Therefore, the change agent can never "accept" a research report as it is and expect it to be immediately useful and relevant for his purposes. You may ask yourself the question, "What does this mean *for my setting* and *for my client*?" This is a difficult question to ask because you have to know how to ask it and usually you need to have a good deal of practice before you can ask it well. Nevertheless, it is worth the effort. A great deal of research *is* relevant and can be useful if you work hard to think through what it means in terms of the situation you are confronting. It is also worth the effort because research-based information is more likely to be *valid* and *reliable* than information from non-research sources. Research findings deserve more attention than opinions and conjectures since they are (or should be) based on systematic observation and measurement of *real* events.

It is wise to approach the task of derivation systematically, starting from the retrieval of relevant materials and proceeding to the formulation of solution ideas. One possible sequence would be as follows: 1) retrieving summary statements; 2) reformulating and checking for understanding; 3) establishing relevance to your setting; and 4) stating implications for action. To help you in following the discussion of these four steps, we have provided an example of an actual derivation sequence on the right-hand side of the page.

1. *Retrieve Summary Statements*

A research report can have all kinds of purposes (see STAGE III for D-A-E-T-E-I-M), but when you are looking for solution ideas *the most important part of a research report is the summary*, particularly the statement of conclusion. The change agent cannot afford to spend countless hours checking through procedures and data analyses, and it is inappropriate for him to use his time in this way at this stage. What he needs are *ideas* stated as concisely as he can get them. Therefore, he should focus his acquisition efforts on abstracts or review articles which give the most abbreviated statements of "findings." If you cannot lay your hands on

STEVE AND HIS COLLEAGUES WOULD HAVE DONE WELL TO READ THROUGH SOME RESEARCH REPORTS ON ATTEMPTS TO INSTALL SENSITIVITY TRAINING PROGRAMS IN SCHOOL SETTINGS. SUCH STUDIES ARE AVAILABLE AND A "DERIVATION" ACTIVITY ON SUCH STUDIES WOULD PROBABLY HAVE BEEN USEFUL. IT WOULD NOT NECESSARILY HAVE LED TO DISCARDING THE PROGRAM BUT IT MIGHT HAVE LED TO THE REDESIGN OF CERTAIN FEATURES TO MAKE THE TOTAL PROGRAM MORE POWERFUL AND MORE ACCEPTABLE.

HENRY'S AGENCY HAD A "RESEARCH TEAM" WHICH HAD THE SKILLS TO RETRIEVE AND EVALUATE RESEARCH REPORTS. SUCH A TEAM WOULD BE A VALUABLE RESOURCE GROUP FOR OTHER CHANGE AGENTS BECAUSE IT COULD GENERATE THIS TYPE OF SUMMARY STATEMENT IF CALLED UPON TO DO SO. A NUMBER OF INFORMATION CENTERS, SUCH AS THE ERIC CLEARINGHOUSES, HAVE THIS CAPACITY.

good summaries, you should try to get someone to help you who has a good grasp of the literature and can find and organize such summary statements for you.

SAMPLE DERIVATION OF IMPLICATIONS: The Diagnosed Problem in This Case Was: "Student alienation from the school and indifference to learning."

The following research summary statements were retrieved from a search with the help of the ERIC center.

1. "One set of research findings pictures the typical student as alienated from any significant contact with or commitment to the school as a community. Another set, based on different inquiry methods, found 'superior' students to be highly involved and to like their school and teachers. However, their high involvement was 'in the wrong aspects of life,' i.e., getting good grades instead of having meaningful educational experiences . . . There is nonalienation in spite of triviality of work and powerlessness of role."

2. "There is a high correlation between self-perception of potency to influence one's environment and openness to learn from it."

3. "Most school administrators and teachers do not see students as relevant resources for collaboration in educational program planning and decision-making."

4. "The majority of high school students do not view student government as a significant channel of influence on the school administration."

2. *Summarize in Your Own Words*

Once you have a good list of "findings" generally relevant to your concern, you should discuss with your client what the research is trying to say. Try to summarize what is being said in your own words. It is only in this way that you will really learn and begin to have a feel for what these findings mean. If you can get the client actively involved in the process of summarizing for himself, so much the better.

The staff summarized the above statements as follows:

1. Although the superior student is not alienated from his school, the majority of students do exhibit such alienation. Moreover, regardless of whether or not a student *feels* alienated, he is able to report no significant educational experiences from the educational establishment.

2. The student is open to learning from the adult-managed educational system to the degree that he perceives this system as open to influence from him.

3. It would probably not occur to most teachers and administrators to collaborate with students in planning the educational program of their school. If the idea were suggested to these educators, they would probably not see the students' participation as relevant to the process of program planning.

4. a) Most high school students view the influence exerted on the school administration by the student council as insignificant; or

    b) Most high school students would not use the student council as a channel for their influence attempts on the administration and, therefore,

        (1) the administration would not "feel" the students' influence . . . or

        (2) the administration would feel their influence through other channels (e.g., violence, personal confrontation, etc.).

3. *Establish Relevance to Your Setting*

When you have figured out what the researcher was trying to say (Step 2), you should then begin to match these statements with your diagnosis. The question now becomes, "How does this finding relate to, or explain, what we have observed as a problem in the client system?" Again it is a good idea to proceed systematically from point to point, discussing each finding and writing down summary statements of these points of relevance. This exercise will further serve to internalize and concretize your understanding of the research findings.

These research findings were then discussed in the context of the immediate situation:

1 & 2. Many of the school staff felt that they were unable to "reach" their students or to supply them with classroom experiences that were relevant to the students' real lives. Even more painful (i.e., more frequently mentioned) than this personal inadequacy in the instructor role was the aggressive hostility expressed by many students toward their teachers.

3. The discouragement voiced by many teachers was augmented by the fact that they *had* been making a concerted effort to increase the relevance of the curriculum for their students. For over a year they had been contributing hours of their free time to committee work on redesigning the school program offerings. The apparent antagonism with which the students greeted the new program was puzzling and disillusioning to the exhausted teachers. Many complained bitterly of the students' "lack of appreciation" and "uncooperative attitudes" and suggested reinstituting former, less demanding, course offerings "since it didn't seem to make any difference anyway and, at least, with the traditional program descriptions it was easier to measure a student's progress."

4. Students had been informed of the impending curriculum change through their student council representative who reported back to the homeroom the information given by the assistant principal at a student council meeting. With the help of the council, the administration had sponsored several "career days" and "community development" projects, but school-wide student support and participation were typically unenthusiastic.

4.   *State the Implications for Action*

The most important part of derivation is stating implications in concrete behavioral terms as ideas for action and problem solution. This is a challenging and difficult assignment and researchers usually do not give us much help with it. The researcher tends to be very cautious in drawing conclusions, in part because he wants to make sure that what he says is thoroughly based on observed fact. Nevertheless, change agents and their clients can use research-based generalizations to stimulate their own thinking. Again it takes some practice to learn how to derive action possibilities from research, but it is usually worth the effort.

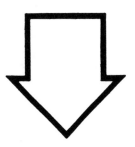

These findings from research and from the diagnosis of the system helped the staff to generate action steps such as:

- hold a staff meeting to review the program and to discuss alternative courses of action:
    - surface feelings of fatigue and disillusionment
    - present research findings

- incorporate student participation, e.g., through a joint planning session on "where do we go from here?"

- utilize student energies in subsequent efforts
    - will alleviate the current pressure on overworked staff
    - will permit students to become meaningfully involved in their own educational process.

In this chapter we stress the utility of abstracts and brief summary statements of research findings as the raw material for building research-based solutions. Although many other parts of research reports (procedures, data analysis, interpretations, etc.) may sometimes stimulate our thinking about solutions, *the summary is the best starting point for deriving implications.*

STEP B *IN SELECTING A SOLUTION: GENERATING A RANGE OF SOLUTION IDEAS*

Ideas for solutions can come from a variety of sources. They may come from research findings as discussed above; they may also come from other client systems or from commercial sources. Some solutions will be suggested more or less directly by the diagnosis or by the statement of objectives, while others will be suggested by the kind of resources we have available. Where good solutions are readily available from other programs and projects, it is probably wise to use them, but it is also possible and sometimes advantageous for a client system to generate its own solutions. This may not be a matter of "reinventing the wheel" but, rather, a matter of adapting and combining ideas from various sources to produce something that is appropriate for one's own situation.

Regardless of the sources of these solution ideas, it is important to generate *more than one* alternative. A range of alternatives gives the client freedom of choice and an opportunity to make rational and meaningful decisions. In assembling this range of alternatives, practicality or *feasibility should not be the first consideration*. Rather this should be a mind-stretching experience for the client. He should be led to start thinking of possibilities that may never have occurred to him before. Foremost in his thinking should be the question, "What would be the ideal solution?" or "What would do the most good?"

Also in beginning to generate solution ideas, you should not be too concerned for details of how something works, how much it costs, and how hard it is to install and maintain. You are really looking for "awareness" information, i.e., information which will give a rough idea of what the innovation can do or is supposed to do. For this purpose films, live demonstrations, field trips, and even testimonials from other change agents may be appropriate. At the earlier stages of selecting the innovation, alternatives should not be ruled out too quickly even if they seem to come from nonobjective sources.

Two strategies discussed in STAGE II as a part of diagnosis are particularly relevant in generating solution ideas. One was the emphasis on "opportunities" in contrast to problems. As noted earlier, a focus on areas of internal strength adds a new and hopeful dimension for many clients. These "opportunities" may suggest solution possibilities already available within the client system but not previously seen as relevant to problem areas.

The second strategy recommended as part of diagnosis was the construction of an "ideal model." Members of the client system should be given the chance to think through an "ideal" solution to their problems even if they have no immediate prospect of attaining such a solution. The exercise is mind-stretching: it opens up new vistas for the client and gives him the notion that solutions to his particular problems are at least conceivable; this can be a tremendous stimulus to constructive thinking.

Brainstorming is a specific technique for generating solution ideas in a small group. There is probably no faster way of freeing up thinking and creating bright images of potential solutions. Brainstorming involves four steps: (1)

STEVE, MIKE, AND LINDA ALL COMMITTED THEMSELVES TO ONE "SOLUTION" EARLY IN THE GAME ALTHOUGH FOR MIKE THERE WAS SOME FLEXIBILITY WITHIN THAT SOLUTION.

FOR STEVE'S CASE WAS SENSITIVITY TRAINING THE **ONLY** POSSIBLE SOLUTION FOR FACULTY INBREEDING AND TRADITIONALISM?

FOR MIKE WAS SEX EDUCATION THE **ONLY** WAY TO GET A COURSE FOR STUDENTS TO DISCUSS PERSONAL PROBLEMS?

FOR LINDA WAS BLACK STUDIES THE **ONLY** WAY TO INCREASE SUBURBAN WHITE AWARENESS AND UNDERSTANDING OF BLACK CULTURE?

*Fox, Lippitt and Schindler-Rainman have written a book which suggests a number of ideal models and mind-stretching ideas for school reform (**Humanizing School and Community: Images of Potentiality**, NTL Institute for Applied Behavioral Science, 1972). Such a book might be a good starting point for a brainstorming activity.*

IT IS UNFORTUNATE THAT NO BRAINSTORMING ON SOLUTION ALTERNATIVES WAS UNDERTAKEN IN ANY OF THE CASES CITED. SUCH AN ACTIVITY WOULD HAVE BEEN ESPECIALLY HELPFUL FOR STEVE AND LINDA IN UNFREEZING THE SITUATION AND GENERATING COLLECTIVE ACTION.

preparing the group with background information; (2) stage setting; (3) establishing and maintaining ground rules; and (4) summarizing and synthesizing.

(1) *Preparing.* Those who are to participate should be briefed or stimulated with information about the problem area, including diagnostic data, research derivations, etc. Before starting a brainstorming session participants should be reasonably well informed although they do not all have to start from the same information base. Laying this groundwork is very important. Even though participants in brainstorming may feel that their ideas are spontaneously generated, in actuality they are almost always based on knowledge they already possessed. Hence prior *acquisition* of resources lays the basis for brainstorming.

(2) *Stage Setting.* To be useful, brainstorming sessions should have a specific focus, which is usually the problem or the diagnosis which has been previously determined. However, a mere statement of the problem may not be enough to trigger creative thought processes. The change agent should try to set the stage by suggesting an image of some future time or set of circumstances that releases the participants from the reality constraints of the here-and-now. For example, he might ask them to think of the kind of school they would like to have in the year 2000 or the kind of educational environment they would build if they were suddenly granted several million dollars without strings. Of course, the stage set will vary with the type of problem and should be directly relevant to the problem. The more vivid and imaginative the stage setting by the change agent, the more likely the brainstorming will take hold.

(3) *Ground Rules.* Brainstorming literally shows the power of positive thinking. Brainstorming groups consciously strive to inhibit critical or negative thinking about a problem. Hence the most important ground rule is "no criticism" of ideas (your own or others) on grounds of feasibility. The only criterion is relevance to the problem or to the stage set. This kind of free associating to solutions does not come easily; it requires practice and discipline-in-the-service-of-freedom to ward off the natural tendency to slip back into a traditional task set. Comment on the ideas of others is allowed but it

"Not only the romanticizing biographer, but also the individual artist-scientist himself, reports creative experience in terms of inexplicable insight, neglecting the workday routine that has given the insight an underpinning."

Gordon[2]

A stage set for "the kind of school we'd like to have" might be:

"The educational program will be very finely tuned to the needs of the children in the school—it will truly be a pupil-centered school; an atmosphere of freedom will pervade the school; it will exemplify the ideals of our democratic system; and the life of the school and the life of the community will be seen as inseparable, the one serving and depending upon the other—it will truly be a public school."

Schrag[3]

105

should be in the form of "piggybacking," i.e., adding to a previous idea or suggesting another variation on the same theme.

It is also important to include a *recording* function as part of the ground rules. In other words, it is just as important to "get it down" as to "get it out." The change agent may want to appoint a recorder or to assume this task himself so that at the conclusion of the session, a list has been generated which adequately represents the thinking of the group. This "recorder" function is vital and should not be slighted; the written record is the principal "product" and the key element in linking "brainstorming" to the overall problem-solving enterprise.

(4) *Summarizing and Synthesizing* are really post-session activities but are necessary in making the brainstorm truly productive. Members of the group should try to put together their various ideas in a series of more-or-less coherent solution possibilities. This fourth step is necessary to reduce redundancy and to make the product manageable. *Feasibility* questions are still out of bounds, however, at this point.

Brainstorming had its earliest applications in the field of advertising, a fact which may have inhibited its use by other groups. Nevertheless, it is a very useful "unfreezing" method which is applicable in all kinds of situations. There is no one method of brainstorming and probably any method will have to be adapted or modified for working with particular types of clients. This process can be the turning point of a change program and is well worth trying, particularly if you feel reasonably secure in your role and in your relationship with the client.

STEP C *IN SELECTING A SOLUTION:* *FEASIBILITY TESTING*

When the change agent and the client have several potential solutions before them, they can begin the task of choosing in earnest. "Choosing" really means testing and comparing, applying criteria, eliminating some possibilities, accepting others, and modifying still others on the basis of comparative judgments. There are three broad categories of measurement which should concern us during this phase. The first is *benefit*: Will the potential solution really do a lot of good if it works? The second is *workability*: Will the potential solution really work, regardless of how much good it is supposed to do? Is it practical for us in this setting at this point in time? The third is *diffusibility*: Will the solution (the innovation) be accepted by the client system regardless of benefit and workability?

There is a considerable body of research literature on the characteristics of innovations. Such research is relevant to the task of selection. These studies provide us with a number of criteria, yardsticks against which to measure and compare potential solutions. The following listing summarizes the main factors that should be considered in evaluating any possible solution or innovation.

1. POTENTIAL BENEFIT

    a. *How many* people will it help?
    b. *How long* will it help them?
    c. *How much* will it help them?
        (1) Will it solve the problem or fill the diagnosed need adequately?
        (2) Might it have additional positive effects besides filling *diagnosed* needs?
    d. Does it have any *negative effects*?
        (1) Might it make the problem worse?
        (2) Might it have negative side effects (apart from its need-filling value)?

2. *Workability*

    a. Will the proposed innovation *actually provide* the promised benefits? (Do you have concrete evidence such as evaluation data, convincing testimony from other users, or demonstration results in natural settings and conditions similar to your own?)
    b. Will the innovation *perform reliably*?* Is there any proof of durability and precision?
    c. Can the client meet the *dollar cost* and the *human costs*:
        for trial?
        for initial purchase and installation?*
        for maintenance* over the long haul?
    d. Are the costs reasonable in proportion to the

"In the absence of good measures of output, educational organizations tend to stress cost reduction, since other potential rewards of the innovation remain only vaguely seen."

Miles[4]

"The most successful innovations are those which increase the autonomy and initiative of the users."

Woods[5]

"... we are discovering the principle that a change in a simple technology or a new procedure may become completely intertwined with wider factors in the client system."

Chin[6]

PRIMUM NON NOCERE is a well-known physicians' motto which means "above all, do no harm!"

MIKE'S PILOT EXPERIMENT AP-PARENTLY SHOWED A VERY HIGH "POTENTIAL BENEFIT" BUT DID IT REALLY SHOW "WORKABILITY" FOR OTHER TEACHERS? WHAT WAS THE FLAW IN HIS DESIGN?

NONE OF OUR FOUR CHANGE AGENTS ATTEMPTED ANY COST-BENEFIT ANALYSIS FOR THEIR INNOVATIONS. COULD ANY OF THEM MAKE SUCH AN ANALYSIS MEANINGFULLY?

---

*Many readers may feel that terms like "performance reliability," "installation," "maintenance," and "servicing" apply only to technological change, but increasingly in recent years this same terminology has been used to describe all kinds of innovations. There is a growing recognition that social, behavioral, and technical innovation can be described using similar concepts.

expected benefits? (Is there a good "*cost-benefit ratio*"?)

e. Does the client have the *staff* to operate the innovation successfully? Do they have the time, skill, training, experience, and desire to make it work?

f. Is the innovation *adequately developed*? Is all the necessary hardware and software available and ready for use? Does the innovation come with adequate information on how and when to install,* to use, to alter, to maintain,* and to replace? Does installation* include training in how to use? Do the suppliers provide adequate servicing* and help to the users over time?

3. *Diffusibility*

a. Is the innovation *acceptable*? Is it congruent or compatible with the attitudes and values of most members of the client system?

b. Can it be *demonstrated* easily and convincingly? Is it easy to describe and understand? Are results visible?

c. Can it be *tried out* on a *limited basis* before the client system is committed to adoption? Can it be tried a little bit at a time? Can it be tried out by a few members at a time?

d. Is it adequately *packaged* and *labelled*? (Ideally, an innovation should be familiar enough to be understood but different enough to be seen as something genuinely new; this is partly a packaging-labelling problem.)

These are all questions which should be asked before final decisions are made on the selection of innovations. However, all questions need not be answered affirmatively. Choosing usually is a matter of compromise and trade-off among a number of advantages and disadvantages. There is as yet no precise way of evaluating these criteria. The advantages will be different for different clients in different situations and, in large part, the determination of advantages and disadvantages is something only the client himself can judge; he knows what questions are most important and least

---

*Many readers may feel that terms like "performance reliability," "installation," "maintenance," and "servicing" apply only to technological change, but increasingly in recent years this same terminology has been used to describe all kinds of innovations. There is a growing recognition that social, behavioral, and technical innovation can be described using similar concepts.

"The most successful innovations are those which are accompanied by the most elaborate help to teachers as they begin to provide the new instruction."

Brickell[7]

"It matters little whether or not an innovation has a great degree of advantage over the idea it is replacing. What does matter is whether the individual perceives the relative advantage of the innovation."

Rogers[8]

STEVE'S PILOT PROGRAM HAD SOME VERY VISIBLE NEGATIVE RESULTS IN THE PSYCHIATRIC PROBLEMS IT BROUGHT TO THE SURFACE. WERE THERE VISIBLE POSITIVE RESULTS?

"Direct experience with a particular device and any associated materials seems essential for an adoption decision."

Miles[9]

DID STEVE CONSIDER "DIFFUSIBILITY" IN CHOOSING HIS INNOVATION?

IN BOTH MIKE'S AND LINDA'S CASES THE PROGRAM COULD BE AND WAS TRIED OUT ON A LIMITED BASIS BY A FEW TEACHERS BEFORE COMPLETE SYSTEM-WIDE ADOPTION AT ALL LEVELS.

important for the people in his system.

Even though precision is impossible, it is important to ask these questions in some form. All too often when we survey the wreckage after an innovation has failed, we find that some critical feasibility question was not even asked prior to the decision to adopt.

STEP D *IN SELECTING A SOLUTION: ADAPTATION*

Because a selected innovation will not meet all criteria, you may want to consider further changes and redesigning to make the innovation "better." You may want to make improvements either to increase benefit, increase workability, or increase diffusibility. If the change team has a lot of resources at its disposal (dollars, time, and staff with creativity and appropriate skills in research and development), you may be able to reshape the innovation completely so that it is "custom made" to fit your client and his specific problem. Usually, however, you will not have such resources so that the *less* adaptation you have to do, the better off you are. This is why it is so important to be a good utilizer, taking maximum advantage of the R & D efforts of others.

There are a large number of university centers and laboratories now putting effort into *educational "development"* so that change agents and their clients will have a range of fully developed and pretested innovations to choose from in the future. Unfortunately, these efforts are just beginning, largely spurred on by the federal education acts of the early and middle 1960's. Therefore, in many areas, the would-be user may still have to do a great deal of adaptation because the development has not caught up to the needs of the educational community. Sometimes the user may have to "invent" the innovation but before he does, he should make sure he has done his resource acquisition job as well as he can (STAGE III) so that he has some assurance that he is not "reinventing the wheel."

Whenever you have the opportunity you should plan a pilot test of an innovation before making a final decision on selection. Limited tryouts on several innovations can give additional data on several of the criteria listed above to help in making rational choices. Above all, the trial demonstrates the degree of relevance and suitability to the problem at hand. Because the trial phase can also be seen as an aspect of "installation" and "gaining acceptance," it will be discussed again in STAGE V.

HENRY'S CHANGE AGENCY HAD THE RESOURCES TO DO A LOT OF SCREENING AND ADAPTATION FOR LOCAL SCHOOL CLIENTS. HIS PLANS TO COMBINE ELEMENTS OF "TABA" AND "MINNESOTA" (P. 35) ILLUSTRATE ONE TYPE OF ADAPTATION.

IN USING THE **SIECUS** MATERIALS, MIKE AND HIS COLLEAGUES TOOK MAXIMUM ADVANTAGE OF THE R&D WORK OF OTHERS, BUT THEY DID NOT ADOPT **SIECUS**, THEY ADAPTED IT, DESIGNING A SET OF COURSES WHICH THEY FELT WAS MOST SUITABLE TO THEIR OWN COMMUNITY.

BECAUSE OF HER STRONG STANCE AS AN ADVOCATE OF THE BLACK STUDIES PROGRAM, LINDA FOUND IT DIFFICULT TO ACCEPT THE PROGRAM EVENTUALLY ADOPTED AS A LEGITIMATE AND NECESSARY ADAPTATION OF HER IDEA.

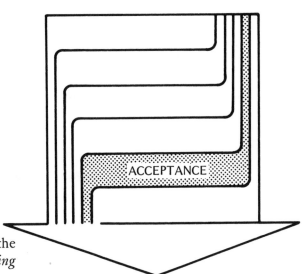

Stage V:

GAINING ACCEPTANCE

In the preceding four chapters we have discussed the procedure which the change agent should follow in *preparing* for a program of change. During these early phases you have established a working relationship with your client; you have worked with the client system to diagnose the relevant problem areas, and on the basis of information which has been retrieved from diverse resources, you and your client have decided on a potential innovative solution.

At this point the groundwork has been laid for the actual installation of the innovation in the client system. Now is the time for transforming intentions into actions. This is the heart of the plan for change; during this phase all the preparatory work is put to the test, and it is in this phase that you find out whether or not you have a workable solution that can be accepted and used effectively by *all* the members of the client system.

In the present chapter we will consider how the change agent should proceed with the actual installation of the innovation in the client system. In the sections of this chapter we will consider four issues which are of particular importance during this process:

A. *HOW **INDIVIDUALS** ACCEPT INNOVATIONS*
B. *HOW **GROUPS** ACCEPT INNOVATIONS*
C. *HOW TO CHOOSE A **COMMUNICATION STRATEGY** WHICH IS EFFECTIVE FOR INDIVIDUALS AND GROUPS*
D. *HOW TO MAINTAIN A FLEXIBLE PROGRAM FOR GAINING ACCEPTANCE*

A. *Acceptance by the Individual*

During the period of installation each individual who will be involved in the change program must be allowed to become familiar with the innovation; he must learn how to use it, and he must come to accept it as a part of his routine behavior. This process usually follows a six-step sequence:

"In addition to providing for innovators and creating the conditions under which innovation thrives, we must also take care of the needs of the 'acceptors'—the majority of educators, those who must learn to accept and use the new resources. We must not be content with lamenting the fact that most people are heel-dragging resistors to change, suspicious of the new, and not very much interested in creating new things."

Caffrey[1]

awareness, interest, evaluation, trial, adoption, and integration. We will also discuss the role which a change agent should play in helping and supporting the individual through each of these steps.

B. *Acceptance by the Group*

The individuals involved in the adoption process do not function independently but, as we pointed out in STAGE I, as members of social groups (family, neighborhood, school, community). Therefore, to understand how to coordinate the adoption activities of the individual members of the client system we must also have an understanding of the process by which an innovation is adopted by a social system. We shall also discuss in this section the role which the change agent should play in facilitating this process of innovation acceptance by the system.

C. *How to Communicate*

The key to success of the change effort may well lie in the effectiveness with which the new ideas are communicated. The relevant "facts" about the innovation must be conveyed to the relevant audiences clearly and accurately. In addition to the "facts" the change agent must effectively convey his *support* and *approval* as attempts are made to carry out the change plan. In this section we will discuss the most appropriate style and means of communication for the change agent to employ for different purposes and at different stages in the adoption process.

D. *Keep Your Program Flexible*

In planning the adoption schedule and procedures, the change agent must make an effort to be realistic and to take into account all the elements involved in the change process. He probably will not think of everything, however, and very often there are contingencies which arise which could not possibly have been foreseen. It may be that a change in plans is forced upon the system by events taking place in the external environment, or it may be that the internal situation itself changes, forcing a change in plans. In any case, the change agent must be willing to review and reassess any or all aspects of the change program, including the choice of the innovation itself.

Therefore, every attempt should be made to prepare a schedule which is both *flexible* and *schematic*—a difficult balance to strike, but a crucial one.

A. *HOW INDIVIDUALS ACCEPT INNOVATIONS*

Full acceptance and adoption rarely come when an individual first learns about an innovation. A person reaches the decision to adopt by a very complex process, but we have learned through research that this process usually follows a predictable pattern. The time period required to reach adoption can be broken down and described in terms of "phases."

These adoption phases can be used as a guide for the change agent in planning his activities. After describing each phase briefly, we will point out the types of activity which the change agent can best employ during each adoption phase to facilitate individual acceptance of the innovation.

1. The Adoption Process: Six Phases

Researchers have identified six phases in the process of individual adoption of an innovation: *"awareness," "interest," "evaluation," "trial," "adoption,"* and *"integration."*

a. *Awareness*

During the initial "awareness" stage, the individual is exposed to the innovation and becomes aware of it. As yet he has only a *passive* interest and he does not necessarily seek further information. The way in which the innovation is presented to him at the beginning may well determine whether or not he is motivated enough to move on to the second and subsequent stages.

HENRY'S AGENCY WAS ABLE TO DEVELOP **AWARENESS** IN INDIVIDUAL TEACHERS AND ADMINISTRATORS IN THEIR REGION BY PUBLISHING A NEWSLETTER AND GENERATING NEWS STORIES IN THE LOCAL MEDIA. BY HOLDING MEETINGS, CONDUCTING DEMONSTRATIONS, AND REPORTING TO SUPERINTENDENTS THEY WERE DEVELOPING **INTEREST**.

b. *Interest*

The "interest" stage is characterized by active information seeking about the innovation. Although he has an interest in the innovation and a generally open attitude toward it, at this stage the individual has not made a judgment as to whether or not the innovation would be suitable for his own particular circumstances. As he gathers more information and learns more about the innovation, the individual's first positive or negative attitudes toward it begin to emerge. These feelings may prompt him to decide against adoption, or they may motivate him to move on to the next phase in the adoption process.

PRINT MATERIALS FROM **SIECUS** WERE PROBABLY ENOUGH TO ESTABLISH **INTEREST** IN THEIR SERVICES BY MIKE'S GROUP.

c. *Evaluation*

The third stage, "evaluation," is generally described as a period of "mental trial" of the innovation, a necessary

WHEN HENRY'S AGENCY CONDUCTED IN-SERVICE TRAINING AND HELD WORKSHOPS, THEY WERE ALLOWING MEMBERS OF THE CLIENT SYSTEM TO MAKE IN-DEPTH BEFORE-TRIAL EVALUATIONS OF THE PROGRAMS THEY WERE PROPOSING AND THEY WERE ALSO PROVIDING CRUCIAL INFORMATION AND SKILL PRACTICE THAT TEACHERS NEED TO MAKE TRIAL EFFORTS.

preliminary to the decision to make a "behavioral trial." In his mind, the individual applies the innovation to his own situation and decides whether or not it is worth the effort to try it out.

d. *Trial*

In the "trial" stage the individual uses the innovation on a small scale in order to find out how it will actually work in his own situation. An alternative method of conducting a trial is to use the innovation on a temporary or probationary basis before moving on to true adoption.

e. *Adoption*

In the "adoption" stage, the results of the trial are weighed and considered and, on the basis of this post-trial evaluation, the decision is made to adopt (or reject) the innovation.

f. *Integration*

Even when a favorable decision is made, however, true adoption cannot be considered to have taken place unless use of the innovation becomes routine. It must be integrated into the day-to-day working life of the teacher, or the administrator, or the user, whoever he may be.

2. Matching the Change Agent's Activities with the Individual User's Adoption Process

The change agent should try to facilitate each of these six processes. Therefore, in dealing with the individuals in the client system, you should try to coordinate your activities with the adoption stages of the potential adopters. You should try to understand where potential adopters are in terms of these six phases so that you can try to be with them, not ahead or behind. You should be prepared to go back as individual adopters slip back and to keep up as other adopters jump ahead; and you should know when to switch from one mode of communication to another with each adopter.

You may want to use the following guidelines in choosing the behavior most appropriate to each of the individual adoption stages:

a. *Awareness*

At the beginning of your contact with a potential adopter, your primary objective should be exposure. You

LINDA'S SCHOOL SYSTEM ADOPTED BLACK STUDIES ON A LIMITED "TRIAL" BASIS FOR THE FIRST YEAR: AN ELECTIVE COURSE AVAILABLE ONLY TO THOSE ELEVENTH AND TWELFTH GRADERS WHO HAD THE TIME AND WHO HAD FULFILLED THEIR HISTORY REQUIREMENTS.

114

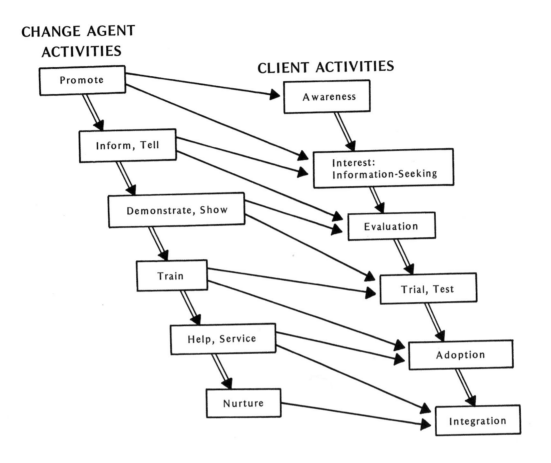

CHANGE AGENT ACTIVITIES

CLIENT ACTIVITIES

want to make sure that he hears and sees and that he develops some conception of what the innovation is all about. The image should be clear and positive. Most of all you want to instill *curiosity*, a motivation to seek more information. There needs to be something in this initial message that will turn him on. Therefore it should be *brief, interesting, easy to understand*, and *rewarding* in some way.

b. *Interest*

During the "interest" stage you should expect and *encourage* the individual to come to you for facts and to become actively involved in the search for information. If he is really interested, the individual will also seek information from any other source available, most commonly from his associates within the client system. You should promote

A good "soft-sell" TV commercial will follow all the rules of a good "awareness" message: it is short (15 seconds to one minute), it is interesting (usually featuring a well-known comedian or attractive model in a strange get-up or a bizarre situation), it is easy to understand (the product brand name and some indication of its function is all you get: "Blors are good to eat," "Zaz makes your clothes cleaner," ... "your breath fresher," etc., without any technical details about why and how), and it is rewarding (it makes you laugh).

115

group discussion, not only as a means of satisfying the need for information but also as an opportunity to air doubts and to mold positive attitudes about the innovation. Group discussion can be used to support individual risk taking.

c. Evaluation

As the individual begins to make his "mental trial," he will continue to seek information, but now an attempt should be made to provide information which will enable him to envision the innovation applied to his own situation. An aid to this type of communication is a *demonstration of the innovation* in his home environment under conditions that are natural to him. If the individual is shown how the innovation will work for him, he will be more inclined to make a favorable evaluation.

d. Trial

Further demonstration will be necessary as the individual begins his behavioral trial. In addition, he will need *training* in order to fulfill his new role or to carry out these new activities. At this stage the possibility of experiencing failure becomes very real; now the potential adopter needs maximum *support* and encouragement from the change agent. You should also do what you can to help the user evaluate his own experience; the results of his trial may not be immediately apparent or clearly appreciated unless you can point them out.

e. Adoption

After trial the client is in a position to decide whether to adopt or reject the innovation, but a decision to adopt is not the end of the story. The adopter may still encounter difficulties in trying to carry out his intention, and the change agent must be prepared to provide further training and encouragement. He must *help the individual to adjust* to the new situation, and he must be ready to provide his services when problems and unexpected obstacles arise.

f. Integration

After adoption there are a number of things a change agent can do to nurture integration of the new skills or materials into the day-to-day behavior of the client. Practice sessions, reminders in newsletters, and brief follow-up questionnaires on frequency of use and usefulness will all serve

"Resistance will be reduced if it is recognized that innovations are likely to be misunderstood and misinterpreted, and if provision is made for feedback of perceptions of the project and for further clarification as needed."

Watson[2]

MIKE'S PILOT COURSE WAS A "TRIAL" FOR MIKE, BUT FOR HIS FELLOW TEACHERS IT WAS A DEMONSTRATION WHICH GAVE THEM INFORMATION FOR THEIR OWN "MENTAL TRIAL" BEFORE COMMITTING THEMSELVES TO ACTION.

"The load on teachers at all levels and at all times is heavy, and it is difficult enough for them to conduct existing programs, much less carry out new ones. With a busy person every little bit helps—workshops, materials, guides, consultants—and any one of these may make the difference between adoption and rejection."

Woods[3]

". . . the change manager is considering introduction of an overhead projector which the school agreed to buy and make available for teacher use. Purchasing the projector and putting it in the audio-visual room does not implement the change. Several more steps must be taken to ensure that the projector becomes part of the working system. Instruction in the operation of the projector must be given to all

the purpose. Nowhere is the need for inside change agents more apparent than at this stage (see again discussion, pages 50-53).

3. Taking Advantage of Your Knowledge of Adoption Phases to Prevent Failure

It should be clear that *rejection* can take place at any stage along the way. Indeed, a decision to *reject* sometimes may be a good decision; the innovation may not be appropriate for this or that particular client. Assuming, however, that the innovation is, in fact, suitable, there are some things you can do to reduce the chances of rejection:

a. *Individuals Must Be Allowed and Encouraged to Progress Through All the Adoption Steps in Sequence.* The six steps provide a natural process through which the individual becomes familiar with new ideas and, at the same time, gives up old ways of doing things. Specifically, the change agent should keep these hazards in mind:

(1) Skipping steps (e.g., *trial* without *evaluation* or *adoption* without *trial*).

(2) Changing the order of steps (e.g., *trial* before getting sufficient information or commitment to try).

(3) Hurrying through the stages just to meet a schedule. (Most people need time to think things over before they make a change that will affect their lives in a significant way.)

(4) Ignoring individual differences in adoption rates (e.g., assuming that everyone in the client system is *aware* of the innovation).

You will have worked with some members of the client system in your initial planning and they may be ready for trial; others will not yet have enough information, while still others may not even be aware of the innovation.

b. *Individuals Must Be Allowed and Encouraged to Make a Personal Commitment;* let them come to you once their interest is aroused, and do not help them when they do not need it.

c. *Individuals Must Be Allowed and Encouraged to*

the teachers. Examples of different ways in which the projector can be used should also be illustrated. Scheduling the use of the projector as well as check-out procedures may also be required. Part of the strategy may involve a campaign to promote usage among the teachers. Although these steps seem obvious, the fact is that there are schools where audio-visual equipment gathers dust in the audio-visual room because the teachers are not sure how to use it, they have not been encouraged to experiment with it and check-out procedures are too complicated."

Rogers and Svenning[4]

LINDA AND STEVE DID NOT HAVE A CLEARLY MAPPED OUT STRATEGY FOR GAINING ACCEPTANCE. STEVE WENT AHEAD WITH A TRIAL BEFORE HIS GROUP HAD DONE A COMPLETE JOB OF PRE-TRIAL EVALUATION.

BOTH MIKE AND STEVE MADE SOME FALSE ASSUMPTIONS ABOUT THE SPEED WITH WHICH THEIR COMMUNITIES WERE MOVING TOWARD ACCEPTANCE OF THEIR INNOVATIVE PROGRAMS.

117

Discuss Their Doubts About the Innovation. Everyone has these feelings; they must be worked through and it is best to bring them out in the open.

d. *The Change Agent Should Try to Acquire and Offer the Client Resources* relevant to each adoption phase (see again STAGE III and discussion of D-A-E-T-E-I-M).

e. *Individuals Need Greater Support from the Change Agent When the Actual Behavioral Trial Begins.* This may be the point of greatest resistance since the implications of the change become apparent at this point, and such feelings as fear of failure and loss of previous security become salient and threatening. Be prepared to offer this *extra support at the time of trial.*

B. HOW GROUPS ACCEPT INNOVATIONS

It is impossible to understand how individuals adopt without also considering the social relationships and group structures which bind individuals together. The communication of innovations depends upon a vast network of social relationships, both formal and informal; *a person's position in that network is the best indicator of when he is likely to adopt an innovation.*

1. Common Things and Key People

One overriding characteristic of groups could be called "commonality." A group can be defined as a number of people who have something *in common.* Typically they have common backgrounds, common interests, common circumstances, common values, common problems, and, most of all, common needs. A social system is a group of people who have pooled their resources to satisfy needs they have in common. These common things bind them together psychologically so that "mine" becomes "ours" and "self-interest" becomes "our common interest." This arrangement is usually very beneficial for all concerned but sometimes it gets in the way when *new* ideas and new ways of doing things are introduced from outside. When this happens, the members of the group have to decide individually or collectively whether or not the new thing threatens the common good. At this point, all these common values, beliefs, interests, and backgrounds become potential *barriers.*

Social organization, by its very nature, is conservative and protective; it is supposed to keep some potential "innovations" out for the preservation of the common good, and when it lets them come in they are supposed to be

ISSUES LIKE SEX, PERSONAL SENSITIVITY TO OTHERS, AND RACIAL ATTITUDES COVER VERY TROUBLESOME AND GUILT-RIDDEN FEELINGS IN MANY PEOPLE. IF THEY DON'T UNDERSTAND THE PROGRAMS OFFERED IN THESE AREAS VERY CLEARLY, THEY ARE LIKELY TO REACT WITH FEAR AND AVOIDANCE. DID MIKE, STEVE, AND LINDA FULLY APPRECIATE THE "LOADED" NATURE OF THE INNOVATIONS THEY WERE TRYING TO INTRODUCE?

". . . one of the principal petty barriers to innovation in instruction is the reliance of the mature teacher on filing cabinet drawers full of excellent lesson plans, developed over years and refined by experience, which now must be consigned to the burn barrel to make way for the new math, the new biology, the new English. Older teachers especially do not have the energy they once had, and we have to respect this and understand it and help them forge new tools if we are properly to exploit the chance to change the old ways."

Caffrey[5]

WHEN THE TEACHER IN MIKE'S SYSTEM SAID, "WE CAN'T TEACH MORALS," HE WAS EXPRESSING A VALUE AMONG EDUCATORS, BUT AT THE SAME TIME HE WAS REJECTING AN ESTABLISHED VALUE POSITION OF HIS COMMUNITY.

"acceptable," which usually means "what we are accustomed to." Therefore, the structure of the group is a kind of filtering mechanism. Various members are needed to "sniff out" new ideas, to expel dangerous ones, or to make the final decisions about "acceptability" for the group as a whole. Sometimes different people are appointed or self-appointed to fill each of these filtering functions.

The first step for the change agent who wants to gain the acceptance of the group is to find out what kinds of barriers are most important and what kinds of filters are used to maintain the status quo. We cannot generalize too much beyond this for *all* groups because some are very open to new ideas while others will admit almost nothing new.

Diffusion of an innovation begins with the acceptance of the idea by a few key members of a community. From there on, it begins to spread more rapidly, usually through word-of-mouth contacts between friends, neighbors, and relatives. This person-to-person process is very effective; once it has started and there are clusters of people who accept the idea and are "talking it up," it gathers momentum. A chain reaction seems to be generated once this "critical mass" of key individuals has formed, and there is a rapid upswing in the rate of acceptance until a large majority has been won over.

Three types of people play a significant part in generating group acceptance. These are the "innovators," the "resisters," and the "leaders." Because the characteristics of these three types of people have been studied extensively by social scientists, we are in a position to understand who they are and how they work regardless of the particular innovation we are concerned with.

a. The Innovators

The innovators tend to be intelligent and risk-taking; they travel a lot, they read a lot, they depend on outside sources of information, and they are usually very receptive to influence by outside change agents. They also tend to be marginal to their home communities. They may be viewed as "odd balls" or mavericks, and they do not usually have a great deal of direct power or influence. Hence, they can be both an asset and a liability to the change agent. These people will have commitment to a new idea and are willing to stand up and be counted even though they may be risking the scorn and ridicule of others, but if they have stood up too often for lost causes they may not be an effective ally. Usually, inside members of inside-outside change agent teams can be recruited from this group.

"In promoting school improvement projects, school leaders have not always used effective political strategies. In many cases of public school referenda there has been no formally prescribed strategy. Many school elections are lost because the educator had no well-defined strategy or because the strategy used ignored the unique nature of the political system in which it was used."

Kimbrough[6]

THE GROUP OF LEADING CITIZENS IN MIKE'S COMMUNITY WHO WERE BELATEDLY MOBILIZED IN SUPPORT OF THE INNOVATION REPRESENTED THE "CRITICAL MASS" FOR ACCEPTANCE OF SEX EDUCATION BY THE ENTIRE SYSTEM.

" . . . Traditionally, the innovator is not popular; he is an annoying minority, a gadfly, an irritant who nevertheless likes to think he will stimulate a pearl within the establishment's hard shell."

Guskin[7]

FROM THE POINT OF VIEW OF AN OUTSIDE CHANGE AGENT TRYING TO INTRODUCE BLACK STUDIES, LINDA MIGHT HAVE BEEN VIEWED AS BOTH AN ASSET (FOR HER ENERGY AND PERSISTENCE) AND A LIABILITY (FOR BEING SEEN AS A "FLAMING RADICAL").

b. The Resisters

Many social systems also contain some members who assume the active role of resisters or critics of innovation. They are the defenders of the system the way it is, the self-appointed guardians of moral, ethical, and legal standards. Although these people are "conservative" in a strictly logical sense, they may wear all kinds of labels from "radical" and "liberal" to "reactionary."

Resisters of various orders have been very successful in preventing or slowing down such diverse innovations as the fluoridation of community water supplies, urban renewal, the integration of neighborhoods, and the invasion of certain civil liberties by such means as wire tapping and indiscriminate school testing. From the diversity of these issues it should be evident that the resisters do not all march under the same banner. They are a mixed group ideologically even though they tend to function in the same way. As preservers of a social order these innovation resisters play a big part *and a useful part* in our society by resisting intrusions from alien influences; they are the antibodies in our social blood stream.

c. The Leaders

Many studies of how groups accept innovations have singled out one very important social role which they have identified as the "opinion leader." Opinion leaders are found in any community and they are the key to the growth of any movement. Study after study has shown that there are certain influential people who are held in high esteem by the great majority of their fellow men. They tend to have control of the wealth and power of society. They are usually not the first people to try out new ideas because they need to maintain their standing with their followers. The opinion leaders listen to both the innovators and the resisters so that they can better size up a developing situation. They watch the innovator to see how the idea works, and they watch the resister to test the social risks of adopting the idea. Indeed, in many cases they are eager to observe these changes because their continuance in power rests upon their ability to judge innovations. They want to be the champions of the *innovation whose time has come.* In other words, they must be able to adopt new ideas at the point at which those new ideas become popularly feasible.

Leadership of any kind has critical strategic importance in a change program whether that leadership be formal, informal, administrative, or elective. The school superintendent, the principal, the esteemed senior teacher will all have a great deal of "opinion leadership" on a wide range of innovations. Some act as *legitimators,* making the majority

"The most common resistance to educational improvements which would cost money comes from organized or unorganized taxpayers... A few powerful political or financial interests can block programs desired by a large majority of ordinary citizens... The closer any reform comes to touching some of the taboos or rituals in the community, the more likely it is to be resisted."

Watson[8]

STEVE SAID THAT THE EXTREMISTS WHO OPPOSED HIS PROGRAM WERE FROM RURAL AREAS OUTSIDE OF TOWN BUT HE ADMITS THEY HAD INFLUENCE WITH THE MEDIA AND WITH THE "POWER SOURCES." YET HE DOESN'T ASK HIMSELF WHY THESE "POWER SOURCES" WERE RECEPTIVE LISTENERS.

"Some resistance to change may be quite logical and may have well-supported evidence to support resistance. Such opposing persons are often viewed by the proponents of change as impossibly intractable and dismissed as 'rabble-rousers' or 'crack-pots.'"

Klein[9]

BOTH STEVE AND MIKE HAD A TENDENCY TO DISMISS RESISTERS AS FEW IN NUMBER, IGNORANT, SICK, AND ISOLATED FROM THE MAINSTREAM OF COMMUNITY LIFE (e.g., COMING FROM RURAL AREAS). IN SOME RESPECTS, OF COURSE, THIS WAS AN ACCURATE PICTURE BUT WAS IT **COMPLETE**LY ACCURATE?

feel that it is o.k. to try something out without having the axe fall. Others serve as *facilitators*, approving and rewarding the innovators and encouraging others to follow their example, getting clearance, providing funds and release time, and generally making it easier to be an innovator. Still others serve as *gatekeepers*, opening up (or closing off) access to needed resources, funds, outside consultants, training courses, etc. The gatekeeper is often not the top man in an organization and he may be function-specific, e.g., the business manager, the training director, etc.

2. How the Change Agent Can Work to Gain Group Acceptance

The change agent can use his knowledge of the group to plan and carry out an effective strategy for gaining group acceptance. But in order to plan a strategy he must first have the knowledge. This means once again making a diagnosis of the client system.

a. *Diagnosing the Forces For and Against the Innovation*

In STAGE II we described the diagnostic process in which the change agent and the client define needs and objectives. However, you may find that you have to make another kind of diagnosis when you already have an innovation which fills these needs and you want to win the support of large numbers of people. Broadly speaking, you now want to address yourself to two questions:

What are the most important *common things*?
Who are the most important *key people*?

To answer each of these questions you may find it helpful to draw up a rating form on which you can identify and compare the forces which are acting for and against the desired change. To analyze the "common things" you might make two columns on a sheet of paper, one marked "forces probably favoring this innovation" and the other marked "forces probably opposing this innovation." Under these headings you would then list as many of the group characteristics as you can think of which might affect acceptance: commonly held values and beliefs, characteristic modes of thought and behavior, shared circumstances, common needs, and commonly perceived group objectives.

Having identified a number of such characteristics, you will then want to rank-order them in terms of relative

"An innovation will not be spread until the opinion leaders give their 'stamp of approval.'"

Woods[10]

THE LEADERS OF STEVE'S COMMUNITY WERE PROBABLY STILL WATCHING AND WAITING UNTIL THE PSYCHIATRIST SPOKE UP. REGARDLESS OF HIS INTENT, HE SHOWED THE LEADERS THAT THE INNOVATION WAS "HIGH RISK" AND SEALED ITS FATE.

STEVE IMPLIES THAT THE PASSIVE ENDORSEMENT OF HIS SUPERINTENDENT WAS NOT ADEQUATE LEADERSHIP SUPPORT. HE NEEDED MORE LEGITIMATION AND FACILITATION FROM THAT OFFICE.

....

HENRY'S AGENCY MADE SURE THEY GOT SUCH SUPPORT FROM THE SUPERINTENDENT **IN WRITING**.

"At each stage of innovation, from its inception to its defense as status quo, wise strategy requires perceptive analysis of the nature of resistance."

Watson[11]

importance and the relative ease with which they could be altered. Such a list would then provide some good guidelines for an action program to improve the chances of acceptance.

From your previous diagnosis of the client system (STAGE II) you should also be able to draw up a list of individuals who could fit under each of the headings, "innovator," "resister," and "leader." The innovators are probably the easiest people to identify. Some of them will already be working with you as "inside" members of the change team. Others will have been in touch with you and will have been vocal in their support. Still others may be identified as leading spokesmen for one or another of the issues listed under "forces favoring."

Your "innovator" list should be rated on a number of characteristics such as (1) their degree of understanding and sophistication in using the innovation, (2) the extent to which they are representative or typical of the client system as a whole, (3) the amount of direct influence ("opinion leadership") which they can exert on other members of the client system and, most importantly, (4) their extent of contact and influence with the leadership.

"Resisters" may be identified for having spoken out previously on the innovation or from having come to you with objections. They may also be identified as spokesmen who personify some of the issues which are "forces against." It is important, however, to try to identify resisters *before* they become vocal and committed on this particular innovation. Resisters, like innovators, should be judged for relative sophistication and influence.

Finally, as part of your diagnostic analysis of the acceptance problem you should take an inventory of the leadership. Who are the *formal* leaders and *gatekeepers* for this type of innovation? Who are the informal leaders? the example-setters? the facilitators? the legitimizers? The leaders should be rated on such dimensions as (1) their attitude towards both innovators and resisters, (2) their visibility, (3) their relationship to one another, and (4) their ability to lead.

b.   *Using the Key People as*
     Stepping Stones

A number of social scientists have described innovation-diffusion as a two-step process. In the first step, outside information about the innovation reaches the opinion leaders. In the second step, the opinion leaders pass on the information to their followers by word or example. This process sounds simple but such a process will only work if two conditions are present in the client system: first, the opinion leaders must be innovators or innovation-minded;

AS AN EXERCISE, IMAGINE YOURSELF AS AN OUTSIDE CHANGE AGENT CONSIDERING HOW A SENSITIVITY TRAINING PROGRAM MIGHT BE INTRODUCED TO THE SCHOOL SYSTEM IN **MIKE'S** CITY. FROM WHAT YOU KNOW ABOUT HIS STORY YOU SHOULD BE ABLE TO DRAW UP A PRETTY GOOD "FORCE" CHART. YOU MIGHT ALSO TRY SEX EDUCATION OR BLACK STUDIES WITH **STEVE'S** COMMUNITY.

"It should be recognized at the outset that resistance to a change is not the fundamental problem to be solved. Rather, any resistance is usually a symptom of more basic problems underlying the particular situation. To focus attention on the symptom alone will achieve at best only limited results."

Judson[12]

122

and second, these leaders must have very good follower connections throughout the client system.

As a change agent, you usually cannot count on either of these conditions and it would be dangerous to assume them. However, you can use this basic concept of "steps" effectively if you put together all the information from your diagnosis and analysis of roles. An adequate strategy may have to include not one but four stepping stones to gain group acceptance.

How this type of stepping stone strategy might work is suggested in Figure 11.

(1) First, introduce the innovation to a core group of "innovators." Get them to try out the innovation, to become sophisticated in its use, and to demonstrate it to others.

(2) Second, begin to work with some of the concerned citizens who are potential but not-yet-vocal resisters, answering their questions and showing them by demonstration that the innovation does not violate established values and does not threaten the survival of the system as they know it. If you are not able to receive any cooperation from resisters and if they are already vocal and mobilized, you should at least do what you can to protect the innovators and to make the innovation less vulnerable. This means being hard-headed, realistic, and scientific in your approach and having sound and well-reasoned answers for legitimate questions. With these safeguards, you may not be able to silence your detractors but in many cases you may be able to disarm them and prevent them from turning the rest of the community against you.

(3) Third, bring the innovation to the attention of the leaders, allowing them to observe live demonstrations by the innovators and to sound out the reactions of potential resisters.

(4) Allow the leaders to lead the way to acceptance by the rest of the system. If possible, get them to publicly commit themselves and organize themselves into supporting and endorsing committees.

In following any strategy to gain group acceptance do not forget that groups are made up of individuals and that each individual has his own step-by-step process of moving toward acceptance. Thus, while you are working on "evaluation" or "trial" with innovators, you may need to be

"In certain situations the participation of defenders in the change process may even lead to the development of more adequate plans and to the avoidance of some hitherto unforeseen consequences of the projected change . . . He should encourage the interplay of advocates of change and defenders of the status quo."

Klein[13]

BOTH MIKE AND HENRY IMPLIED THAT STEPPING STONE STRATEGIES WERE EMPLOYED TO INTRODUCE INNOVATIONS TO THEIR COMMUNITIES.

IN MIKE'S COMMUNITY IT WAS FINALLY POSSIBLE TO AROUSE OPINION LEADERS TO CONCERTED DIRECT ACTION ON BEHALF OF THE INNOVATION.

FIGURE 11:   A Stepping Stone Strategy for Gaining Group Acceptance

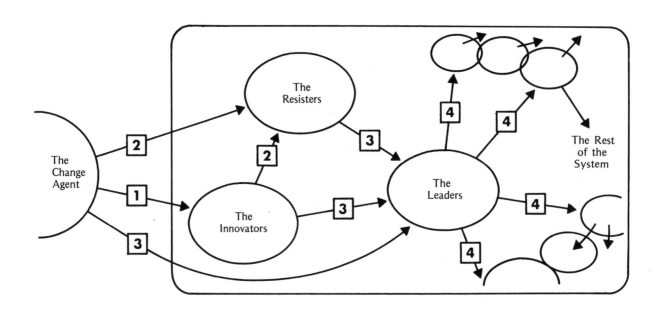

working on "awareness" and "interest" with leaders. A good program should be planned to provide each set of individuals with the kind of information they are ready for at a given point in time.

C.   HOW TO COMMUNICATE

Gaining acceptance of innovations is, in large part, a matter of effective communication. If you can get the right message across to the right people in the right way, acceptance will follow. But this is not a simple matter. Communication is a complicated process which is strongly influenced by the personality of both the senders and receivers, the message and the medium. In a few pages, we cannot say very much about all these factors but we can note some special advantages and disadvantages of various media and suggest how a multi-media communication strategy could be put together.

1.   Choosing the Right Medium for the Right Job

The effective change agent cannot limit himself to one medium. You should be aware of the possibilities of various methods of presentation and you should be prepared to use several in combination as circumstances warrant. Of the six types discussed below, three (*written-oral presentation, films, and demonstrations*) are primarily one-way media: they allow you to send a message to your client but they do not allow him to send any counter-message to you. The other types, *person-to-person, group discussion,* and *training events* are two-way media: they give the client a chance to tell you what his needs and his objections are. The best type of program probably has both one-way and two-way media in various combinations, but it is important to recognize at the outset that one-way media, by themselves, rarely provide an adequate vehicle for gaining acceptance of innovation.

a. *Written and Oral Presentations*

Lectures and textbooks are still standard fare in college teaching but they should be used more sparingly and judiciously by the change agent. These traditional message forms are effective only when the audience is thoroughly "tuned in" and "turned on." This will only apply to a handful of innovators who are already aware and interested. For the majority of potential adopters, written and oral communications can only serve to provide awareness and, even then, only if the message is brief and to the point.

In more progressive communities, opinion leaders will be media-oriented; e.g., some of them will read about the innovation in the local newspaper and may even get to a PTA meeting to hear a lecture. This kind of exposure may create awareness *and* interest but it may also create awareness *and* resistance if the message is not carefully composed. A major difficulty with written communications is the fact that the change agent has no control over the conditions of exposure. Words and phrases can be torn out of context and meanings badly distorted with no assurance that the receiver even heard or read the important parts of the message.

b. *Film*

Because of these and other drawbacks to the traditional written and oral message forms, we have seen a trend in recent years toward carefully packaged audio-visual presentations, of which the TV commercial is perhaps the most notorious. Such presentations are primarily effective in creating awareness and perhaps interest. At their worst, film presentations are simply lectures on celluloid, but if the medium is used to best advantage various visual effects can be created to make the message more attractive. Films only work if the film maker invests a tremendous amount of time, money, and creative energy in the production. Most change agents will not have the resources to make their own films,

"AWARENESS-AND-RESIST-ANCE" WAS THE RESULT OF THE INITIAL EFFORTS OF MIKE'S GROUP IN EXPOSING COMMUNITY OPINION LEADERS TO THE PROPOSED SEX EDUCATION PROGRAM. BE-CAUSE THEIR INITIAL MES-SAGE ABOUT THE PROGRAM AND ITS GOALS WAS NOT CAREFULLY COMPOSED, THEY WERE TEMPORARILY RE-STRAINED FROM IMPLEMENT-ING THE CURRICULUM CHANGE.

but it is well worth a check to see if any films are available which might help you introduce the innovation to the client system in an interesting and lively way. If films are available, it is always wise to *preview* to make sure production quality is high before you risk exposure to a large or important audience. Some films are also useful as means of getting a group started on thinking about their problems. It is sometimes possible to make 8mm films in the client system itself, to illustrate various problems. In any case, films should almost always be used in conjunction with group discussion and as a prelude and stimulus to group interaction on the problem or the situation.

c. *Demonstrations*

Sometimes it is possible to put on live demonstrations of the innovation for potential adopters, or to take potential adopters to other settings where the innovation is already installed. This approach can be effective for building interest and for pre-trial evaluation but, as a technique, it should be handled carefully. There are two conditions which must apply before a demonstration is advisable. First, *the setting and the conditions must appear to be natural and similar* to those prevailing in the client system. Second, the change agent must know that *the demonstration will work* and will clearly illustrate the positive features of the innovation. A demonstration that fails through clumsy execution can be a disaster for a change project.

d. *Person-to-Person Contacts*

It is important for the change agent to make personal contacts with leaders, opinion leaders, potential resisters, and other key people. Such contacts have several advantages over the one-way approaches discussed above. First, they give you feedback on the reactions of the client system, including some idea of the kinds of resistance which you are likely to encounter and which you must plan to overcome. Second, the personal contact is very helpful in increasing the "reality" of the innovation. It forces the person contacted to start thinking about it seriously. Furthermore, it gives him an opportunity to express feelings of doubt and difficulty; it allows him a chance to talk about his own needs in personal terms.

Personal contact with the change agent is probably most vital at the time when the potential adopter is about to make a trial. Your presence is required then (1) to legitimize and reinforce the decision to try; (2) to provide needed information and help in the trial itself; and (3) to applaud and otherwise reward the trial effort, once made. This last is

". . . Commissioner Allen has announced the possibility of creating a state-sponsored, centrally located education center for the demonstration of novel programs. During the interviews people from all across the state flatly rejected the idea. 'Too artificial,' they said, 'what can we learn from a "show-off" school where specially selected teachers and specially selected kids, using the best equipment and materials, perform in a sort of convention atmosphere?' "

Brickell[14]

MIKE MADE A LARGE NUMBER OF PERSONAL CONTACTS WITH STUDENTS AND PARENTS AS WELL AS TEACHERS. THESE CONTACTS SEEMED TO BE CRUCIAL IN CREATING A POSITIVE AND TRUSTING ATTITUDE TOWARD THE KIND OF PROGRAM HE WAS INTRODUCING.

especially important when the results of the innovation trial effort are not immediately visible.

On the other side it should also be said that person-to-person contact is a very slow and costly method if you plan to reach each and every member of a large client system. It is therefore sometimes necessary to restrict these personal contacts to key people and, wherever possible, you should try to multiply yourself by training and encouraging insiders to take on this change agent task. Actually, personal contacts from insiders are probably more effective for legitimizing innovation, especially if these insiders have some degree of opinion leadership. They help get the innovation around the "NIH" syndrome (see opposite).

e. *Group Discussions*

Group discussion meetings of various sizes can be used to mobilize popular support but, like the demonstration, they can also mobilize resistance if not adequately handled. Group discussion serves many of the same functions as person-to-person contact, but you can reach more people and you can use the group to promote individual acceptance. Groups have these special advantages if they are well handled.

(1) They increase the feeling of safety and the willingness to take risks.

(2) They help the individual user move toward a commitment to try out the innovation.

(3) They legitimize feelings of doubt about the innovation and about one's own ability to try it out. Once these feelings are thus legitimized they can be spoken. Out in the open they can be discussed frankly and considered in a rational light. Some of these feelings do have a rational basis, some do not. Those that do must be answered by the change agent and/or the promoters of the innovation. Those that do not will probably dissipate if they are handled in an open and honest way.

(4) They give the client system an opportunity to move toward a consensus on the innovation. Individuals who favor it will begin to find others who favor it.

(5) They give potential adopters the feeling that they are actually participating in a decision with the freedom to say "yes" or "no."

"If persons regard the change as coming from an outside source, it may receive only half-hearted support which is sometimes called the NIH treatment—NOT INVENTED HERE."

Watson and Glaser[15]

127

If possible, a group discussion should be an enjoyable experience which is rewarding in itself. People who come to a meeting are usually extending themselves, making a real effort to get involved; their effort should be rewarded.

f. *Conferences, Workshops and Training Events*

When complex innovations are under consideration, it will usually be necessary to arrange conferences or workshops which involve key members of the client system. Such meetings can be used for diagnostic sessions (STAGE II), for identifying relevant resources (STAGE III), for brainstorming and choosing alternative solutions (STAGE IV), for facilitating individual awareness, interest, and evaluation, for providing a protected environment to allow practice of new skills and trial use of the innovation, and to mobilize social forces (leaders, opinion leaders) on behalf of the change. Any one conference could conceivably accomplish all of these goals but it is probably advisable to specify in advance the particular subset of change goals you want to achieve in a particular meeting.

The design and management of such conferences is an art, not a science, and it deserves a handbook of its own. Here we can only suggest some general outcomes that conference planners should strive for. The ideal conference:

(1) is an enjoyable experience in itself for *all* participants.

(2) leaves *all* participants with some *new* learning of:
      ideas
      problems
      findings
      solutions
      or skills.

(3) leads to diffusion of such learning beyond those participating (which usually means that opinion leaders in the client system have to participate).

(4) leads to subsequent self-training, self-practice back home, further inquiry activities by participants back home.

(5) multiplies itself (causes participants to initiate similar meetings for others).

(6) leads to more permanent linkage (liking, trust, and respect) among individual members and the groups they represent.

2. Orchestrating a Multi-Media Program*

One medium among those listed above may be just right for one particular audience at one point in time, but this does not constitute a total program for gaining the acceptance of the client system as a whole. A complete program will inevitably require the use of several different media approaches to reach various groups with the kinds of messages they are ready to hear. Four principal considerations should enter into your planning for a multi-media program:

a. *Think of the type of people you wish to reach.* What kinds of media are they accustomed to, and what kinds will they respond to?

b. *Plan to use different media approaches at different stages* of individual acceptance. (Section A of this chapter.)

c. *Plan to use different media approaches to reach different key individuals* (the *innovators, resisters,* and *leaders* discussed in Section B of this chapter).

d. *Build Redundancy into Your Program.* Never assume that anybody gets the message the first time. Review it with them again and again via different media.

"The aim is to develop an awareness about print and newer media so that we can orchestrate them, minimize their mutual frustrations and clashes, and get the best out of each."

McLuhan[16]

HENRY'S AGENCY TRIED TO DEVELOP A MULTI-MEDIA PROGRAM. HOW COULD SUCH A PROGRAM HAVE BEEN DEVELOPED BY MIKE AND HIS GROUP? STEVE AND HIS TEAM? LINDA AND THE PEOPLE WHO SUPPORTED HER?

D. KEEP YOUR PROGRAM FLEXIBLE

Throughout this handbook we have stressed the value of planning for innovation, utilizing a systematic step-by-step approach based on what you know about how people change their attitudes and behavior. However, once you have a plan, you should not be overly rigid in the way you carry it out. You must remain flexible, ever willing and able to change your plans as you gather more data on the client system and its reactions to the innovation. As you proceed you may, for example, find that the innovation is completely unacceptable to a large minority and that it divides the community and causes unhealthy conflict. Such a reaction should lead you either to revise the strategy of gaining acceptance, to readapt (redesign, repackage, etc.) the innovation so that it is more

---

*This is not a text on the use of media. The reader should consult Appendix B for more specific advice, particularly the ERIC Clearinghouse on Educational Media and Technology at Stanford University, Stanford, California.

acceptable, or perhaps to abandon the innovation altogether in favor of another which diffuses more readily.

To maintain a flexible posture, you should always be prepared to (1) readapt the innovation, (2) shift gears (up, down, reverse), and (3) change your implementation strategy.

1. Adaptation of the Innovation

Even when you have done a very careful job of selecting and adapting the innovation prior to introducing it to the client system, you may still find that more adaptation is necessary. You should be prepared to give concessions to meet various client objections in order that the major portion of the change be accepted. In order to ensure greater understanding of the nature of the innovation, you should be prepared to translate the relevant information to make it more meaningful.

2. Shifting Gears

Timing and proper pacing are important factors in gaining acceptance. Therefore, you should always be ready to shift gears, to move faster or slower than you had originally planned, depending on the readiness of your clients.

a. *Shifting Up*

Sometimes you may over-anticipate resistance to the innovation and may have an overly elaborate and extended program for introduction. When you sense that your clients are more sophisticated or more open than anticipated, you should accelerate your program.

b. *Shifting Down*

You may also find that you have expected too much of your clients and that they are unable to absorb information and to adapt to the innovation as rapidly as you had planned. Therefore, there should be enough flexibility in your planning to allow for a relatively long period of time for diffusion of the innovation. For example, you should be prepared to reset the projected date of final adoption in the light of unforeseen problems that may arise in the various stages of the change process.

c. *Reversing Gears*

The common belief that "if at first you don't succeed, try, try again" may not always be true in gaining acceptance of innovations. Sometimes, more pressure and more hard

FURTHER ADAPTATION WAS NECESSARY BEFORE MIKE'S AND LINDA'S INNOVATIONS WERE FULLY ACCEPTABLE. THE SAME WAS PROBABLY TRUE FOR HENRY ALTHOUGH HE DOES NOT SAY TOO MUCH ABOUT THIS.

MIKE'S GROUP WAS ABLE TO SLOW DOWN AND REVERSE GEARS WITHOUT SCUTTLING THEIR PROGRAM. APPARENTLY IN STEVE'S CASE THE PROJECT HAD TO BE ABANDONED. WAS THERE ANY WAY STEVE COULD HAVE REVERSED GEARS WITHOUT ABANDONMENT?

"When a new idea is first introduced to us, we begin to think about and consider it from many different viewpoints. In time, its novelty and strangeness disappears. Eventually, it becomes familiar ... When sufficient time is not allowed for such adjustment, those involved in a change could become bewildered or apprehensive and develop feelings of opposition."

Judson[17]

"More new methods, hell! I can't farm half as well as I know how already."

Anonymous Farmer

130

salesmanship will only *increase* the resistance. This is why your diagnosis of opposing forces is so important. Frequently you will be more successful in the long run if you retreat in the face of strong opposition, concentrating instead on reducing the motivation for this resistance.

3. Changing Your Implementation Strategy

Throughout this handbook we have urged change agents to adopt an open and collaborative strategy with their clients. *This posture is more likely than any other to ensure the best use of new knowledge.* Collaboration works for three reasons: First, it gets the client involved and motivated; second, it improves the *quality of the adoption* because the client understands it better; and third, it may improve the *quality of the innovation* itself, because the client can make valuable contributions *in adaptation* to his setting. However, there is an additional reason for choosing collaboration, which is purely ethical: to choose to be purposefully non-collaborative is to break faith with a client; such a stance presumes that the client is unwilling and unable to innovate on his own initiative and must be coerced, cajoled, or tricked into acceptance.

After all this is said, it must be admitted that *sometimes* collaboration just will not work and, when it fails, there are a number of alternatives that should be considered, ranging from complete abandonment to complete deception. The quotation opposite suggests a strategy of "fait accompli," one approach which might be employed when you think collaboration will not work. However, Watson and Glaser's message is basically the same as ours: *be flexible about your strategy for gaining acceptance;* use collaboration wherever you can, but remember that other approaches are possible, and sometimes, perhaps, these other approaches are necessary to achieve an end which all desire.

"A natural impulse of many people is to meet force with force; that is, to overcome the opposing forces by exhorting, appealing, arguing, urging, inducing, and scolding. Increasing pressure against the opposing forces usually will increase the resistance pressure, and as a result, tension will be heightened. Frequently (but not always), the wisest and most effective course of action is to focus on ways of understanding and reducing resistance rather than trying to overwhelm it."

Watson and Glaser[18]

"Some social psychological studies have shown that it is sometimes more effective to introduce the changed operation first, before attempting to bring about the desired attitude change. This is the fait accompli technique: The situation is changed by responsible management decision, then workers are helped to understand and accept it.

"This technique runs directly counter to much that has been said, here and elsewhere, about enlisting participation in planning for change. There are situations, however, where it presents marked advantages. As long as a change seems merely hypothetical, many persons find it difficult to come to grips with it. They are beset by vague fears and discomforts. When the change has been actually experienced, its advantages may be more apparent.

"The frequent success of both the participative method of decision-making and the fait

accompli technique raises the question, 'When is each preferable?' Generally, if the consequences of the change can be realistically understood by the people at the working level, their cooperation in designing change is helpful and the participative method is more effective. If, however, the results of a change are not clearly and rationally predictable—if there is a heavy 'loading' of irrational prejudice—then experience may be the best teacher. Under these conditions, if earnest and skillful efforts to understand and reduce resistance are fruitless, and the legitimate and responsible authorities still believe the action to be essential, the change may be more likely to come about if imposed from the top. If, in a limited area of the organization, or for a limited time in the organization as a whole, it proves successful, attitudes may be more effectively changed than they would be by many hours of advance argument."

Watson and Glaser[19]

Stage VI:

STABILIZING THE INNOVATION AND GENERATING SELF-RENEWAL

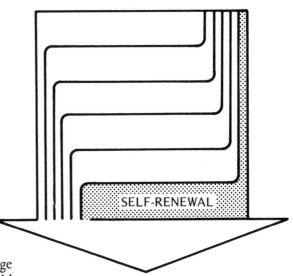

SELF-RENEWAL

It is probably not accidental that two of the four change agents who reported cases at the beginning of this book could find nothing to say about stabilization and termination. When the change agent has succeeded in gaining acceptance, he is very much inclined to think that his job is done and that it is now up to the client to take over the task of long-term maintenance. This is, indeed, a reasonable assumption; the responsibility of the change agent must end somewhere. His time and energy are not unlimited and there are clients in other places with problems waiting for his help. In this final chapter we will, therefore, try to suggest when and how the change agent can leave the project feeling reasonably sure that his client has been well served and has the capacity to carry on alone.

If you have been able to develop a change program along the lines suggested in previous chapters, your task will now be relatively simple. Because you have worked collaboratively with the client and involved him directly in all phases of the change process, by this time he should be well trained in helping himself; he will have a good understanding of diagnosis, retrieval, selection, and so forth. *That* is the *ideal*, but we know that it is *not* usually the *reality*; hence this chapter had to be added.

STAGE VI is divided into three sections. In the first we consider the problem of how to *insure the continuance of a particular innovation* once it has been accepted by the client system. The second will introduce the concept of *system self-renewal* and suggest ways in which the change agent can move the client toward a self-renewal capacity. In the third brief section we will explore some of the problems related to the *act of disengagement,* the final termination of the relationship with the client.

> *"Many an innovation brought in with great fanfare is superficially accepted, and months or years later, things have drifted back to the way they were before. Nobody may have openly resisted the change. Nobody revoked it. It just didn't last . . ."*
>
> Watson and Glaser[1]

always train the client towards being self sufficient.

WHICH OF THE FOUR CASE STUDY INNOVATIONS HAS THE BEST CHANCE OF LONG-TERM SURVIVAL? WHY?

A. *INSURING CONTINUANCE**

The key word in insuring continuance is "internaliza-

*Some of these points have already been made in STAGE V but they bear repeating.

tion." Where possible, the change agent should lead the client toward self-help and responsibility in the maintenance of the innovation. There are at least six important considerations in insuring continuance. These are:

1. *Continuing **Reward***
2. *Practice and **Routinization***
3. ***Structural Integration** into the System*
4. *Continuing **Evaluation***
5. *Providing for Continuing **Maintenance***
6. *Continuing **Adaptation** Capability*

1.   Continuing Reward

Positive reinforcement is the most important influence on human behavior. The client must feel that the innovation pays off in one way or another and he must see that it continues to pay off over time. You should do all you can to make sure that the rewards are visible to the client and that they continue to be visible.

Rewards for innovation can come in a number of ways. The innovation may pay off directly in improved performance, reduced costs, saved time and labor, etc., but when these direct benefits are not clear immediately the *indirect* rewards, such as the continuing encouragement and approval of others, become very important. One major reason for follow-up by the change agent is to provide this kind of support; the knowledge that "someone out there really cares" can be a crucial factor in promoting continued use.

"*Guidance and encouragement, not power control, fosters creativity and innovativeness.*"

Woods[2]

2.   Practice and Routinization

True adoption of an innovation does not come automatically with acceptance. The would-be user must become familiar with it, trying it out repeatedly in the situations which are natural to him. Early trials take a lot of time and effort because new things do not come easy. For a long time the user is likely to feel awkward and artificial even if he believes that the innovation is right for him. He must get through this period before the change agent can be sure that the innovation will really work.

Ideally the innovation should eventually become a routine part of everyday life for the client. It should be something he can do or use automatically without an excessive amount of concentrated effort.

3.   Structural Integration into the System

Innovations which last are those which become a part of the way of life of the client system, embedded in its everyday

"The members of the organization participate in determining the rate of change and the amount of effort to be devoted to development in light of the importance they give to the effort and the day-to-day pressures to which

behavior. For this to happen the innovation must also be integrated within the existing structure: there must be room for it. Provision must be made for people to have time to use it and money to buy it, or run it, or maintain it. The willingness of the leaders to make room for an innovation is probably the best index to their real attitudes toward it, regardless of the lip service that is paid to "accepting" it.

4. Continuing Evaluation

Some provision should be made for reinspection and reevaluation of the innovation over time. This type of activity insures against slippage in the *quality* of the innovation as well as providing an added incentive and reminder that the innovation is still supposed to be in operation.

Evaluation need not be in the form of rigorous and detailed measurement and analysis, but it should be a self-consciously objective inspection and reappraisal, preferably performed by someone who is informed but not personally invested in the innovation. Obviously, the larger the investment in the innovation and the greater its presumed impact, the more attention should be paid to reevaluation.

Evaluation is one of the many tasks which the change agent should encourage *others* to undertake, partly because it is time consuming, but mainly because the change agent may be too subjectively invested in the innovation. If you have expended much energy in gaining acceptance for an innovation you may not be an objective judge of its effectiveness because you will *want* to believe that it is being used widely in an efficient and beneficial way.

5. Providing for Continuing Maintenance

Whether we are talking about hardware innovations (such as sound 8mm film equipment) or social innovations (such as new patterns of management), breakdowns and misapplications are bound to occur after initial installation. There must be some sort of maintenance system to deal with these situations. There must be someone to show us where the innovation went wrong and how we can make it right. Again because you cannot predict when a breakdown will occur and you cannot remain on the scene indefinitely, maintenance probably should be a built-in function provided by someone you have trained for this purpose. If there is no provision for maintenance, you may get a rapid erosion of acceptance after failures begin to occur. The inability to correct errors and breakdowns rapidly breeds distrust of the innovation and a spread of negative reactions and rumors that

they must respond. The pressure of other tasks, we have found, is one of the most difficult barriers to surmount—although it is also a socially acceptable reason cited by those who are uneasy about becoming involved in change or have encountered a difficult phase of the process. Allowing participants to help decide how they will allot their time, however, appears to have this advantage: When they do devote effort to development, they are doing so because it makes sense to them and not merely because 'it satisfies the boss' or an outside expert."

Buchanan[3]

"Part of any program of change should be a procedure for periodic review and revision. Again, the role of the members of the organization is vital. By inviting them to participate in the review, we deepen their commitment to the enterprise. If they know that the experiment has been inaugurated with the intention of re-evaluating it after a reasonable period of trial, they will accept some initial inconvenience, aware that they will have a chance to air their complaints and to modify the program. If they know that they themselves will be called upon to take part in this review, they will observe more carefully and prepare themselves to offer better suggestions."

Watson and Glaser[4]

135

the innovation will not work and will be more trouble than it is worth.

6. Continuing Adaptation Capability

As noted in the previous chapter, sophisticated acceptance and adoption requires flexibility and an ability to adapt as well as adopt. This continues to be true over time because the client's circumstances may change. If the client is able to reshape the innovation to meet his changing needs he will be more likely to continue using it effectively.

If these six points are considered in formulating your strategy, you are likely to succeed in stabilizing the innovation. But complete stabilization of a particular innovation may not always be in the best interest of your client in the long run, as one of the case study change agents noted (see opposite).

A sophisticated consumer accepts innovations only so long as they benefit him more than competing innovations. Thus, stabilization should only be partial, never total. The client should retain the flexibility and the freedom to discontinue an innovation when something better comes along.

B. *CREATING A SELF-RENEWAL CAPACITY*

A great deal of what has been said so far in this chapter contains an implicit message: *the client should learn to be a change agent for himself.* This is what we mean by "self-renewal."

A self-renewing client system will have to have four built-in features. First, it should have a *positive attitude* toward innovation in general. Second, it should have an *internal subsystem* which is specifically devoted to bringing about change. Third, it should have an active *inclination to seek external resources.* Fourth and finally, it should have a *perspective on the future as something to plan for.* Each of these features deserves some discussion.

1. A Positive Attitude to Innovation

The reason that many "successfully adopted" innovations seem to fade and disappear in time is that the systems which adopted those innovations failed to fully incorporate innovative norms and attitudes which are fundamental to innovative behavior. Consider the history of your clients in this regard. Are they typically on the forefront of new developments in education? Do they seem to look forward to

HENRY'S AGENCY, BECAUSE IT SERVES A LIMITED REGION WITHIN ONE STATE, IS IN A POSITION TO PROVIDE FOLLOW-UP AND MAINTENANCE FOR ITS CLIENT SCHOOLS.

"Many educational approaches to change in the past have been directed at a single change. This tends to result in thinking of change as product introduction rather than as a process of adaptation. This approach is dysfunctional in any long term view since it tends to lead to an attitude of 'we innovated last year.' "

Howsam[5]

"Following any important change comes a period during which the new equilibrium is being stabilized. Yet that condition, too, is only temporary. The organization that has accepted an innovation may need a breathing spell in which to consolidate what it has learned. But if the organization is geared to continued growth, its members will value forward-moving change as a recurrent and desirable phenomenon. From the plateau on which equilibrium is regained, the cycle of change can be launched again."

Watson and Glaser[6]

"Perhaps change agents should seek to provide their clients with a more favorable basic attitude toward new ideas and spend fewer efforts in campaigns to secure the adoption of single innovations."

Rogers[7]

change as potential improvement rather than potential threat?

If you answer these questions in the negative, then the major issue becomes: "How can I instill an innovative attitude?" Adequate answers to this question are hard to come by but there are some partial answers. First, make the positive results of innovating as visible as possible. Second, provide as many secondary rewards (praise, financial aid, recognition of achievement) as possible to people in the client system who do innovate. And third, encourage and assist the innovators in becoming more influential and in assuming more leadership. Some additional ideas are suggested by Chesler and Fox (see opposite).

2. An Internal Change Agency

It was not until after World War II that a number of large corporations decided they should have their own research departments to do advance planning and design on new products. These early "R & D" units were the first attempt to create a change agency within the organization, a group of people who were supposed to work on innovation as a full-time job. Now with the help of federal legislation of the 1960's and the project funding which it has generated, there is the possibility of developing an internal change agency in every school district. Such an agency would give structural legitimacy and reality to the concept of self-renewal.

A subsystem for innovation ideally should incorporate such features as:

a. full-time change agents or consultants who understand the innovation process and can work easily with other members of the client system.

b. built-in competence to train all members of the client system in the skills of diagnosis, retrieval, selection, and evaluation of innovations.

A fully developed change agency such as that described by change agent "Henry" has all these features and more; we doubt that most change agents will be able to bring together all the resources that Henry was able to muster, but, at a minimum, a self-renewing system should be one that includes *some* sort of structural entity (e.g., an office, a part-time staff member, a budget line item, etc.) especially set aside for innovation.

3. An External Orientation

"Innovativeness" cannot simply be viewed as a passive receptivity to new ideas. Self-renewing systems are habitually aggressive in seeking out new solutions. They have an active faith that outside resources will be useful and a willingness to

"Work in a situation where one feels liked and respected by peers and supervisors is obviously more satisfying and fulfilling than work where one feels ignored; furthermore, it predisposes one to be positive and supportive to others. Thus, such a setup fosters a continuing cycle of change and support, invention and sharing of ideas.

"To establish a healthy climate for change we need first to develop ways for individual teachers to share new ideas with other staff members and to gain support for worthy innovations. Further, we need to make teachers feel that they have had some influence in developing changes by adopting new administrative styles which decentralize decision-making.

"The growing body of research findings about change processes in the schools makes clear, however, that the development of an open and supportive climate of personal and professional relationships among the members of the school faculty carried high priority."

Chesler and Fox[8]

137

walk the extra mile to get them. Rural sociologists discovered a long time ago that innovative farmers took more trips to town. They were more "cosmopolite," willing and able to go outside their immediate environment. The same is true for educators. If your clients have a habit of visiting other systems, attending all sorts of meetings and training programs, they will keep coming home like Marco Polo, bringing all kinds of new ideas and new products to their colleagues.

There are many ways in which the change agent can encourage an external orientation in the client system. Above all, he can encourage and facilitate travel and outside visiting. The important thing is to get clients used to the idea that visiting and conferencing are not only legitimate but are enjoyable activities. Developing this cosmopolite orientation is a good reason for taking the time to set up site visits and demonstrations away from home. What the client learns about the specific innovation may turn out to be less important in the long run than the fact that he got out of his rut and began looking at the rest of the world.

4. Future Orientation

A self-renewing system believes in progress. It believes that things can be better in the future, especially if we plan for the future carefully and conscientiously. This means developing a capacity to forecast community needs and desires five and ten years hence. It also means setting aside time and resources to think about the future and to draw up tentative programs to meet future needs. (See again our discussion of brainstorming in STAGE IV.)

This sort of planning is not simply an intellectual exercise or a pleasant escape into science fiction. On the contrary, a perspective on the future helps us to put the present in focus and may suggest things that we can do today that we would not have thought of in other, more time-bound contexts.

C. *DISENGAGEMENT (AFTER A SUCCESSFUL INNOVATION PROJECT)*

A change agent can make a career out of one innovation and one client system. Depending on the size of the client system and the significance and complexity of the innovation, this may be quite a reasonable decision to take. For such a change agent disengagement is not an important issue because it never comes. For most change agents, however, it should and will come. You should think about the consequences of disengagement and plan for them well in advance

"It is a sad fact, that few school systems have full-time training directors and training staff, whereas no industrial concern would feel it could maintain its competitive position without a fully developed, continuing program of manpower training and retraining. When one member of a school board, who also happened to be president of a paper company, discovered this fact recently, he exclaimed, 'You mean to tell me we use better intelligence in producing better paper than we do in raising better kids!' "

Lippitt[9]

"Narrow time-perspective within the decision-making processes—a lack of perception of long-range consequences of action as relevant to immediate decision—tends toward a pattern of living from crisis to crisis in the life of the system."

Benne[10]

138

of actual termination. The two questions that should concern you are "*when?*" and "*how?*"

1. When Do You Begin to Disengage?

You can begin to think about disengagement when you start to observe signs of internalization of the innovation or, preferably, when you see signs that self-renewal capacity is beginning to build. There are three basic conditions which allow withdrawal on happy and honorable terms: (a) there is good evidence that the originally diagnosed problem is on its way to solution; (b) the innovation has been accepted by the leadership and is beginning to diffuse rapidly among other system members; (c) there is evidence that the system is generating a self-renewal capacity. Which of these three criteria you choose will depend upon your own objectives. Alternatives "a" and "b" are obviously more limited than "c," but you may not be able to wait for "c" to develop if you have competing demands and obligations from other client systems. Moreover, it probably takes a good deal of experience and clinical insight to sense the moment when the client is ready to step out on his own.

2. How Do You Disengage?

Because of the need for follow-up and continuing aid in adaptation, the disengagement process should be gradual. You should not leave the client without fully thinking through with him how he will carry on without you. Discussions and specific commitments to continued work on the innovation should be a part of these closing phases of the relationship.

In addition you should not be blind to psychological problems which may surround the act of disengagement. Remember that you have worked to create a strong relationship in which there has been some degree of mutual dependency. If you have done your job right, you now have many good friends throughout the system. They will be reluctant to have you go and you will be reluctant to leave on this account alone. Talking to them about the necessity of termination and discussing how they will carry on the project will smooth the transition.

Complete termination, however, is neither necessary nor advisable in most situations. Even after you have departed you should be available for emergency help and scheduled annual reunions. These continuing friendships and formal and informal contacts with former clients are an important part of *your* reward system. This is one of the great satisfactions of being a change agent.

"I would like to suggest that finding a means of freeing planning talent from executive responsibilities is an urgent necessity if long-range planning is to get beyond the talking stage. There is a level of planning between the 'big idea' and the level of detailed planning that requires extended analytical attention, and the time given to this level of planning often determines the quality and worth of an entire endeavor."

Barnes [11]

"If the client system has come to depend heavily on the change agent for support and guidance throughout the process of diagnosis, change, and evaluation, then naturally the end of the relationship is likely to be a somewhat painful affair."

Lippitt, Watson and Westley [12]

NOTES

Notes to Stage I:

1. Ronald Lippitt, Jeanne Watson, and Bruce Westley, *The Dynamics of Planned Change* (New York: Harcourt, Brace and World, Inc., 1958), p. 170.

2. Goodwin Watson, "Resistance to Change," in *The Planning of Change*, 2nd ed., eds. Warren G. Bennis, Kenneth D. Benne, and Robert Chin (New York: Holt, Rinehart and Winston, 1969), p. 492.

3. *Ibid.,* p. 494.

4. Henry M. Brickell, "State Organization for Educational Change: A Case Study and a Proposal," in *Innovation in Education,* ed. Matthew B. Miles (New York: Teachers College, Columbia University, 1964), p. 502.

5. Goodwin Watson and Edward M. Glaser, "What We Have Learned About Planning for Change," *Management Review*, November 1965, p. 36.

6. *Ibid.,* p. 36.

7. *Ibid.*

8. Ronald Lippitt, "Dimensions of the Consultant's Job," in *The Planning of Change,* eds. Warren G. Bennis, Kenneth D. Benne, and Robert Chin (New York: Holt, Rinehart and Winston, 1961), p. 160.

9. John C. Glidewell, "The Entry Problem in Consultation," in *The Planning of Change,* eds. Warren G. Bennis, Kenneth D. Benne, and Robert Chin (New York: Holt, Rinehart and Winston, 1961), p. 657.

10. Lippitt, Watson, and Westley, *op. cit.,* pp. 95-96.

11. Alinsky, Saul, *Rules for Radicals* (New York: Random House, 1971).

12. Glidewell, *op. cit.,* p. 659.

13. Lippitt, Watson, and Westley, *op. cit.,* p. 169.

14. *Ibid.,* p. 171.

15. *Ibid.,* p. 134.

16. Lippitt, *op. cit.,* p. 160.

17. Donald Klein, "Some Notes on the Dynamics of Resistance to Change: The Defender Role," in *Concepts for Social Change,* ed. Goodwin Watson (Washington, D.C.: National Training Laboratories, NEA, for the Cooperative Project for Educational Development 1967), pp. 29-30.

Notes to Stage II:

1. Ronald Lippitt, Jeanne Watson, and Bruce Westley, *The Dynamics of Planned Change* (New York: Harcourt, Brace and World, Inc., 1958), p. 66.

2. *Ibid.,* p. 66.

3. Robert Chin, "The Utility of System Models and Developmental Models for Practitioners," in *The Planning of Change,* eds. Warren G. Bennis, Kenneth D. Benne, and Robert Chin (New York: Holt, Rinehart and Winston, 1961), p. 203.

4. Henry M. Brickell, "State Organization for Educational Change: A Case Study and a Proposal," in *Innovation in Education,* ed. Matthew B. Miles (New York: Teachers College, Columbia University, 1964), pp. 503-504.

5. Matthew B. Miles, "Some Properties of Schools as Social Systems," in *Change in School Systems,* ed. Goodwin Watson (Washington, D.C.: National Training Laboratories, NEA, for the Cooperative Project for Educational Development 1967), p. 22.

6. Ralph B. Kimbrough, "Power Structures and Educational Change," in *Planning and Effecting Needed Changes in Education,* Designing Education for the Future, No. 3, eds. Edgar L. Morphet and Charles O. Ryan (New York: Citation Press, 1967), pp. 128-129.

7. Lippitt, Watson, and Westley, *op. cit.,* p. 42.

8. *Ibid.,* pp. 65-66.

9. Warren G. Bennis, Kenneth D. Benne, and Robert Chin, "Conceptual Tools for the Change Agent: Social System and Change Models," in *The Planning of Change,* eds. Warren G. Bennis, Kenneth D. Benne, and Robert Chin (New York: Holt, Rinehart and Winston, 1961), p. 197.

10. Lippitt, Watson, and Westley, *op. cit.,* p. 65.

Notes to Stage III:

1. William Paisley, *Sources of Information on Social Issues: Education, Employment, Public Health and Safety, Population, etc.* A brief guide for journalists and others. An occasional paper from ERIC Clearinghouse on Educational Media and Technology, Institute for Communication Research, Stanford University, Stanford, California, September, 1969.

2. *Ibid.*

3. *Ibid.*

4. *Ibid.*

5. W.C. Wolf, Jr. reporting on his research on the diffusion of educational innovations, *Educational Researcher*, XXI, January 1970.

6. Thomas Clemens, "Information Transfer and Research Utilization in Education" (Address presented to the staff of the Michigan Department of Education, Lansing, Michigan, July 14, 1969), p. 11.

7. Richard Lanham, "Marian the Technologist," *SDC Magazine,* 11, No. 10, (November 1968): 2.

8. Clemens, *op. cit.,* 11.

Notes to Stage IV:

1. Ronald Lippitt, Jeanne Watson, and Bruce Westley, *The Dynamics of Planned Change* (New York: Harcourt, Brace and World, Inc., 1958), p. 198.

2. William J.J. Gordon, *Synectics: The Development of Creative Capacity* (New York: Harper and Row, 1961), p. 9.

3. Peter Schrag, *Village School Downtown* (Boston: Beacon Press, 1968), p. 132.

4. Matthew B. Miles, "Innovation in Education: Some Generalizations," in *Innovation in Education,* ed. Matthew B. Miles (New York: Teachers College, Columbia University, 1964), p. 635.

5. Thomas E. Woods, *The Administration of Educational Innovation* (Eugene, Oregon: Bureau of Educational Research, School of Education, University of Oregon, 1967), p. 54.

6. Robert Chin, "Models of and Ideas about Changing," in *Media and Educational Innovation,* ed. Wesley C. Meierhenry (The University of Nebraska Extension Division and the University of Nebraska Press, 1964), p. 3.

7. Henry M. Brickell, "State Organization for Educational Change: A Case Study and a Proposal," In *Innovation in Education,* ed. Matthew B. Miles (New York: Teachers College, Columbia University, 1964), p. 505.

8. Everett M. Rogers, *Diffusion of Innovations* (New York: The Free Press, 1962), p. 124.

9. Miles, *op. cit.,* p. 636.

Notes to Stage V:

1. John G. Caffrey, "The Innovational Matrix" (Paper presented at the Institute for Government and Public Affairs Conference on Educational Innovations, UCLA Lake Arrowhead Center, December 17-29, 1965), p. 14.

2. Goodwin Watson, "Resistance to Change," in *The Planning of Change*, 2nd ed., eds. Warren G. Bennis, Kenneth D. Benne, and Robert Chin (New York: Holt, Rinehart and Winston, 1969), p. 497.

3. Thomas E. Woods, *The Administration of Educational Innovation* (Eugene, Oregon: Bureau of Educational Research, School of Education, University of Oregon, 1967), p. 57.

4. Everett M. Rogers and Lynne Svenning, *Managing Change* (San Mateo, California: Operation PEP, 1969), pp. 70-71. [Prepared under contract to USOE, Title III, ESEA 1965.]

5. Caffrey, *op. cit.*, pp. 10-11.

6. Ralph B. Kimbrough, "Power Structures and Educational Change," in *Planning and Effecting Needed Changes in Education*, Designing Education for the Future, No. 3, eds., Edgar L. Morphet and Charles O. Ryan (New York: Citation Press, 1967), p. 124.

7. Alan Guskin, "The Individual: Internal Processes and Characteristics Which Inhibit and Facilitate Knowledge Utilization," in *Planning for Innovation Through Dissemination and Utilization of Knowledge*, Ronald G. Havelock *et al.* (Ann Arbor, Michigan: Institute for Social Research, University of Michigan, 1969), Chapter 4, p. 10.

8. Watson, *op. cit.*, p. 495.

9. Donald Klein, "Some Notes on the Dynamics of Resistance to Change: The Defender Role," in *Concepts for Social Change*, ed. Goodwin Watson (Washington, D.C.: National Training Laboratories, NEA, for the Cooperative Project for Educational Development 1967), p. 31.

10. Woods, *op. cit.*, p. 56.

11. Watson, *op. cit.*, p. 11.

12. Arnold S. Judson, *A Manager's Guide to Making Changes* (New York: John Wiley and Sons, 1966), p. 69.

13. Klein, *op. cit.*, p. 33.

14. Henry M. Brickell, "State Organization for Educational Change: A Case Study and a Proposal," in *Innovation in Education*, ed. Matthew B. Miles (New York: Teachers College, Columbia University, 1964), p. 499.

15. Goodwin Watson and Edward M. Glaser, "What We Have Learned About Planning for Change," *Management Review,* November 1965, p. 36.

16. Marshall McLuhan, "Introduction," in *Explorations in Communications,* eds. Edmund S. Carpenter and Marshall McLuhan (Boston: Beacon Press, 1969), p. xii.

17. Judson, *op. cit.,* p. 80.

18. Watson and Glaser, *op. cit.,* p. 42.

19. *Ibid.,* pp. 44-46.

Notes to Stage VI:

1. Goodwin Watson and Edward M. Glaser, "What We Have Learned About Planning for Change," *Management Review,* November 1965, p. 45.

2. Thomas E. Woods, *The Administration of Educational Innovation* (Eugene, Oregon: Bureau of Educational Research, School of Education, University of Oregon, 1967), p. 37.

3. Paul C. Buchanan, "The Concept of Organization Development, or Self-Renewal, as a Form of Planned Change," in *Concepts for Social Change,* ed. Goodwin Watson (Washington, D.C.: National Training Laboratories, NEA, for the Cooperative Project for Educational Development, 1967), p. 3.

4. Watson and Glaser, *op cit.,* p. 46.

5. Robert B. Howsam, "Effecting Needed Changes in Education," in *Planning and Effecting Needed Changes in Education,* Designing Education for the Future, No. 3, eds. Edgar L. Morphet and Charles O. Ryan (New York: Citation Press, 1967), p. 72.

6. Watson and Glaser, *op cit.,* p. 46.

7. Everett M. Rogers, *Diffusion of Innovations* (New York: The Free Press, 1967), p. 281.

8. Mark A. Chesler and Robert Fox, "Teacher Peer Relations and Educational Change," *NEA Journal,* 56, No. 5 (May 1967): 26.

9. Ronald Lippitt, "Improving the Socialization Process," in *Change in School Systems,* ed. Goodwin Watson (Washington, D.C.: National Training Laboratories, NEA, for the Cooperative Project for Educational Development, 1967), p. 45.

10. Kenneth D. Benne, "Deliberate Changing as the Facilitation of Growth," in *The Planning of Change,* eds. Warren G. Bennis, Kenneth D. Benne, and Robert Chin (New York: Holt, Rinehart and Winston, 1961), p. 233.

11. Melvin W. Barnes, "Planning and Effecting Needed Changes in Urban and Metropolitan Areas," in *Planning and Effecting Needed Changes in Education,* Designing Education for the Future, No. 3, eds. Edgar L. Morphet and Charles O. Ryan (New York: Citation Press, 1967), p. 221.

12. Ronald Lippitt, Jeanne Watson, and Bruce Westley, *The Dynamics of Planned Change* (New York: Harcourt, Brace and World, Inc., 1958), p. 142.

PART THREE:

SUPPLEMENTARY RESOURCE INFORMATION

Appendix A

THE STRATEGIES AND TACTICS OF INNOVATION
Including
a Glossary and Guide to Selection

APPENDIX A
TABLE OF CONTENTS

THE STRATEGIES AND TACTICS OF INNOVATION

Including
a Glossary and Guide to Selection

As evidenced in many of the contents of this *Guide*, there has emerged in the last generation a solid conception of innovation based on realistic diagnosis of educational needs and systematic planning, development, and evaluation. "Strategy" is a key aspect of this new concept of innovation because it is now becoming recognized that change will only lead to real progress if it is brought about in an orderly sequence of goal-setting, planning, and systematic execution. Clearly, therefore, there is a need for educators to spell out in detail their "innovative" plans and activities in terms of overall "*strategies*" and in terms of the explicit sequences of action steps ("*tactics*") that make up these strategies.

This handbook would not be complete without a listing of specific strategies and tactics which experienced change agents have recommended for use at various stages of a change program. Our prime purpose is to impress upon the reader the very broad range of alternatives available to him in the selection of innovation strategies. Hence, the more useful part of this Appendix may be the listing and brief description of tactics which have been included, because each educational innovator does not have to belong to any of the three strategic schools we will describe. Rather, he can be his own strategist; he can be perfectly pragmatic and eclectic in choosing tactics that fit his own style and experience and the situation in which he finds himself.

In a two-page chart we have also tried to show which strategies and tactics might be applicable to specific stages in the process described in the handbook. It is not easy to make such a listing because there is considerable overlap. Most strategies have multiple purposes that stretch across two or more stages and nearly *all* strategies and tactics have *some* relevance to *every* stage.

CONSIDERATIONS IN CHOOSING THE BEST STRATEGY

We have stressed throughout this handbook the need for the educational change agent to formulate his own strategies to suit his own peculiar background and circumstances. The specific strategies and tactics discussed below may provide a number of additional ideas to help in this task, but there are some general considerations which should always be a part of strategy building.

1. The change agent should evaluate his *own style and skills.* Most of the tactics discussed below cannot simply be picked up casually from a manual. They are skills which have to be learned. A good tactic badly executed may be worse than no tactic at all. (*PRIMUM NON NOCERE!*)

2. The change agent should consider the *type of relationship* which he has with his client system. If he enters the relationship as a superior or "expert" with considerable influence, the number of strategic and tactical options are greater than if he enters as a peer. If the original

relationship to the client system is ill-defined or misperceived, the early focus of activity should be exclusively on altering and clarifying the *relationship*. Relationships not only to the intended target audience but also to other social forces which impinge directly upon this audience (e.g., political and economic tensions in the community) also have to be considered.

3. The *special characteristics of the client system* always have to be weighed carefully in choosing a strategy. If, for example, human relations tactics are totally foreign to the experience of your clients, some of the more sophisticated H-R tactics should probably be held in abeyance. The change agent needs to make a good diagnosis of his client, learn of his special weaknesses and prejudices and his special talents and areas of high capacity and openness.

4. The *characteristics of the innovation* itself also should be analyzed carefully on a number of dimensions. How much adaptation will be required by the user? How much practice and trial? How long a delay before positive results are apparent (reward)? How much training is required? "User-proof" innovations may not require elaborate innovative diffusion strategies; perhaps they can even succeed via the "fait accompli" method; but if the innovation is not "user-proof," then a collaborative problem-solving approach is the best way to proceed.

5. Similar questions should be asked of the *medium.* Is the medium one with which the intended receiver will be familiar? (E.g., Does he actually spend time watching educational TV? Does he customarily pick up new ideas from reading about them in print? etc.) Is the medium capable of transmitting your message clearly and accurately? Are you, as the change agent, sufficiently experienced and sufficiently comfortable in using this particular medium in this particular way?

6. A strategy should also be adapted to the specific *situational factors* of time, place, and circumstances. The kind of tactics that can be employed in teaching a course or conducting a weekend workshop may be totally inappropriate for a one-hour slot in a convention program.

7. The change agent should make a thorough accounting of *resources* to which he and his client have access, internal and external, human, material, and informational. A *good library* in the community, the availability of *volunteer help,* or a strong *motivation to change:* these are all examples of resources which may suggest one approach over another. *Existing capacities* of the system should be mobilized and utilized whenever and wherever possible.

THREE MAJOR STRATEGIC ORIENTATIONS AND SOME EMERGING ALTERNATIVES

There is a considerable bulk of literature dealing explicitly with strategies of innovation in education.* Most of the strategies discussed in these sources can be grouped conveniently under three headings, which roughly fit the designations "Problem-Solving" (P-S), "Social Interaction" (S-I), and "Research, Development, and Diffusion" (RD & D). It is not our desire in this Appendix to recommend any one of these strategic orientations over any other, nor will we be able to thoroughly explore the relative merits of each. But in the discussion below, we want first to

*See Appendix C for an annotated bibliography of the major sources.

154

highlight the major positive features of each; second, to indicate the specific strategies that are derived from each; and third, to list the tactics most frequently associated with such strategies.

1. **Problem-Solving (P-S)**

   a. *The P-S Strategic Orientation*

This orientation rests on the primary assumption that innovation is a part of a problem-solving process which goes on inside the user. Problem-solving is usually seen as a patterned sequence of activities beginning with a *need*, sensed and articulated by the client, which is translated into a *problem* statement and *diagnosis*. When he has thus formulated a problem statement, the client-user is able to conduct a meaningful *search* and *retrieval* of ideas and information which can be used in formulating or selecting the *innovation*. Finally, the user needs to concern himself with *adapting* the innovation, *trying out* and *evaluating* its effectiveness in *satisfying* his original need. The focus of this orientation is the user himself, his needs and what he does about satisfying his needs. The role of outsiders is therefore consultative or collaborative. The outside change agent may assist the user either by providing new ideas and innovations specific to the diagnosis or by providing guidance on the *process* of problem-solving at any or all of the indicated stages. Figure A-1 illustrates this relationship.

FIGURE A-1:   The Problem-Solver Strategic Orientation

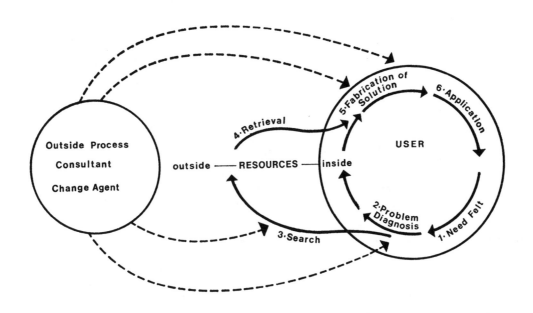

At least five points are generally stressed by advocates of this orientation: first, that *user need* is the paramount consideration and the only acceptable value-stance for the change agent; second, that *diagnosis* of need always has to be an integral part of the total process; third, that the outside change agent should be *nondirective,* rarely, if ever, violating the integrity of the user by placing himself in a directive or expert status; fourth, that the *internal* resources, i.e., those resources already existing and easily accessible within the client system itself, should always be fully utilized; and fifth, that *self-initiated and self-applied innovation* will have the strongest user commitment and the best chances for long-term survival.

A few of the major advocates of this orientation are Lippitt, Watson, and Westley,[1] Goodwin Watson,[2] Charles Jung,[3] and Herbert Thelen.[4] Most of those who belong to this school are social psychologists in the group dynamics-human relations tradition.

b. *P-S Derivative Strategies*

(1) *System self-renewal.* Several strategies originally developed by organizational psychologists to improve communication and decision-making in business and government are now being applied to educational systems. One such project is reported by Benedict *et al.,*[5] and a large and ambitious program of this type was undertaken in the mid-1960's by an inter-university team which included Lake, Lippitt, Jung, Mial, Miles, Thelen, and others.[6] In essence the strategy proposes that school systems can develop an atmosphere favorable to innovation and an internal problem-solving capacity through collaboration with an inside-outside team which gives training in various "process" skills. To date the most thoroughly developed and systematic approach to organizational self-renewal is that proposed by Blake and Mouton[7] for industry.

(2) *Action Research.* In this approach, university social scientists can collaborate with school personnel in diagnosis and evaluation of existing problems, utilizing research methods to collect and systematically analyze data on the system.[8] Presumably the researcher benefits by gaining access to field sites and generating generalizable (and publishable) findings. School personnel gain by receiving self-evaluation data and an increasing sophistication in scientific approaches to diagnosis and evaluation.

(3) *Collaborative Action Inquiry.* This strategy, as elaborated by Thelen,[9] goes well beyond "action research" in the extent to which it builds a team relationship between outside expert and inside school staff. There is a clearer focus on the target system as the *beneficiary* rather than the field site for a university research project. Practitioners and researchers collaborate in defining change goals and in conducting all phases of the research and intervention activities.

(4) *Human Relations Laboratory.* The National Training Laboratories of the NEA (now renamed the NTL Institute for Applied Behavioral Science) have developed several models for improving the problem-solving capacities of individuals, groups, organizations, and communities.[10] These "laboratory" strategies employ a variety of the tactics listed below in combination. They stress the development of greater openness and interpersonal competence as the prerequisites of both effective problem-solving and meaningful innovation by individuals and systems. Laboratories may be conducted for individual self-renewal ("stranger" labs) or for team and system development ("cousin" and "family" labs) and they may be conducted on-site or at off-site "retreats." The most elaborate laboratory strategies employ all these variants in various combinations.

(5) *Consultation.* This term has so many referents that it may be well-nigh useless as the designation of a specific strategy. Nevertheless, it does have special meaning when used as a derivation of "mental health consultation," a technique of helping a client system to define its own helping role and to work through its own problems by means of reflection and authentic feedback (see below under "Tactics"). Caplan[11] has evolved this technique from its psychotherapeutic origin into a systematic method for the helping professions. Its relevance to school settings is manifest. The specific rationale developed by Caplan may differ in detail from those employed by human relations consultants who work in other settings, but the basic elements and tactics appear to be similar.

(6) *Sharing of Practice Innovations.* Because the P-S viewpoint stresses the user and user-involvement, it places special value on user-originated innovations. Lippitt and his colleagues, for example,[12] have developed elaborate strategies by which teachers can share new classroom teaching practices with each other. The program includes systematic screening and evaluation by teachers themselves.

c. *Tactics Associated with P-S Strategies*

Tactics, as we have said previously, have no necessary or logical connection to particular strategies. However, the nine tactics listed and briefly noted below are typically associated with the P-S Tradition.

(1) *T-Group, Sensitivity Training Group.* Most variants of human relations training include an extended series of more-or-less unstructured group sessions which give members a chance to examine group dynamics in the "here-and-now." Such groups are designed to build sensitivity to others and to the way others react to oneself. Members learn how to establish norms of trust and openness to giving and receiving new ideas. The T-group is an essential ingredient of laboratory training (P-S strategy #4 above) and many organizational self-renewal programs.[13]

(2) *Reflection.* This is a specific tactic used by trainer-leaders in T-groups and by consultants generally. The change agent guides the user toward a more careful *self*-examination by reflecting back to him his own spoken thoughts and actions. The change agent carefully avoids placing himself in an "expert" or directive role even when asked to do so by the user. Initial reactions to this procedure may be confused or hostile, but usually the client begins to recognize that he contains the best answers to most questions within himself. The change agent should not be seen as merely a passive bystander in this process, however; in fact, to be effective, reflection must be a very *active form* of listening in which the change agent expresses to the user that he sincerely is involved, cares, and is making a mighty effort to understand. Reflection is also a skill which can be taught to users as a means of making them more effective listeners and helpers to others. A specific application of the "reflection" principle to interpersonal communication is suggested by Carl Rogers.[14]

(3) *Authentic Feedback.* Often confused with reflection, feedback represents non-evaluative perception and interpretation of behavior as it affects the receiver. Training in giving and receiving feedback gives the client system a more realistic view of itself and hence a greater capacity for self-diagnosis, for objective evaluation of innovations, and for a better understanding of its own resistances to innovation.

(4) *Role Playing.* This is an effective method for gaining understanding of ourselves as others see us and for modeling various aspects of problem-solving and innovating prior to behavioral commitment. Role playing of the client by the change agent and the change agent by the client may help in the creation of greater trust and understanding of their respective roles (see discussion of "linkage" below). The variants of role playing now in currency are enormous, and applications extend far beyond these human relations and P-S traditions.[15]

(5) *Group Observation and Process Analysis.* Members of work groups can gain considerable insight and develop greater openness by self-consciously examining their own interaction processes at frequent intervals. This analysis of "here-and-now" behavior (a major feature of the T-group) helps to legitimize discussion and to bring to the surface objections and resistances to "work" activities that would normally be repressed. The authentic consensus and constructive self-criticism that results from process analysis is another important element which may facilitate the introduction and successful adaptation of complex innovations, especially those which require extensive organizational and behavioral adjustments.

(6) *The Derivation Conference.* As developed by Lippitt and by Jung,[16] the "derivation" conference is a systematically designed temporary system which includes research resource persons and client system representatives at various levels in a series of collaborative activities beginning with definition of a problem area, retrieval of relevant findings from research and from the practice setting, derivation of implications for action, and the laying down of specific plans for application with commitment to tryout. The derivation conference combines group process analysis, diagnostic activities, research retrieval activities, and collaborative problem-solving in one package.

(7) *Survey Feedback.* Organizational survey research can be applied directly to changing organizations through a method known as "survey feedback." As developed by Mann and his associates,[17] this tactic includes systematic collection of data from the staff or employees of an organization on a wide range of issues, including supervisor perceptions, work motivations, aspirations, communication patterns, and satisfactions. This data is summarized and fed back to administrators and their subordinates as a means of confronting *real* perceptions and performance. This process helps to unfreeze the organization by revealing real but heretofore unspoken conflicts and problems. The client system is then able to generate an accurate self-diagnosis and specific remedial actions, with consultative help from social scientist change agents.

(8) *Brainstorming.* Most of the tactics listed up to this point have stressed either diagnosis, evaluation, or application phases of the problem-solving process. Brainstorming, in contrast, is a type of free *search and retrieval* activity in which group members are asked to imagine and articulate problem solutions while holding all questions of validity and practicality in abeyance.[18] These exercises in uncritical creative expression are probably valuable not only in themselves as means of bringing new ideas to the surface, but also as ways of training users to think in terms of new possibilities. While they may increase the danger of jumping to premature solutions, they mitigate the opposite danger of becoming mired in problems and obsessive diagnosis. To work successfully, brainstorming may need some structuring or stage-setting by the change agent.

(9) *Synectics.* Gordon[19] suggests that brainstorming can be systematized and combined with experiment and other problem-solving steps to produce a systematic invention and innovation technique for which he has coined the term "synectics." Whether this process has wide applicability in educational settings remains to be seen, but its possibilities are enticing.

2. Social Interaction (S-I)

a. *The S-I Strategic Orientation*

A second strategic orientation places emphasis on the patterns by which innovations diffuse through a social system. This perspective, supported by the rich empirical research tradition of rural sociology, views the innovation as something relatively fixed and concrete. Such a presumption makes the phenomena of diffusion more susceptible to quantitative empirical analysis. Usually the "innovation" is a concrete item such as a fertilizer, a new kind of seed, a new drug, or a new curriculum package.

The overwhelming body of research associated with this social interactionist school tends to support five generalizations about the process of innovation diffusion: (1) that the individual user or adopter belongs to a *network of social relations* which largely influences his adoption behavior; (2) that his *place in the network* (centrality, peripherality, isolation) is a good predictor of his rate of acceptance of new ideas; (3) that *informal personal contact* is a vital part of the influence and adoption process; (4) that *group membership* and *reference group identifications* are major predictors of individual adoption; and (5) that the rate of diffusion through a social system follows a *predictable S-curve pattern* (very slow beginning followed by a period of very rapid diffusion, followed in turn by a long late-adopter or "laggard" period).

FIGURE A-2: The Social Interaction Perspective

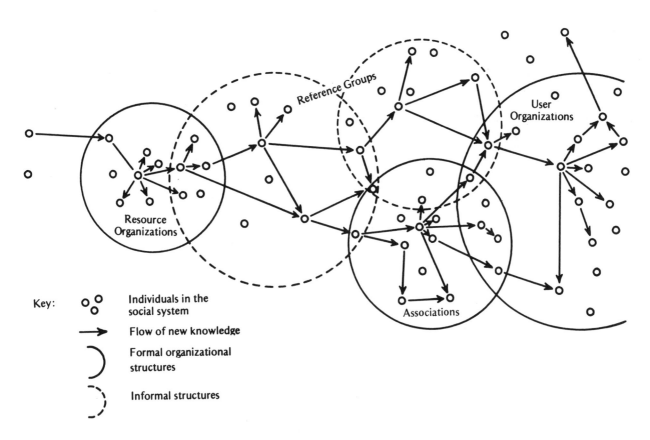

159

Although the bulk of the evidence comes from rural sociology, these five propositions have been demonstrated in a remarkably wide range of situations in every field of knowledge and using every conceivable adopter unit, including individuals, business firms, school systems, and states.

Figure A-2 suggests the type of variable usually considered by the social interactionists. In education, major advocates of the S-I approach have been Mort,[20] Ross,[21] and Carlson.[22]

b. *S-I Derivative Strategies*

Because of the strong empiricist orientation of the S-I approach, it has generated relatively few explicit strategies or action alternatives. S-I theorists generally prefer to sit back and ponder the "natural" process without meddling in it. Nevertheless, four quasi-strategies can be identified with this school.

(1) *Natural Diffusion.* One derivation from S-I research suggests that innovations will diffuse through a natural and inevitable process. After a very extended early period [23] of testing, development, trial and error, and sporadic localized adoption, innovations diffuse in a remarkably regular pattern. Indeed, when 10 to 20 per cent have accepted an innovation, the forces of social interaction are such that the vast majority of the rest of the society will soon follow.[24]

(2) *Natural Communication Network Utilization.* Most change agents undoubtedly rely on S-I principles in planning and carrying out dissemination activities. Such a strategy would include identification of opinion leadership and circles of influence within the social system, and channeling of information to such key points.

(3) *Network Building.* More ambitious and self-conscious applications of S-I principles are found in such massive diffusion networks as the Cooperative Extension Service,[25] and in the marketing networks of large commercial enterprises, notably drug companies. These systems use informal contact by agents or salesmen, enlisting of natural opinion leaders as "demonstrators," and group meetings of various sorts as integral parts of an innovation diffusion program.

(4) *Multiple Media Approaches.* Effective commercial marketing practice is consonant with S-I findings not only in utilizing the social interaction network but also in employing a variety of media to approach the user, including mass-media advertising, package advertising, salesmen, demonstrators, neighborhood "parties," free home trials, etc. S-I research suggests that different media are effective at different stages in the adoption process (awareness, interest, evaluation, trial, and adoption).[26] Hence a successful program would involve the phasing of different media approaches to synchronize with progressive stages of user involvement.

c. *Tactics Associated with S-I Strategies*

(1) *Mass-Media Dissemination.* S-I research tends to show that mass media are effective means for reaching opinion leaders in the social system. They may be particularly effective at initial stages in spreading awareness of innovation to all system members very rapidly and in giving interested innovators and early adopters the leads which they need to seek out further information for themselves.

(2) *The "County Agent."* Locally based full-time experts on innovation (for which the "county agent" of agricultural extension is a commonly cited model)[27] are crucial adjuncts to the "natural diffusion process" because they serve as the feed-in points and personal contacts for the earliest adopters and opinion leaders. They have to be there to get the ball rolling. They also play a major facilitative role at later stages by organizing group meetings and setting up demonstrations where S-I forces can have maximum impact.

(3) *The Salesman.* The county agent typically does not have the time or resources to reach every member of the social system but the salesman can. Driven by profit motivation, both personal and corporate, the salesman utilizes personal and informal contact to the maximum. Moreover, he may be more effective than the "expert" county agent in reaching the less progressive and more isolated sectors of the community.

(4) *Prestige Suggestion.* Most S-I strategies employ various forms of prestige suggestion. The potential adopter is told of the neighbors, peers, and local, regional, and national leaders who have adopted and endorsed the innovation. If these persons are perceived by the user as significant leaders and representatives of personally relevant reference groups, then presumably the suggestion will be effective.

(5) *Opinion Leadership Utilization.* If opinion leaders can be found and influenced, then presumably the rest of the social system will adopt through the natural workings of S-I forces. There are some pitfalls with this approach, however: first, opinion leaders tend to be area-specific[28]; hence, for example, opinion leadership for curriculum innovation may be entirely different from that for school building design. Secondly, coherent opinion leadership may not exist in certain areas, or it may be so diffused or so divided that it cannot be reached effectively, and when reached it cannot effectively influence a significant number of followers. Finally, the enlistment of opinion leaders on behalf of a controversial innovation may undermine their leadership effectiveness.

3. Research, Development, and Diffusion (RD & D)

a. *The RD & D Strategic Orientation*

The most systematic conceptual categorization of processes related to educational innovation is that evolved first by Brickell[29] and later by Clark and Guba,[30] under the headings "Research, Development, and Diffusion." This orientation is guided by at least five assumptions. First, it assumes that there should be a *rational sequence* in the evolution and application of an innovation. This sequence should include research, development, and packaging before mass dissemination takes place. Second, it assumes that there has to be planning, usually on a massive scale over a long time span. Third, it assumes that there has to be a *division and coordination of labor* to accord with the rational sequence and the planning. Fourth, it makes the assumption of a more-or-less *passive but rational consumer* who *will* accept and adopt the innovation if it is offered to him in the right place at the right time and in the right form. Fifth and finally, the proponents of this viewpoint are willing to accept the fact of high initial development cost prior to any dissemination activity because of the anticipated long-term benefits in *efficiency* and *quality* of the innovation and its suitability for *mass audience dissemination.*

FIGURE A-3:   *The Research, Development, and Diffusion Perspective*

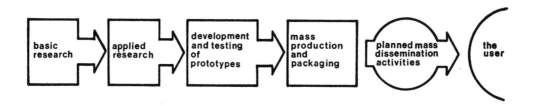

Prototypes of this RD & D model are presumed to exist ·in industry and agriculture. Figure A-3 provides an outline of its major components.

b.   *RD & D Derivative Strategies*

In broad terms, RD & D is itself a grand strategy for planned innovation, but in practice this model has been spelled out in a number of different forms, each of which stresses one or another of these steps. A few of the most commonly expanded variants are listed below.

(1) *Development of High-Performance Products.* Many authors see RD & D as a process whereby ideas and tentative models of innovations can be evaluated and systematically reshaped and packaged in a form that ensures benefit to users and which eases diffusion and adoption. In this process most of the *adaptation* and translation problems of the user are anticipated and adjusted for. The final outcome is therefore *"user-proof,"* guaranteed to work for the most fumbling and incompetent receiver. To some degree the regional laboratories of the U.S.O.E. have been established to carry forward this strategy of high-performance product development.[31]

(2) *Information System Building.* Sometimes the "product" of development will itself be a system for diffusion and innovation. Some of the regional laboratories are experimenting with the design and creation of information systems which take into account the many known barriers and translation problems that separate researchers and developers from potential users.[32] These experimental information systems, when fully developed, will presumably have the same "user-proof" characteristics as the other high-performance products discussed above. Hence, they will form a new and effective channel for the continuous funnelling of innovations and innovative ideas to practitioners.

(3) *Engineered Diffusion Projects and Programs.* A few thoroughly planned and systematically executed and evaluated diffusion projects can be cited from the literature, but in spite of tremendous variations in design and context they may be classified together as one "strategy" on the basis of certain common elements: e.g., (1) careful advance planning, (2) innovative packaging, (3) careful identification, selection, and preparation of the target audience, (4) multi-media presentations (written and oral material, group discussion, demonstration, etc.), (5) some sort of active user involvement, (6) systematic follow-up, and (7) experimental evaluation and documentation. The most successful program of this kind was developed by Bell Labs to diffuse transistor technology to other industries.[33] Well-documented recent ventures of this general type are Richland's "traveling seminar and conference for the implementation of educational innova-

tions,"[34] and Glaser's project to diffuse results of a successful vocational training program for the mentally retarded.[35] Probably the most outstanding *failure* of this strategy is that reported by Cumming and Cumming.[36] A well-conceived and well-designed program to diffuse new mental health concepts to a Canadian community backfired in large part because of the disturbing nature of the information itself.

(4) *Experimental Social Innovation.* Fairweather[37] suggests a method whereby innovative social science projects can be designed as field experiments which include many of the features of laboratory experimentation so as to insure valid and readily interpretable results. Although his method is costly and perhaps impractical for many field situations, it seems to be one which should always be attempted when very large resources are invested and where results are going to be widely publicized (as, for example, in the evaluation of Headstart programs and hard-core unemployed training projects). Fairweather's procedure calls for research, development, and utilization as activities to be carried on simultaneously.

(5) *Administered and Legislated Change.* One presumption that is sometimes implicit in RD & D strategies is that the resulting high-performance product can reasonably and legitimately be diffused through legislative or administrative fiat. If the leadership has assurance from evaluation data that the innovation will be successful and beneficial, then they may feel that they are on safe ground in deciding that all the users under their direct control shall receive it. This is a very common "diffusion" pattern for innovations. Examples range from safety devices required in automobiles to desegregation guidelines for school systems.

(6) *Fait Accompli.* Related to the above is what Watson and Glaser[38] call the strategy of innovation by "*fait accompli.*" When anticipated initial resistance to an innovation is extremely great, the change agent may opt for immediate installation without consultation or the building of advance awareness. The presumption in this case is that the actual benefits from use of the innovation are so great and so apparent *after trial* that the long-run good of the user is well served. The ethical problems inherent in this approach are obvious.

(7) *"Systems Analysis" Approaches to Innovation.* "Systems analysis" usually refers to a systematic strategy of innovation which begins with the careful construction of an optimum but detailed *ideal model* of the problem area. Comparison of this ideal model with current operational reality highlights various shortcomings and focal points for change effort. The problem foci are then systematically tackled on a priority basis so that steady progress is made in approaching the ideal. (See also the tactic of "successive approximation" discussed below.)

c. *Tactics Associated with RD & D Strategies*

To a large extent the tactics of RD & D are the tactics of *research* itself: e.g., hypothesis building and operationalizing, design, sampling, instrumentation, measurement, statistical analysis and inference, derivation of implications, etc. A detailed listing and discussion of such tactics can be found in numerous sources.[39] Of more unique interest may be some of the tactics of *development* and of experimental *diffusion* which set them off from traditional research. A few of these tactics are listed below, but a more thorough codification of such mechanisms is badly needed.

(1) *Experimental Demonstration.* RD & D diffusion specialists take to heart the old saw that

"seeing is believing." The demonstration model or demonstration site where potential users can see the innovation in operation seems to be a common feature of most RD & D strategies. More often than not the demonstration is rigged or loaded to show the innovation in its best light, under ideal circumstances, in the hands of a skilled user, in a highly enriched setting, etc. The demonstration of a "lab" school attached to a school of education is likely to have such exceptional features.[40] In spite of such obvious biasing factors, demonstrations are useful in indicating the potential of an innovation.

(2) *Research Evaluation of Adoption Success and Failure.* The biasing effects of the experimental demonstration model are partially overcome when the strategist includes careful documentation and evaluation of the success of diffusion of the innovation *over time*. The best RD & D programs incorporate this evaluation in the design of the overall diffusion program, and use the evaluation data to redesign the diffusion program or the innovation or both.

(3) *User Need Surveys.* The most sophisticated RD & D strategies include systematic data collection on the needs of the target population, and use this data in the design and development phases.[41] By so doing they partially account for some of the factors stressed by the P-S strategists discussed earlier.

(4) *Successive Approximation.* Development is usually seen as an extended process which may start with an elaborate model or initial prototype which is carefully constructed on the basis of theory and presumed performance specifications, but there is no expectation that this original model will actually work very well. Rather, it is assumed that the innovation can gradually be shaped into a useful product through a long series of informal evaluations and redesigns. The most explicit formulation of this recycling process as applied to educational development will be found in a paper by Carter and Silberman[42] of the System Development Corporation.

(5) *Translation.* Much of the important work of development can be summed up under this one word, "translation." Development requires the translation or transformation of research findings, theory, and design ideas into usable artifacts. Terms such as "simplifying," "recoding," and "generalizing" all suggest different aspects of the translation process. At least one major study[43] suggests that this may be the key neglected function in RD & D systems.

(6) *Packaging for Diffusion.* Educational developers seem slow to learn what advertisers learned years ago: that the package is a critical and integral part of development and may be more critical to successful diffusion than the merits of the innovation. Interesting printed, audio, and visual formats are all part of packaging. The richness, variety, and potential power of this tactic can barely be conceived at this early stage of the packaging revolution.

4. Other Strategic Orientations

It is certain that the three orientations discussed above do not exhaust the real and potential models of the innovative process, and they are suggested only as potentially useful guideposts for ordering much of the literature. It appears that we are witnessing the rebirth of *conflict and crisis models* of innovation, and although these have not yet been fully articulated, they may soon receive the same formalization and elaboration that distinguishes the preceding three. Conflict models, of course, are not new and can be traced back at least to the "dialectic" theories of Hegel and Marx, but the late-twentieth-century version is likely to be quite different from classical versions.

Chesler and Franklin[44] suggest ten strategies for resolving interracial and intergenerational conflicts in school systems. Although many of these fit within the P-S orientation discussed above, some clearly go beyond that formulation. For example, one strategy they suggest is "training for negotiation," by which they mean not only how to carry on discussion but also how to equalize power relations so that genuine give-and-take bargaining is possible.

They also suggest a general strategy of "crisis intervention," by which they mean a concentration of effort by outside change agent-consultants at the time when the client system is most disrupted and hence most motivated to make *sincere* change efforts.

5.   Linkage: A Unifying Concept

Although the various orientations to innovation discussed above are espoused by different authors and represent different schools of thought, the pragmatic change agent should see them each as elucidating different but equally important aspects of a total process. In attempting to build a synthesis from these various schools, the author has derived the concept of "linkage," which is illustrated in Figures A-4 and A-5 on the following pages.[45] According to this principle, the internal problem-solving process of the user is seen as the essential starting point, but the process of searching for and retrieving new outside knowledge relevant to the problem-solving cycle is spelled out in greater detail. To coordinate helping activities with internal user problem-solving activities, the outside resource person (or system) must be able to recapitulate or *simulate* that internal process. Technically speaking, the resource person needs to develop a good "model" of the user system in order to "link" to him effectively. Clinically speaking, we could say that he needs to have empathy or understanding.

At the same time, the *user* must have an adequate appreciation of how the *resource system* operates. In other words, he must be able to understand and partially simulate such resource system activities as research, development, and evaluation.

In order to build accurate models of each other, resource person and user must provide reciprocal feedback and must provide signals to each other which are mutually reinforcing. This type of collaboration will not only make particular solutions more relevant and more effective but will also serve to build a lasting relationship of mutual trust, and a perception by the user that the resource person is a truly concerned and competent helper. In the long run, then, initial collaborative relations build effective channels through which innovations can pass efficiently and effectively.

Linkage is not seen merely as a two-person process, however. The resource person, in turn, must be linked in a similar manner to more and more remote expert resources, as indicated at the left-hand side of Figure A-4 and in Figure A-5.

As the RD & D school holds, there must be an extensive and rational division of labor to accomplish the complex tasks of innovation building. However, each separate role-holder must have some idea of how other roles are performed and some idea of what the *linkage system as a whole* is trying to do. In particular, the government has a primary task of "modelling" the total innovation-building and disseminating system so that it can act as a facilitator and coordinator, seeing to it that the "system" is truly a system, serving the needs of the user (or, as some would have it, the "public interest"). Hence a prime strategy for government would appear to be "systems analysis," as briefly noted earlier.

FIGURE A-4: A Linkage View of Resource-User Problem-Solving

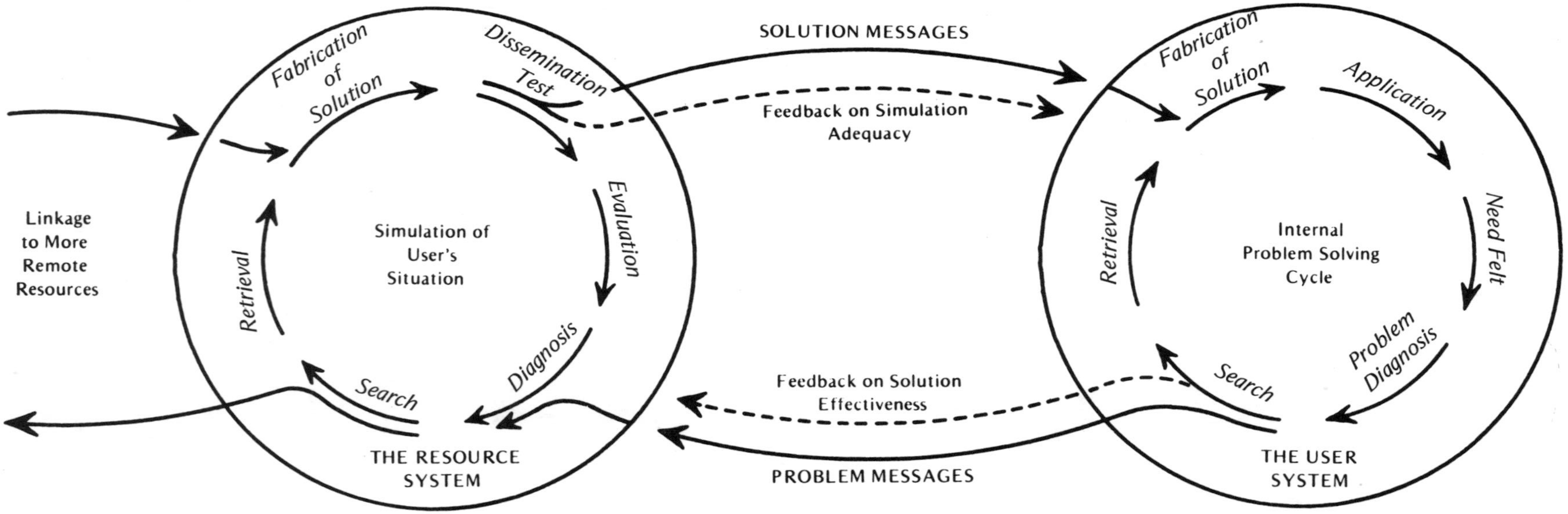

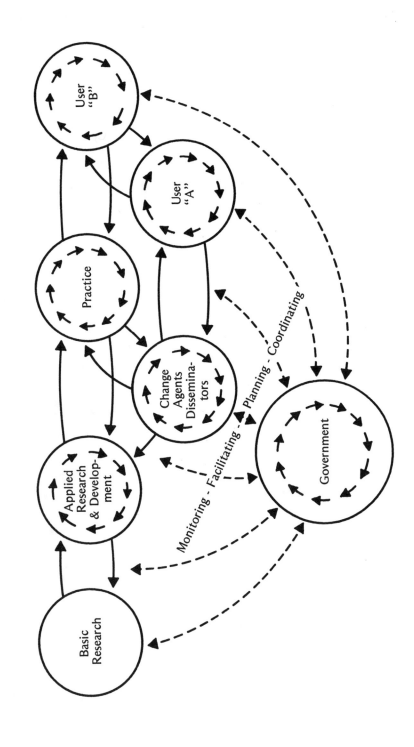

FIGURE A-5: *The Macrosystem of Knowledge Linkage*

All sub-systems of the society must be able to simulate each other's problem-solving process and exchange messages concerning needs, problems, and solutions; but the efforts of all need to be monitored and, where necessary, coordinated and facilitated by a government which has an evolving concept of what the total dissemination and utilization system should become. This concept of a "total system" must be clearly oriented toward a definition of "the public interest" which safeguards, as much as possible, the special interests of the sub-systems involved.

It is too early to say whether this linkage concept can be the generator of uniquely different strategies and tactics. Certainly simulation, role-playing, and feedback all appear to be very relevant, as do the various mechanisms which facilitate social interaction. To initiate linkage between researchers, developers, and practitioners, we probably need to bring them together in what Miles[46] calls "temporary systems," where they can experiment with such reciprocal interactions. The "derivation conference" tactic mentioned earlier is one example of such a temporary system.

GLOSSARY OF MAJOR INNOVATION STRATEGIES AND TACTICS
(Alphabetic listing)

ACTION RESEARCH: an approach which involves the collaboration of university social scientists and school personnel in diagnosing and evaluating existing problems. The use of research methods in collecting and analyzing data from the system benefits the scientist because it provides him with access to field sites and the raw data for later publications. It benefits the school system by providing it with self-evaluation material—and an increasing knowledge of scientific methods of diagnosis and evaluation.

AUTHENTIC FEEDBACK: a non-evaluative perception and interpretation of an individual's behavior as it affects the person who receives it. The use of feedback allows for easier self-diagnosis, objective evaluation of innovations, and an understanding of the reasons for resistance to change.

BRAINSTORMING: a group retrieval technique in which members suggest innovative problem solutions while they deliberately restrain critical judgment. Questions about feasibility, practicality, negative side effects, etc., are set aside until all potential solutions are on the table.

COLLABORATIVE ACTION INQUIRY: similar to "action research" (see above), but the collaboration between social scientists *outside* and school personnel *inside* is more emphasized than in action research, and a true team effort results.

CONSULTATION: a widely used and variously defined change strategy, based on the assistance of an outside expert(s) in helping a system work through its own problems and define its own needs, primarily through the use of reflection and authentic feedback.

DERIVATION CONFERENCE: usually comprised of resource persons and client system representatives meeting on a temporary basis to collaborate on problem definition, information retrieval, derivation of implications for action, and planning for implementation. This tactic combines group process analysis, diagnosis, retrieval, and collaborative problem-solving all in one.

DIFFUSION, NATURAL: "diffusion," in the social context, refers to the spread of the adoption of an innovation; usually there is an extended early period of testing, development, trial-and-error, and sporadic localized adoption; but after 10 per cent to 20 per cent have adopted, the vast majority of potential adopters will shortly follow, due to the forces of social interaction.

EXPERIMENTAL DEMONSTRATION: in the hands of a skilled demonstrator, and under ideal circumstances, a demonstration of an innovation can be quite powerful for adoption. Remember the old saw, "seeing is believing." To be effective a demonstration must look convincing. First, it must show clearly and dramatically that the innovation makes a difference, that it changes things for the better. Second, it must look natural, something that the client can really use in his own setting with his own resources.

FAIT ACCOMPLI: this strategy of change consists of installing an innovation *without* consulting users or without informing them in advance. It has been recommended for use with innovations which would arouse excessive initial resistance and whose actual benefits would not become apparent until after "tryout." Various ethical issues are relevant in a consideration of this approach.

GROUP OBSERVATION AND PROCESS ANALYSIS: self-conscious examination by a group of its own on-going interaction processes in order to understand group processes and to enhance group trust and openness. The self-criticism and group consensus which often arise from such analysis help to facilitate behavioral adjustment to change.

HUMAN RELATIONS LABORATORY: a "temporary system" strategy for improving problem-solving skills which can be adapted for use by individuals, groups, organizations or communities; originated by the National Training Laboratories (a part of NEA, now called the NTL Institute for Applied Behavioral Sciences). The core of human relations training is the sensitivity or T-group. However, a variety of other mechanisms are enlisted in the development of greater openness and interpersonal competence, the prerequisites of effective problem-solving and meaningful innovation.

LEGISLATED (OR ADMINISTERED) CHANGE: a change strategy which assumes that an innovation can be effectively diffused through legislative or administrative fiat; i.e., if the leadership is convinced that an innovation will be successful and beneficial, they may feel that they can—and should—decide that all users under their control shall receive it (e.g, automobile safety devices and public school desegregation guidelines).

MASS-MEDIA DISSEMINATION: the dissemination of new ideas through television, radio, and the popular press. It is usually most effective (a) for reaching *opinion leaders* who are media-oriented, (b) for creating *awareness* of new ideas, (c) for conveying *simple* ideas, and (d) for disseminating in *crisis* situations. Effective utilization usually requires that mass media be combined with other approaches.

MULTIPLE MEDIA APPROACHES: effective innovation strategies, as well as effective advertising campaigns, employ a variety of media to reach potential users (e.g., newspapers, pamphlets, TV, radio, demonstrations, free samples, etc.). Researchers have verified that different kinds of media are optimally effective at different stages in the adoption process (i.e., awareness, interest, evaluation, trial, adoption). A successful strategy of media use would synchronize different media with the progressive stages of user involvement.

NETWORK BUILDING: a complex strategy which results from the use and enhancement of informal social relationships in a client system by a change agent. Through informal personal contact the support of opinion leaders in the system is enlisted in the first phase of network building. Demonstrations and other forms of group meetings are emphasized in the diffusion program. A network, once established for one innovation, may provide a speedy and effective medium for the diffusion of many other related innovations.

OPINION LEADERSHIP UTILIZATION: it has often been asserted that if opinion leaders can be influenced, then the rest of the social system will follow. Since there are many variables that determine the effectiveness of this approach, it should be used with caution. For example, it is predicated on the assumption that opinion leaders do exist for a given innovation, that they can be identified, and that they can be persuaded earlier than most of their followers.

PACKAGING FOR DIFFUSION: clear, attractive, and effective labelling, printing, and formatting of the innovation can add a richness and a potential power for future adoption.

PRESTIGE SUGGESTION: identifying use of the innovation with leaders and other well-known personalities on the assumption that these individuals have true opinion leadership. Effects of this type of influence-by-association are probably very temporary and limited. The high prestige source must be seen as a very salient leader to the user's reference group, or must be seen as having legitimate expertise relevant to the innovation, or both.

PROBLEM-SOLVING: a term used widely and loosely to describe various activities which represent a step-by-step, or systematic, or rational approach to filling human needs. It usually includes distinct phases of problem definition or diagnosis, setting and "prioritizing" of objectives, search for and selection of solution, and tryout of solutions with evaluation of the tryout.

PRODUCT DEVELOPMENT: according to the RD & D model of planning change, ideas and prototypes of an innovation can be systematically evaluated, adapted, and packaged so that when it finally reaches the user all problems have been anticipated and corrected—and the innovation is guaranteed against even the most fumbling and incompetent adopter. Most currently available educational "innovations" have *not* resulted from such a comprehensive RD & D process. Therefore, it is not safe to assume that an innovation is "user-proof" in this sense unless ample evidence to this effect is provided.

REFLECTION: many change agents and consultants are able to help a client by restating the client's problems. By listening to his own words and actions "reflected" back to him by the change agent, the client can begin to move toward serious self-examination and self-diagnosis. Reflection is a very active form of listening in which the change agent must feel and express genuine concern and genuine willingness to understand the client. Although initial reactions to a "reflection" procedure may be confused or hostile, the client eventually begins to recognize that he contains the best answers to most questions within himself.

RESEARCH EVALUATION: in lieu of using an "experimental demonstration" with its potential bias, one may perform a careful documentation and evaluation *over time* to measure the success or failure of the innovation. Some clients will only be persuaded by scientific evidence that the innovation has succeeded in their own setting. Continuing research evaluation is an important aspect of an RD & D strategy.

ROLE PLAYING: acting out roles of other members of a system in "simulations" of real situations. This is an effective method for gaining understanding of ourselves as others see us and for modeling various aspects of problem-solving and innovating prior to behavioral commitment. Role playing of the client by the change agent and the change agent by the client may help in the creation of greater trust and understanding of their respective roles. The variants of role playing now in currency are enormous; it has been used successfully as a learning tool in virtually every type of client system in introducing and training for a variety of innovations and change programs.

SENSITIVITY TRAINING GROUP ("T-GROUP"): most variants of human relations training include an extended series of more-or-less unstructured group sessions which give members a chance to examine group dynamics in the "here-and-now." Such groups are designed to build sensitivity to others and to the way others react to oneself. Members learn how to establish norms of trust and openness to giving and receiving new ideas. The T-group is an essential ingredient of laboratory training and many organizational self-renewal programs.

SUCCESSIVE APPROXIMATION: through a series of evaluations and contingent redesigns, an innovation can gradually be shaped into a more useful product.

SURVEY FEEDBACK: involves a systematic collection of data from the members of an organization on such questions as job satisfaction, supervisory behavior, work motivations, etc. This data is summarized and fed back to administrators and their subordinates as a means of confronting *real* perceptions and performance. This process helps to unfreeze the organization by revealing real but heretofore unspoken conflicts and problems. The client system is then able to generate an accurate self-diagnosis and specific remedial actions, with consultative help from social scientist change agents.

SYSTEM SELF-RENEWAL: refers to the development of an atmosphere favorable to continuing innovation and an internal capacity for problem-solving through the collaboration of an "inside-outside" team in the training of various "process" skills.

SYSTEMS ANALYSIS: usually refers to a systematic strategy of innovation which begins with the careful construction of an optimum but detailed *ideal model* of the problem area. Comparison of this ideal model with current operational reality highlights various shortcomings and focal points for change effort. The problem foci are then systematically tackled on a priority basis so that steady progress is made in approaching the ideal.

TRANSLATION: in order that potential users understand fully the innovation and its theoretical basis, the change agent may often be required to translate such information into language familiar to his client.

USER NEED SURVEYS: systematic collection of information on the needs of the client system on the assumption that such "diagnostic" data will be used in problem-solving or in the design and development of useful innovations.

TABLE A-1:

*Relevance of Strategies
and Tactics for Stages of Change*

TABLE A-1: Relevance of Strategies and Tactics for Stages of Change

This table is only suggestive and is designed to show a number of *potential* uses of various strategies and tactics. It is not a complete list and should be considered only in *conjunction* with the preceding discussion and glossary and the six "stages" described in the main text of the *Guide*.

X = Relevant
XX = Especially Relevant

	Stage I (Relationship)	Stage II (Diagnosis)	Stage III (Resource Acquisition)	Stage IV (Solution Choosing)	Stage V (Acceptance)	Stage VI (Stabilization and Self-Renewal)
Action Research		X		X	X	
Authentic Feedback	X	XX	X	XX	XX	X
Brainstorming			X	XX		
Change Agent: External	X	XX	X	X	X	X
Change Agent: Internal	X	X	X	X	X	XX
Collaborative Action Inquiry	XX	XX	X	X	XX	X
Confrontation	X High Risk	X Some Risk			X High Risk	
Consultation	X	XX	XX	XX	X	X
Derivation Conference	X	X	XX	XX	X	
Diffusion, Natural					X	X
Experimental Demonstration			X	X	X Some Risk	
Fait Accompli					X High Risk	
Financial Support	X	X	X	X	X	XX
Force Field Analysis		XX		XX	X	
Group Observation/Process Analysis	X	X		X	X	X
Human Relations Laboratory	XX	X			X	
Inter-organizational Visiting		X	XX	X	X	
Leadership Change	X	X		X	X	X
Legislated Change					X Some Risk	X

(Continued on next page)

	Stage I (Relationship)	Stage II (Diagnosis)	Stage III (Resource Acquisition)	Stage IV (Solution Choosing)	Stage V (Acceptance)	Stage VI (Stabilization and Self-Renewal)
Linkage	XX	XX	XX	XX	XX	XX
Mass Media Dissemination			X	X	X	
Multiple Media Approaches	X	X	XX	X	XX	X
Network Building			X			X
Opinion Leadership Utilization	X			X	XX	XX
Overlapping Groups			X		X	X
Packaging for Diffusion			X	X	X	
Prestige Suggestion	X Sometimes				X Sometimes	
Problem-Solving	X	XX	X	XX	XX	X
Product Development		X	X	X	X	X
R & D Unit		X	X	X		X
RD & D			X	XX		X
Reflection	XX Some Risk	XX	X	XX	XX	X
Research Evaluation	X	XX	X	X	XX	X
Role Playing	X	X			X	X
Rotation of Roles	X	X	X		X Some Risk	
Sensitivity Training Group	X Some Risk	X		X	X	X
Successive Approximation		X		X		X*
Survey Feedback	X	X	X	X	X	XX
System Self-Renewal	X	X	X	XX	X	X
Systems Analysis	X	XX	X	X	X Some Risk	
Temporary Systems	XX	X		X	X	X
Training					X	X
Translation			X	X	X	X
User Need Surveys		X				X*

*Periodic survey feedback can be a part of building system self-renewal.

NOTES TO APPENDIX A

1. Lippitt, Ronald, Watson, Jeanne, and Westley, Bruce, *The Dynamics of Planned Change*, New York: Harcourt, Brace, and World, Inc., 1958.

2. Watson, Goodwin (ed.), "Resistance to Change," *Concepts for Social Change*, Washington, D.C.: National Training Laboratories, NEA, for the Cooperative Project for Educational Development, 1967, pp. 10-25.

3. Although he is a creative and influential leader in this field, most of Jung's works are not yet available in print. Some of his thinking is reported in Watson, Goodwin (ed.), *Change in School Systems*, Washington, D.C.: National Training Laboratories, NEA, for the Cooperative Project for Educational Development, 1967.

4. Thelen, Herbert A., "Concepts for Collaborative Action-Inquiry," *Concepts for Social Change*, Washington, D.C.: National Training Laboratories, NEA, for the Cooperative Project for Educational Development, 1967, pp. 37-46.

5. Benedict, Barbara A., Calder, Paula Holzman, Callahan, Daniel M., Hornstein, Harvey A., and Miles, Matthew B., "The Clinical-Experimental Approach to Assessing Organizational Change Efforts," *Journal of Applied Behavioral Science*, Vol. 3, No. 3, 1967, pp. 347-380.

6. Watson, Goodwin, *op. cit.*

7. Blake, R.R. and Mouton, Jane S., *The Managerial Grid*, Houston: Gulf Publishing Company, 1961.

8. For an analysis of action research design from the point of view of the social scientist, see French, J.R.P., Jr., "Experiments in Field Settings" in Festinger, L. and Katz, D., *Research Methods in the Behavioral Sciences*, New York: Holt, Rinehart and Winston, 1953. As defined by Stephen Corey, however, in *Action Research to Improve Social Practices*, New York: Bureau of Publications, Teachers College, Columbia University, 1953, "action research" means research done by practitioners for themselves to solve problems in their home setting.

9. Thelen in Watson, *op. cit.*

10. For the most extensive presentation on NTL-IABS approaches see Bradford, L., Gibb, J., and Benne, K.D., *T-Group Theory and Laboratory Method*, New York: John Wiley and Sons, 1964.

11. Caplan, G., "Types of Mental Health Consultation" in Bennis, Warren, Benne, Kenneth, and Chin, Robert (eds.), *The Planning of Change* (Second Edition), New York: Holt, Rinehart and Winston, 1969.

12. Lippitt, Ronald and Fox, Robert, *The Innovation and Sharing of Teaching Practices II: Procedures for Stimulating Adoption and Adaptation of Selected Teaching Practices*, Final

Report, U.S. Office of Education, Cooperative Research Project No. D-137, September 1967, and

Lippitt, Ronald and others, "The Teacher as Innovator, Seeker and Sharer of New Practices," Miller, R.I. (ed.), *Perspectives on Educational Change,* New York: Appleton-Century-Crofts, 1966.

13. Bradford *et al., op. cit.*

14. Rogers, Carl, *Client Centered Therapy,* Boston: Houghton Mifflin, 1951. For a discussion of specific ways to improve listening skills in two-man discussions see Rogers, Carl, "Communication: Its Blocking and Facilitation," *Northwestern University Information,* April 1952, Vol. 20, No. 25, and

Rogers, Carl and Roethlisberger, F., "Barriers and Gateways to Communication," *Harvard Business Review,* 1952, Vol. 30, pp. 46-52.

15. For a general guide to the technique and uses of role playing see Klein, Alan F., *Role Playing in Leadership Training and Group Problem Solving,* New York: Association Press, 1956.

16. Jung, Charles, "A Study of the Derivation Conference: A Collaborative Effort between Social Researchers and Youth-Serving Practitioners to Derive and Use Implications from Research Findings to Meet Action Concerns," Project Proposal, Center for Research on Utilization of Scientific Knowledge, Institute for Social Research, University of Michigan, Ann Arbor, Michigan, 1966.

17. Mann, F.C. and Neff, F.W., *Managing Major Change in Organizations,* Ann Arbor, Michigan: Foundation for Research on Human Behavior, 1961. For an application of survey feedback in a school setting see Miles *et al.,* "The Consequence of Survey Feedback: Theory and Evaluation," in Bennis, Warren, Benne, Kenneth, and Chin, Robert (eds.), *The Planning of Change* (Second Edition), New York: Holt, Rinehart and Winston, 1969.

18. Miles, M.B., *Learning to Work in Groups: A Program Guide for Educational Leaders,* New York: Teachers College, Columbia University, 1959.

19. Gordon, William J.J., *Synectics: The Development of Creative Capacity,* New York: Harper and Row, 1961.

20. Mort, Paul R., "Studies in Educational Innovation from the Institute of Administrative Research," Miles, Matthew B. (ed.), *Innovation in Education,* New York: Bureau of Publications, Teachers College, Columbia University, New York, 1964.

21. Ross, Donald H., *Administration for Adaptability: A Source Book Drawing Together the Results of More Than 150 Individual Studies Related to the Question of Why and How Schools Improve,* New York: Metropolitan School Study Council, 1958.

22. Carlson, Richard O., *Adoption of Educational Innovations,* Eugene, Oregon: Center for the Advanced Study of Educational Administration, University of Oregon, 1965.

23. Originally this period was suggested by Mort (*op. cit.*) to be 50 years for educational innovations, although recent experience indicates a considerably shorter span.

24. Rogers, E.M., *Diffusion of Innovations,* New York: The Free Press of Glencoe, Inc., 1962.

25. Sanders, H.C., *et al., The Cooperative Extension Service,* Prentice-Hall, 1966, 436 pp. A handbook on the CES which describes the network in detail, and provides a history of agriculture extension in the United States.

26. Rogers, E.M., *op. cit.,* page 219.

27. Sanders *et al., op. cit.,* describe in detail the vast range of activities in which the county agent is typically involved.

28. Rogers, E.M., *op. cit.*

29. Brickell, Henry M., *Organizing New York State for Educational Change,* 1961, Commissioner of Education, State Education Department, Albany, New York, 107 pp.

30. Clark, David L. and Guba, Egon G., "An Examination of Potential Change Roles in Education," paper presented at the Symposium on Innovation in Planning School Curricula, Airlie House, Virginia, October 1965.

31. Boyan, Norman J., "Problems and Issues of Knowledge Production and Utilization," in Eidell, Terry L. and Kitchel, Joanne M., *Knowledge Production and Utilization in Educational Administration,* Eugene, Oregon: Center for Advanced Study of Educational Administration, University of Oregon, 1968.

32. Far West Laboratory for Educational Research and Development, *Program Plans,* Berkeley, California: Far West Laboratory, March 1, 1967, 63 pp.

33. The Bell Labs case was described concisely by Professor Robert A. Solo of Princeton University (Department of Economics) in his mimeo paper: "The University in a Science-Based Society."

34. Richland, Malcolm, *Final Report: Traveling Seminar and Conference for the Implementation of Educational Innovations,* Santa Monica, California: System Development Corporation, Technical Memorandum Series 2691, 1965, 140 pp.

35. Glaser, Edward, "Research Frontier: Utilization of Applicable Research and Development Results," *Journal of Counseling Psychology,* 1965, Vol. 12, pp. 201-205.

36. Cumming, E. and Cumming J., *Closed Ranks: An Experiment in Mental Health Education,* Cambridge: Harvard University Press, for the Commonwealth Fund, 1957, 192 pp.

37. Fairweather, George W., *Methods for Experimental Social Innovation,* New York: John Wiley and Sons, Inc., 1967.

38. Watson, G. and Glaser, E., "What We Have Learned About Planning for Change," *Management Review*, November 1965.

39. e.g., Festinger and Katz, *op. cit.*
    Selltiz, C., Jahoda, M., Deutsch, M., and Cook, S.W., *Research Methods in Social Relations* (Revised Edition), New York: Holt, Rinehart and Winston, April 1964.
    Suchman, Edward A., *Evaluative Research*, New York: Russell Sage Foundation, 1967.

40. e.g., see Brickell's critique of the lab school and recommendation that it be abolished (Brickell, *op. cit.*).

41. An example of the self-conscious utilization of a user need study to initiate program development is provided by the Far West Laboratory for Educational Research and Development, *op. cit.*

42. Carter, Launor and Silberman, Harry, *The Systems Approach, Technology and the School*, Professional Paper SP-2025, Santa Monica, California: System Development Corporation, April 1963, 30 pp.

43. Mackie, R.R. and Christensen, P.R., *Translation and Application of Psychological Research*, Technical Report 716-1. Santa Barbara Research Park, Goleta, California: Human Research, Inc., 1967.

44. Chesler, Mark and Franklin, Jan, "Interracial and Intergenerational Conflict in Secondary Schools," presentation made at the Meetings of the American Sociological Association, Boston, Massachusetts, August 1968.

45. This linkage concept is presented in more detail by the author in *Planning for Innovation Through the Dissemination and Utilization of Knowledge*, Ann Arbor, Michigan: Institute for Social Research, University of Michigan, 1969. (Report to the U.S. Office of Education on a Comparative Survey of the Literature.)

46. Miles, Matthew B., "On Temporary Systems," in Miles, Matthew B. (ed.), *Innovation in Education*, New York: Teachers College, Columbia University, 1964, pp. 437-490.

Appendix B

MAJOR INFORMATION SOURCES
IN EDUCATION

APPENDIX B
TABLE OF CONTENTS

MAJOR INFORMATION SOURCES IN EDUCATION

INTRODUCTION:

Sources of educational information are so diverse, far-flung, and numerous that an exhaustive listing of them remains elusive. We have tried in this manual to select the *major* sources relevant to educational innovation, i.e., those that have the largest operations and those with the most growth potential.

We appreciate the helpfulness of the many organizations who provided material for the entries in this Appendix.

We might caution the reader NOT to expect to find *complete* evaluative literature on an educational innovation in any of the resources included here. Few interpretive studies have been carried out thus far, and some of this much needed evaluative information has simply not been written. We have indicated that the evaluative information which *is* available will probably be most easily found in "Information Services" or "Human Resources."

I. PERIODICALS

Audiovisual Instruction

Association for Educational
Communications and Technology
1201 Sixteenth Street, N.W.
Washington, D.C. 20036

Editor: Howard B. Hitchens

10 times/year
$12/year

- reviews the total field of media

Croft Newsletter Services

Croft Educational Services, Inc.
100 Garfield Avenue
New London, Connecticut 06320

- series of brief newsletters for administration, school board, and teaching orientations

Education Recaps

> Educational Testing Service
> Princeton, New Jersey 08540
>
> Editor: Ann Z. Smith
>
> - brief, pithy descriptions of the latest developments in education, educational research and technology, programs, and related issues and areas of interest

Education U.S.A.

> National School Public Relations Association
> 1201 Sixteenth Street, N.W.
> Washington, D.C. 20036
>
> Executive Editor: George W. Neill
>
> Weekly (September-May)
> $21/year
>
> - notes latest developments in educational affairs including related political issues
> - also includes weekly previews of magazines, TV, radio, books, and reports

Educational Product Report

> Educational Products Information
> Exchange Institute (EPIE)
> 386 Park Avenue South
> New York, New York 10016
>
> Editor/Director: P. Kenneth Komoski
>
> 9 times/year
> $35 membership in EPIE which entitles one to subscription and other services
>
> - provides the educational consumer with unbiased information and evaluations of materials related to educational technology (both hardware and software)
> - considered the "Consumers Union" of the educational field

Educational Researcher

> American Educational Research
> Association (AERA)

1126 Sixteenth Street, N.W.
Washington, D.C. 20036

Editor: Richard E. Schutz

Monthly
$10/year—Single copies $1.00

- features news and commentary on events in the field of educational research; editorial focus emphasizes articles which synthesize or analyze matters of general significance to research in education; special features include interviews with prominent individuals in the field and review essays on significant publications

Educational Technology

Educational Technology Publications
140 Sylvan Avenue
Englewood Cliffs, New Jersey 07632

Editor: Lawrence Lipsitz

Monthly
$21/year—Single copies $3.00 or $3.95

- features articles and news of all rigorously applied innovations
- edited primarily for school administrators
- the magazine also conducts an annual conference, featuring seminars and workshops on most aspects of contemporary school innovation, and publishes a full line of books and audio tape cassettes on innovation

EDUCOM

Bulletin of the Interuniversity
Communications Council (EDUCOM)
P.O. Box 364 Rosedale Road
Princeton, New Jersey 08560

Editor: Dave Loye

4 times/year
$5 annually to educators and students—$10 to others
Microfiche $1 per volume

- non-technical bulletin distributed to interested faculty of member institutions and others, demonstrating the latest developments in communication systems related to universities

- includes articles on research and development in the application of technology to higher education, reports on experiences and problems in operating networks, and reports on conferences sponsored by EDUCOM, a consortium founded to promote the sharing of resources in the application of technology to higher education

Evaluation Comment

Center for the Study of Evaluation
University of California Los Angeles
145 Moore Hall
Los Angeles, California 90024

Editor: Marvin C. Alkin

Distributed free of charge to each scholar, researcher, or practitioner on the mailing list. One to five copies may be obtained free of charge

- provides discussion of significant ideas and controversial issues in the study of evaluation of educational systems and programs

General Education Sounding Board

106 Nicholson Hall
University of Minnesota
Minneapolis, Minnesota 55455

Editorial Board: David L. Giese, Mary Ellen Kirchner, Alex Kurak, and Candido P. Zanoni

Issued on an occasional basis by the General College, University of Minnesota

- reports on experimentation in the classroom at the General College

The Individualized Learning Letter

T.I.L.L.
67 East Shore Road
Huntington, New York 11743

Editor and Publisher: James A. Lippke

18 times/year
$40 annually

- newsletter reporting on various methods of individualizing instruction (see also *Educational Technology* Magazine for information on individualized learning)

Inequality in Education

Harvard Center for Law and Education
Harvard Graduate School of Education
Appian Way
Cambridge, Massachusetts 02138

Editor: Eric Van Loon

6 times/year
Distribution free—$6/year to libraries

- reports on research, litigation, legislation, and other news of reform and change
- Center was established to promote reform in education through research and litigation on the legal implications of educational policies affecting equality of educational opportunity

Measurement in Education

National Council on
Measurement in Education (NCME)
Office of Evaluation Service
Michigan State University
East Lansing, Michigan 48823

Editor: Warren W. Willingham

4 times/year
$2/year—Single copies $ .50

- consists of special reports concerned with the practical implications of measurement and related research and their application to educational problems of individuals, institutions, and systems
- emphasis is upon uses of measurement rather than technical or theoretical issues

Memo to the Faculty

Center for Research on
Learning and Teaching
University of Michigan
109 East Madison
Ann Arbor, Michigan 48104

Editor: Stanford C. Ericksen

4 times/year
$1/year—Single copies and back issues $ .25—for off-campus personnel

- keeps faculty abreast of new developments in college teaching, from instructional technology to student attitudes and values

NAEP Newsletter (National Assessment of Educational Progress)

National Assessment of
Educational Progress
300 Lincoln Tower
1860 Lincoln Street
Denver, Colorado 80203

Staff Director: J. Stanley Ahmann

Periodic—Free

- informs the educational community of the progress of the NAEP project. Results of the project will give census-like data on the educational attainments of students and measure any growth and decline which takes place in educational attainment in certain subject areas

NASSP Newsletter (National Association of Secondary School Principals)

National Association of
Secondary School Principals
1201 Sixteenth Street, N.W.
Washington, D.C. 20036

Monthly (September to June)
$2 included in NASSP membership dues

- for junior and senior high school principals

The National Elementary Principal

National Association of Elementary
School Principals
1201 Sixteenth Street, N.W.
Washington, D.C. 20036

6 times/year

- read chiefly by elementary school principals, classroom teachers, university professors, and others concerned with elementary education

New Ways

Charles F. Kettering Foundation
5335 Far Hills Avenue
Dayton, Ohio 45429

4 times/year
(no cost)

- developments one might like to know about in education, science, international affairs, and citizen involvement

Researcher Reporter

Center for Research and
Development in Higher Education
2150 Shattuck Avenue, 5th Floor
Berkeley, California 94704

Editor: K. Patricia Cross

Quarterly
Free subscription

- disseminates latest research findings of the Center to practitioners and professionals in higher education

SLANTS

School Information and Research
Service (SIRS)
100 Crochett Street
Seattle, Washington 98109

Monthly

- disseminates results of surveys, etc., to any well-established educational organization or institution
- reports on school management problems to superintendents and other chief school officers

NTL Institute for Applied Behavioral Science
National Education Association
1201 Sixteenth Street, N.W.
Washington, D.C. 20036

Quarterly
$4/year

- deals with issues that relate to education

II. INFORMATION SERVICES

Information services attempt to organize materials into meaningful collections instead of using the traditional "subject-author" storage system. Their most significant characteristic, however, is not the kind of organization of materials, but the body of information itself. Many information services concern themselves with material that is not usually available in published form. Further, through computerization, information services provide in-depth indexing systems which allow the user to phrase more specific questions and to receive only those materials which are directly relevant to his particular problem area.

Specific information is retrievable from a computerized data bank, through the use of "accession numbers" or key-word listings. This, of course, requires that the resource retriever become familiar with the information system that he wishes to use. Obtaining this orientation to the system will sometimes require patience and persistence. Also, because the materials contained in information systems are usually disseminated on microfiche, there is a cost factor involved for the user: he or his system must buy the fiche and probably also a microfiche reader.

The Educational Resources Information Center (ERIC) is an information system which is emerging as a primary national service. No other national service has comparable organizational support, financial resources, or access to research and development.

On the state level, there is an increasing trend toward locally based information systems to service a defined set of users, e.g., all educators of a region or a special group of educators in the region. Some of these are termed *"one-stop"* information services because they provide many additional services for the user other than simple machine processing of requests. Hopefully, these will form models for future government support. (See RIS and RISE below.)

EPIE (Educational Products Information Exchange)

EPIE is a non-profit professional cooperative that conducts impartial studies of educational materials, equipment, and systems. A membership in EPIE costs $35.00 per year and provides members with a basic service of nine *Educational Product Reports* published during the school year. Five of the nine reports present a review of specific educational material, equipment, or systems which enables the school decision-maker to make a more educated selection of available educational products. Four of the nine present brief evaluations of a variety of products suggested by EPIE members. Areas being covered vary from video tape recorders to materials on drug abuse. Abstracts from selected EPIE research studies are available through ERIC. The studies themselves are available only through EPIE at a cost of $7.00 each to non-members. Membership information may be obtained by writing to:

The EPIE Institute
386 Park Avenue South
New York, New York 10016

Director: P. Kenneth Komoski

ERIC (Educational Resources Information Center)

ERIC is a national information system of the Office of Education dedicated to the progress of education through the dissemination of educational research results, research-related materials, and other resource information that can be used in developing more effective educational programs. Through a network of specialized centers or clearinghouses, each of which is responsible for a particular educational area, the information is acquired, evaluated, abstracted, indexed, and listed in *Research in Education*, the monthly abstract journal of the ERIC system. (See "Directories and Indices" for a description of *Research in Education*.) All the documents cited in the Document Resume section of the journal, except as noted, are available from:

ERIC Document Reproduction Service
P.O. Drawer 0
Bethesda, Maryland 20014

Documents are produced in microfiche (MF) and in hard copy (HC). MF is a 4 x 6-inch sheet of film with up to 70 images, each representing an 8½ x 11-inch sheet of paper. Each microfiche costs $ .65. Microfiche readers, available from many manufacturers, are required to enlarge the images for reading purposes. Hard copy (HC) is a reproduction on paper in easy-to-read form, which costs $3.29 per 100 page increment.

The process of getting at the material that is collected and stored in the ERIC system is explained in "How to Use ERIC," a pamphlet available for $ .35 through:

The Superintendent of Documents
U.S. Government Printing Office
Washington, D.C. 20402

Stock Number: 1780-0796

ERIC Clearinghouses are listed below but individuals desiring additional information concerning ERIC and its functions can contact:

ERIC Central
Room 3013
400 Maryland Avenue, S.W.
Washington, D.C. 20202

ERIC Clearinghouses:

ADULT EDUCATION
Syracuse University
107 Roney Lane
Syracuse, New York 13210

COUNSELING AND PERSONNEL
SERVICES
University of Michigan
School of Education Building
Room 2108
East University
Ann Arbor, Michigan 48104

DISADVANTAGED
Teachers College
Box 40
525 West 120th Street
New York, New York 10027

EARLY CHILDHOOD EDUCATION
University of Illinois
805 West Pennsylvania Avenue
Urbana, Illinois 61801

EDUCATIONAL MANAGEMENT
University of Oregon
320 Hendricks Hall
Eugene, Oregon 97403

EDUCATIONAL MEDIA AND
TECHNOLOGY
Institute for Communication
Research
Stanford University
Cypress Hall
Stanford, California 94305

EXCEPTIONAL CHILDREN
The Council for
Exceptional Children
1411 South Jefferson Davis Highway
Arlington, Virginia 22202

HIGHER EDUCATION
George Washington University
1 Dupont Circle, N.W.
Suite 630
Washington, D.C. 20006

INFORMATION SCIENCE
American Society for
Information Science
1140 Connecticut Avenue
Suite 804
Washington, D.C. 20036

JUNIOR COLLEGES
University of California at
Los Angeles
Powell Library, Room 96
405 Hilgard Avenue
Los Angeles, California 90024

READING
Indiana University
200 Pine Hall
Bloomington, Indiana 47401

RURAL EDUCATION AND SMALL
SCHOOLS
New Mexico State University
Box 3-AP
Las Cruces, New Mexico 88001

SCIENCE AND MATHEMATICS
EDUCATION
Ohio State University
1460 West Lane Avenue
Columbus, Ohio 43221

SOCIAL STUDIES AND SOCIAL
SCIENCE EDUCATION
Social Science Building
University of Colorado
Boulder, Colorado 80302

TEACHER EDUCATION
American Association of Colleges
for Teacher Education
1 Dupont Circle, N.W.
Suite 616
Washington, D.C. 20005

TEACHING OF ENGLISH
National Council of Teachers
of English
1111 Kenyon Road
Urbana, Illinois 61801

TEACHING OF FOREIGN LANGUAGES
AND LINGUISTICS
Modern Language Association
62 Fifth Avenue
New York New York 10011

TESTS, MEASUREMENT AND
EVALUATION
Educational Testing Service
Princeton, New Jersey 08549

VOCATIONAL AND TECHNICAL
EDUCATION
Ohio State University
1900 Kenny Road
Columbus, Ohio 43210

National Audiovisual Center

The National Audiovisual Center serves government, industry, educational institutions, and the general public as a central information, sales, and distribution point for most Government motion pictures, filmstrips, and other audiovisual materials. The Center, a division of the National Archives and Records Service, General Services Administration, provides three main services:

a. *Information*: The Center is the main contact with the public and the Government regarding audiovisual materials available from federal agencies and where and how they can be obtained. Detailed information is gathered on all relevant materials produced by or for the federal agencies and is made available on request.

b. *Sales*: The Center functions as the central sales point for most U.S. Government audiovisual items. Over 6,000 motion pictures and filmstrips are described in a film sales catalog, 1969, and supplement, 1971. The Center is developing a stock footage library and depository.

c. *Rentals and Loans*: The Center provides a uniform, efficient, and economical loan service of 16mm motion pictures, deposited in the Center by various U.S. Government agencies.

National Audiovisual Center
National Archives and Records Service (GSA)
Washington, D.C. 20409

NICEM (National Information Center for Educational Media)

The National Information Center for Educational Media custom-catalogs for AV centers, libraries, colleges, universities, and media centers. NICEM is serving organizations across the country, providing them with custom catalogs of their holdings. NICEM's computerized data bank contains over 170,000 main title entries in the following media:

- 16mm films
- 35mm filmstrips
- 8mm motion picture cartridges
- Records
- Audio tapes
- Video tapes
- Overhead transparencies.

NICEM also maintains a large data base of producers' and distributors' names and addresses. Catalogs are retrieved, photo composed, printed, and bound. In addition to standard titles, annotations, length, producers, and distributors, NICEM catalogs can contain a cataloging of order number, assigned grade levels, rental prices, etc.

National Information Center
for Educational Media (NICEM)
University of Southern California
University Park
Los Angeles, California 90007

(See "Directories and Indices" for a description of *NICEM Indices.*)

NTIS (National Technical Information Service)*

The National Technical Information Service is the nation's principal collector and distributor of Government-sponsored reports. Through agreements with more than 250 organizations it adds about 50,000 reports a year to its collection of unclassified U.S. Government-sponsored research and development reports and translations of foreign technical literature for the scientific, technical, and industrial communities. It also offers a computer-generated abstract search service of the more than 250,000 reports published since 1964. Copies of most of the original reports also are offered for sale. For details send for *NTIS Information Services*, a free brochure listing all products and services available from NTIS. For requests or information write:

National Technical Information Service
U.S. Department of Commerce
Springfield, Virginia 22151

Director: William T. Knox

*Formerly the Clearinghouse for Federal Scientific and Technical Information.

RIS (Regional Information System)

RIS is a concept or model for a regional information linkage system. It is intended to be a "one-stop" tool providing current awareness and reference services for all of the Michigan-Ohio Regional Educational Laboratory (MOREL) projects. This concept was developed at MOREL and the ASSIST Center, a project of ESEA Title III at the Wayne County Intermediate School District, 33030 Van Born Road, Wayne, Michigan 48184. ASSIST and MOREL have been phased out, but the information center concept they developed lives on in ARIS (see below).

ARIS (Association Referral Information Service)

ARIS, operated by the Ohio Education Association, maintains a data bank of resource people and operative school programs in six curriculum areas and two administrative areas. The Resource Bank currently has over 3,000 people and programs listed, most of these limited to Ohio personnel and schools. The Resource Bank is supplemented with a series of publications including ERIC-PREP, eighteen annotated bibliographies, a Research and Practice series, eight seminar reports and six Instructional Focus booklets.

Association Referral Information Service
Ohio Education Association
225 East Broad Street
Columbus, Ohio 43215

Coordinator: Byron H. Marlowe

RISE (Research and Information Services for Education)

Project RISE is a state-wide, responsive information service agency sponsored by the Pennsylvania Department of Education and the Montgomery County Intermediate Unit in cooperation with the National Center for Educational Communication of the U.S. Office of Education. Its services are available to all public schools in Pennsylvania through a network of Resource Utilization Specialists located in each of the 29 Intermediate Units. Its primary activity is the provision of client-tailored literature searching and retrieval services including inquiry negotiation, manual and computer searching, relevance analysis, assembly of the information package, guidance in the use of the material where needed, and evaluation of the package to determine its utility by the client. Other activities include preparation of bibliographies and reviews, assistance in program development and planning, consultation research services (methodology) and acquisition and dissemination of results of research and development activities from federal projects, state, regional, and local efforts, and some higher education activities. RISE is the official dissemination agency for Pennsylvania ESEA Title III programs. It has also developed and conducted training programs for information center personnel.

RISE information resources include complete ERIC materials, some regional lab materials, an in-house collection of some 150 current journal titles (supplemented by access to the additional holdings of a state university library), special collections, a growing non-ERIC fugitive literature collection and access agreements with other information sources such as the ERIC Clearinghouses,

NEA, etc. Hardware capability includes microfiche/film reader/printers, microfiche reproduction, and a computerized search/retrieval system, both batch and on-line.

RISE contracts with agencies not presently included under its diverse funding arrangements, both within Pennsylvania (private and higher education) and outside the state. Questions about services available and contractual arrangements or about RISE publications can be directed to:

Research and Information Services for Education
c/o Montgomery County Intermediate Unit
Colony Office Building
6198 Butler Pike
Blue Bell, Pennsylvania 19422

Phone (215) 825-9141

SRIS (School Research Information Service)

SRIS is an information service sponsored by Phi Delta Kappa to serve its members and other interested educators or educational institutions. Its primary aim is to assist the individual to obtain information related to his educational interests or problems. Reports of research, descriptions of innovative practices with which schools have had experience, and the documents in the ERIC collection make up the library, which is searched for each request for information. A response to a request for information may include microfiche or regular size of reports in the SRIS collection and a listing of relevant ERIC documents.

School Research Information Service
Phi Delta Kappa Research Service Center
Eighth and Union Streets
Bloomington, Indiana 47401

Director: Dr. William J. Gephart

III. LIBRARIES

Most individuals are able to avail themselves of professional or curriculum libraries in their district or county or local university. These resources have the advantage of being familiar and in close proximity to the working environment of the practitioner.

Unfortunately, the organization of library collections does not allow them to be responsive to specific user needs. Information is organized by title and topic, author, and, sometimes, by source (e.g., journals), which means that the library user may have to sift through a substantial quantity of irrelevant material when he is searching for information appropriate to a specific need. The assistance of a good librarian can be particularly valuable at this point.

Often library acquisitions regrettably lag considerably behind the production of new information. Also, their collections of research and development material, perhaps the information most needed by the innovator, are particularly weak.

IV. DIRECTORIES AND INDICES

Directories and indices of relevance to the field of education are published by governmental, professional, and commercial agencies. There is, unfortunately, no single index that lists all the types of written material or all the resource agencies one might want to use (e.g., some include only government publications or agencies; others exclude government resources). Most of the larger directories can be found in any public, university, or ERIC library, and, probably, in the professional library of the local system. There is some need for user-training in the classification scheme of "key-words" used in an index. Subject groupings have some of the same limitations that library organization has: they are often outdated and are, therefore, awkward for handling the newer topics.

Directory of Educational Information Centers

> Division of Information Technology and Dissemination
> Bureau of Research, U.S. Office of Education, 1969

> Order from:
> The Superintendent of Documents
> U.S. Government Printing Office
> Washington, D.C. 20402

> Catalogue Number: FS 5.212:12042 ($1.25) Order OE-12042

This directory, prepared for the U.S. Office of Education by the System Development Corporation, lists a wide range of information centers offering services to educators in communities throughout the United States. Its coverage includes (1) those information centers funded as projects through Title III of ESEA; (2) Research and Development Centers; (3) Instructional Materials Centers for Handicapped Children and Youth; (4) Regional Educational Laboratories; (5) State Research Coordinating Units for vocational and technical education; and (6) State Departments of Education. The general criteria met by those 397 centers included in the directory are (a) provision of at least one information service, such as reference, referral, or bibliography preparation, and (b) possession of or access to a collection of books, periodicals, reports, ERIC materials, or instructional resource materials. Each entry includes the address, director, sponsor(s), services, users, and holdings of the center. The body of the directory is arranged alphabetically by state and by city, and there is a subject index. There are also several appendices: the Regional Offices of the Office of Education, the Research and Development Centers (this list is incomplete), the regional Instructional Materials for Handicapped Children and Youth, the Regional Educational Laboratories, and the State Research Coordinating Units for vocational and technical education.

The directory does not claim to be an exhaustive listing of educational information centers; none of the ERIC Clearinghouses are included. However, subsequent editions of the Directory are planned, and information about other relevant centers is requested.

Published by the Committee on Scientific and Technical Information (COSATI) of the Federal Council for Science and Technology.

U.S. Department of Commerce
National Technical Information Service
5285 Port Royal Road
Springfield, Virginia 22151

Report Number: PB-189-300

This directory will be useful to educators when the specific topic area they are researching transcends the limits of strictly education sources. It is a guide to agencies ranging from ERIC Clearinghouses to the Laboratory Animal Information Center, to the Office of Economic Opportunity Information Center, to the Thermodynamics Research Center... Each entry lists the agency's address, director, sponsor, year of inception, mission, scope, services, staff, and qualified users. This directory of 119 federally supported information analysis centers is descriptive and contains an index of subject areas covered by the listed centers, an index of names of center operators, a list of organizations, and a list of locations. The directory is intentionally selective; inclusion is based on two specific qualifications: (1) the center must operate within a federal government agency or be supported by federal funds, and (2) it must perform a majority of the functions within the scope of the COSATI review panel's definition of an information analysis center; i.e., "a formally structured organizational unit specifically (but not necessarily exclusively) established for the purpose of acquiring, selecting, storing, retrieving, evaluating, analyzing, and synthesizing a body of information and/or data in a clearly defined specialized field or pertaining to a specified mission with the intent of compiling, digesting, repackaging, or otherwise organizing and presenting pertinent information and/or data in a form most authoritative, timely, and useful to a society of peers and management."

*A Directory of Information Resources in the
United States: Social Sciences (1965)*

Published by the National Referral Center for Science and Technology

Available from:
The Superintendent of Documents
U.S. Government Printing Office
Washington, D.C. 20402

($1.50)
(To be revised 1972)

This unique book lists information resources in the United States which will accept and answer questions. Most institutions listed are not information centers; however, they will answer questions because they want to, though their major activity is usually production or research.

This publication is one of a series published by the Library of Congress under the general title "A Directory of Information Resources in the United States."

Directory of Special Libraries and Information Centers

> Anthony T. Kruzas (ed.)
> Gale Research Company
> The Book Tower
> Detroit, Michigan 48226

This is a guide to special libraries, research libraries, information centers, archives, and data centers maintained by government agencies, business, industry, newspapers, educational institutions, non-profit organizations and societies in the fields of science, technology, medicine, law, art, religion, history, social sciences, and humanistic studies. Subject index, geographic index, and personnel index are provided.

The Education Index

> The H.W. Wilson Company
> 950 University Avenue
> Bronx, New York 10452

This index is a cumulative author and subject index to a selected list of educational periodicals, books, and pamphlets. It presents a list of indexed periodicals and a directory of publishers.

Education Directory

> An annual directory available from:

> > The Superintendent of Documents
> > U.S. Government Printing Office
> > Washington, D.C. 20402

This directory consists of four volumes: (1) officers of education programs, by state ($1.00); (2) all public school systems enrolling 300 or more students, by state ($2.25); (3) accredited institutions of higher education, by state ($3.75); and (4) educational associations ($1.25).

Encyclopedia of Associations

> Volume 1, National Organizations of the United States

Gale Research Company
The Book Tower
Detroit, Michigan 48226

The encyclopedia is concerned with information about non-profit American organizations of national scope, covering topics of trade and business, education, religion, agriculture, social welfare, public affairs, health, athletics, veterans, labor, etc. It gives the name of the organization, acronym, address, chief official, founding date, number of members, staff, state and local groups, description, committees, publications, affiliated organizations, and conventions. The names of the organizations are indexed alphabetically and by key word. In the encyclopedia "education" is grouped with "cultural organizations." The section covers associations dealing with such topics as administration, accreditation, and adult education, as well as art, science, biology, etc.

ERIC Publications

a. *Current Index to Journals in Education (CIJE)*

A monthly journal which provides indexing and annotations for articles in over 500 educational periodicals.

For details write to:

CCM Information Corporation
866 Third Avenue
New York, New York 10022

b. *PACEsetters in Innovation*

The Superintendent of Documents
U.S. Government Printing Office
Washington, D.C. 20402

Catalogue Number: OE-20103

PACEsetters was published annually from 1966 through 1969 by the Bureau of Elementary and Secondary Education in cooperation with the Office of Information Dissemination of the U.S. Office of Education and through the services of the Educational Resources Information Center (ERIC). It is a major source of information on the Programs to Advance Creativity in Education (PACE), i.e., Title III of the Elementary and Secondary Education Act of 1965. The volumes rely on two basic formats: indices and resumes. The indices (subject, state and local education agency, and project number) are keyed so that every index refers the reader directly to the corresponding resume.

c. *Research in Education (RIE)*

The Superintendent of Documents
U.S. Government Printing Office
Washington, D.C. 20402

This is an index, compiled monthly by ERIC, of all U.S. Office of Education research projects and other documents of educational significance. Abstracts are provided, as are subject, author or investigator, and institution indices.

Cumulative semi-annual and annual indices to RIE are published separately and may also be purchased from the U.S. Government Printing Office. Subscription rates: domestic, $21.00/year; foreign, $5.25 additional. Send check or money order (no stamps).

National Directory of Newsletters

Gale Research Company
The Book Tower
Detroit, Michigan 48226

($20.00)

This directory contains information about 1500 newsletters and publications in agriculture, conservation, business and industry, education, humanities, public affairs, religion, etc. It lists the title of the publication, editor, publisher, circulation, frequency of issuance, cost, availability, and a description of its scope and content. There are three indices: subject, title, and publisher.

NEA Handbook

National Education Association
of the United States
1201 Sixteenth Street, N.W.
Washington, D.C. 20036

($2.00 single copy, quantity discounts)

This handbook, which serves as a basic reference for local, state, and national associations, is published annually. It is not only a directory of names, professional titles, and addresses, but also a source of information concerning the objectives, structure, and activities of the NEA and affiliated associations. It lists major NEA meetings and outlines the organization of NEA units and departments. It has a subject index, a name index, and an index of commission and committee members and organization officers.

NICEM Indices

National Information Center for Educational Media
University of Southern California
University Park
Los Angeles, California 90007

The following NICEM Indices are available: Index to 16mm Educational Films ($18.50); Index to 35mm Filmstrips ($12.00); Index to Educational Audio Tapes ($12.50); Index to Educational

Video Tapes ($8.25); Index to Educational Records ($9.50); Index to 8mm Cartridges ($8.50); Index to Producers and Distributors ($12.50); Index to Ecology—Multimedia ($9.50); Index to Educational Overhead Transparencies ($8.50); Index to Black History & Studies—Multimedia ($9.50).

Research Centers Directory, 1968
(Third Edition)

Archie M. Palmer (ed.)
Gale Research Company
The Book Tower
Detroit, Michigan 48226

($39.50)

This is a guide to university-sponsored and other non-profit, permanent organizations which have continuing research programs in agriculture, business, conservation, education, engineering and technology, government, law, life science, mathematics, area studies, physical and earth sciences, and social sciences and humanities.

V. REFERENCE BOOKS

Digest of Educational Statistics, Washington, D.C., U.S. Government Printing Office, 1966. This is a kind of statistical abstract of American education. It stresses quantities, i.e., numbers of institutions, number of programs, students, dollars spent, etc.

How to Locate Educational Information and Data: An Aid to Quick Utilization of the Literature of Education, Carter Alexanders and Arvid J. Burke (eds.), New York: Columbia University, Teachers College, 1958. Though dated, this is still a useful guide.

Information Resources: A Searcher's Manual, George Grimes and James Doyle, Regional Information System for Educators. Contact: Dr. George H. Grimes, 5057 Woodward, Detroit, Michigan 48202. This manual discusses the searching process itself, and gives a helpful listing of information agencies.

International Encyclopedia of the Social Sciences, David L. Sills (ed.), New York: Macmillan and Free Press, 1968. Possibly the best of the general encyclopedias dealing with the whole scope of the social sciences. It does not cover raw data.

VI. CONSULTING ORGANIZATIONS

Each consulting organization has its own orientation toward working with client school systems. Details about the extent of their operations and procedures can be obtained by inquiring directly with such an organization.

Basically, they can offer a client system:

- an enlarged research data base for organizational planning and decision-making

- assistance in research and in implementing change

- assistance in diagnosis or evaluation of the client's present state

RELs (Regional Educational Laboratories)

The regional educational labs are private, non-profit corporations which are funded, in whole or in part, under Title IV of the Elementary and Secondary Education Act of 1965. Each lab operates under a contract with the Division of Educational Laboratories, Bureau of Research, U.S. Office of Education. The labs are organized geographically, with some exceptions, dividing the nation into several regions. They are designed to take the product of basic research and develop programs that will link this research with practice in the schools of their respective regions. At this time, most of the laboratories supply direct services only to "demonstration" or project participant schools. However, all will answer specific requests for information about programs which they have under development. The laboratories differ from Research and Development Centers in focus and activities. Centers emphasize *research* and *development* while laboratories stress developmental *design* and *implementation* strategies.

APPALACHIA EDUCATIONAL
LABORATORY (AEL)
P.O. Box 1348
1031 Quarrier Street
Charleston, West Virginia 25325

Region: West Virginia, parts of Ohio, Pennsylvania, Virginia, Tennessee, and Kentucky

Director: Benjamin E. Carmichael

CENTER FOR URBAN EDUCATION (CUE)
105 Madison Avenue
New York, New York 10016

Region: Tri-State metropolitan area cities and suburbs of Greater New York

Director: Robert A. Dentler

CENTRAL MIDWESTERN REGIONAL
EDUCATIONAL LABORATORY (CEMREL)
10646 St. Charles Rock Road
St. Ann, Missouri 63074

Region: Eastern Missouri, southern Illinois, central and western Tennessee, and Kentucky

President: Wade M. Robinson

FAR WEST LABORATORY FOR
EDUCATIONAL RESEARCH AND
DEVELOPMENT (FWLERD)
1 Garden Circle
Hotel Claremont
Berkeley, California 94705

Region: Northern California, Utah, and Nevada (with the exception of Clark County)

Director: John K. Hemphill

NATIONAL LABORATORY FOR
HIGHER EDUCATION (NLHE)
411 West Chapel Hill Street
Mutual Plaza
Durham, North Carolina 27701

Director: Everett H. Hopkins

NORTHWEST REGIONAL EDUCATIONAL
LABORATORY (NWREL)
500 Lindsay Building
710 S.W. Second Avenue
Portland, Oregon 97204

Member States: Alaska, Idaho, Montana, Oregon, and Washington

Associate Member: Hawaii

Executive Director: Lawrence D. Fish

RESEARCH FOR BETTER
SCHOOLS, INC. (RBS)
1700 Market Street—Suite 1700
Philadelphia, Pennsylvnaia 19103

Executive Director: Robert G. Scanlon

AED (Academy for Educational Development)

437 Madison Avenue
New York, New York 10022

770 Welch Road
Palo Alto, California 94304

Embassy Building
1424 Sixteenth Street, N.W.
Washington, D.C. 20036

President: Alvin C. Eurich

SOUTHWEST EDUCATIONAL
DEVELOPMENT LABORATORY (SEDL)
800 Brazos Street
Austin, Texas 78701

Region: Texas and Louisiana

Director: James H. Perry

SOUTHWESTERN COOPERATIVE
EDUCATIONAL LABORATORY (SWCEL)
2104 San Mateo, S.E.
Albuquerque, New Mexico 87108

Region: Portions of Arizona, Oklahoma, Texas and all of New Mexico

Director: James Wilson

SOUTHWEST REGIONAL LABORATORY
FOR EDUCATIONAL RESEARCH AND
DEVELOPMENT (SWRL)
4665 Lampson Avenue
Los Alamitos, California 90726

Region: Southern California, southern Nevada, and Arizona

Director: Richard E. Schutz

206

The Academy for Educational Development, Inc., is a non-profit, tax exempt corporation. It serves schools, colleges, universities, and local, state and federal government agencies, foundations, and other organizations concerned with improving their operations and developing plans for the future.

/I/D/E/A/ (Institute for Development of Educational Activities, Inc.)

Dr. Samuel G. Sava
Executive Director
/I/D/E/A/
5335 Far Hills Avenue
Dayton, Ohio 45429

Dr. John I. Goodlad
Director
Research Division
/I/D/E/A/
1100 Glendon Avenue, Suite 950
Los Angeles, California 90024

Dr. John M. Bahner
Director
Innovative Programs Division
/I/D/E/A/
5335 Far Hills Avenue
Dayton, Ohio 45429

Dr. B. Frank Brown
Director
Information and Services Division
/I/D/E/A/
P.O. Box 446
Melbourne, Florida 32901

/I/D/E/A/ was established in 1965 by the Charles F. Kettering Foundation to accelerate the pace of constructive change in education. A primary focus of the Institute during the past few years has been on developing ways to help schools create an environment and adopt instructional processes that will make education more appropriate for individual learners. The intent is to enable teachers and administrators to learn about and put into practice techniques that will bring about individualization of instruction.

IRS (Information Retrieval System)

(Mrs.) Margaret R. Barry
Wisconsin Department of Public Instruction
126 Langdon Street
Madison, Wisconsin 53702

IRS provides a collection and dissemination bank on current practices and programs in education.

National Referral Center

Library of Congress
Science and Technology Division
10 First Street, S.E.
Washington, D.C. 20540

This national center functions as an intermediary, directing those who have questions about specific areas to individuals or organizations with expertise and specialized knowledge of the particular subject or area. Services are available without charge, by telephone, correspondence or via personal visit. The center's areas of interest include private organizations and institutions, governmental, industrial, academic, and public schools and individuals who have specialized knowledge in any area of the physical, biological, engineering, or social sciences, and are willing to share this knowledge with others. The Center maintains a subject-indexed inventory of information resources, including titles of representative publications, types of information services available, literature and report collections, unpublished data and specimen collections, etc.

National Center for Educational Statistics

400 Maryland Avenue, S.W.
Room 3055
Washington, D.C.

This center will answer inquiries on many aspects of education that have been dealt with in a statistical fashion. Caution is exercised in releasing information about individual schools, school systems, etc.

VII. ACADEMIC INSTITUTIONS

State universities and teachers colleges often provide resource services for school systems in their region. The range of service provided varies greatly among the institutions, but one might explore the offerings of a local institution in terms of the following areas*:

- *Bureaus of School Services*—information and consultants on specified topics

- *Extension Services*—in-service training through classes conducted in the local community

- *Continuing Education*—in-service training through on-campus courses and workshops

- *Educational Research and Development*—may be conducted in the department of education, but also in other bureaus.

- *Consulting Services*—may be organized with the staff of the department of education or education-related research bureaus.

*A related resource, of course, is any publication (journal, newsletter, etc.) put out by any one of these centers.

R & D (Research and Development) Centers

Each Research and Development Center concentrates on a significant problem area in education and conducts activities ranging from basic research through dissemination. The centers are interdisciplinary in organization and maintain cooperative relationships with regional laboratories, state departments of education, local school systems, universities and teacher training colleges, and relevant professional and non-profit organizations:

CENTER FOR THE ADVANCED STUDY OF
EDUCATIONAL ADMINISTRATION
University of Oregon
Eugene, Oregon 97403

CENTER FOR RESEARCH AND
DEVELOPMENT IN HIGHER
EDUCATION
University of California
4606 Tolman Hall
Berkeley, California 94720

CENTER FOR RESEARCH,
DEVELOPMENT AND TRAINING
IN OCCUPATIONAL EDUCATION
North Carolina State University
Raleigh, North Carolina 27607

CENTER FOR SOCIAL ORGANIZATION
OF SCHOOLS
The Johns Hopkins University
3505 North Charles Street
Baltimore, Maryland 21218

CENTER FOR THE STUDY OF
EVALUATION
Graduate School of Education
University of California
145 Moore Hall
Los Angeles, California 90024

CENTER FOR VOCATIONAL AND
TECHNICAL EDUCATION
The Ohio State University
1900 Kenny Road
Columbus, Ohio 43210

LEARNING RESEARCH AND
DEVELOPMENT CENTER
208 Mineral Industries Building
University of Pittsburgh
Pittsburgh, Pennsylvania 15213

RESEARCH AND DEVELOPMENT CENTER
FOR TEACHER EDUCATION
Education Annex
The University of Texas at Austin
Austin, Texas 78712

STANFORD CENTER FOR RESEARCH AND
DEVELOPMENT IN TEACHING
Stanford University
770 Welch Road
Palo Alto, California 94304

WISCONSIN RESEARCH AND DEVELOPMENT
CENTER FOR COGNITIVE LEARNING
The University of Wisconsin
1404 Regent Street
Madison, Wisconsin 53706

Educational Policy Research Centers

    (a)   Stanford Research Institute
            Menlo Park, California

(b) The Policy Institute
Syracuse University Research Corporation (SURC)
723 University Avenue
Syracuse, New York 13210

(c) Educational Policy Research Center at Syracuse
Syracuse University Research Corporation
1206 Harrison Street
Syracuse, New York 13210

VIII. HUMAN RESOURCES

People can be very valuable to the resource retriever. They can serve directly as sources of information, and also as effective guides to other sources of information. The use of "people" resources can help avoid problems resulting from the arbitrariness in the selection and categorization of information in "non-human" resources (libraries, hard-bound collections, information services, etc.). The unique contributions that people can provide are their *ad hoc* evaluations of the probable adaptability of an innovation to the particular needs of the client and the quick referral they can give to other resources. They can be found both inside and outside of the client system.

IX. GOVERNMENT AGENCIES

State Government

The departments of education or of public instruction in the various states provide consultants for their school systems on most topics of pertinence to the educational practitioner, such as curriculum, special services, federal programs, and administration. The state departments can also serve as clearinghouses on the progress of educational innovations in systems throughout the state.

Federal Government

The contributions of the federal government to the development and diffusion of educational information are substantial, as reflected by the involvement of the government in many of the "source" agencies listed in this appendix. The United States Office of Education, as a result of the provisions of the National Defense Education Act, the Elementary and Secondary Education Act, and the Vocational Education Act, is involved in a vast number of programs—many of them innovative—on an operational level. It also sponsors a great deal of research in education and can provide information about or access to relevant projects, completed or on-going. ERIC is the main disseminator of information about these programs. However, the numerous publications of the

Office of Education and other agencies are only one means of gaining access to this vast information source. Most federal agencies have information services of their own; e.g., the Defense Department's Defense Documentation Center and HEW's Children's Bureau.

X. PROFESSIONAL ORGANIZATIONS

Most professional organizations, such as the American Educational Research Association (AERA), the National Education Association (NEA), and numerous others, publish newsletters, conference proceedings, documents, and journals containing educational information. The validity and concreteness of such information varies, and it may be difficult to obtain, especially if one is not a member of the organization. A good technique is to get on their mailing list for newsletters, which announce recent or impending publications. Libraries and information services also collect certain kinds of publications from these organizations (usually the journal). Professional organizations sponsor many workshops and conferences on topics of current interest to educators. Announcements appear in the journal or newsletter of the organization.

American Educational Research Association (AERA)

1126 Sixteenth Street, N.W.
Washington, D.C. 20036

Executive Director: Richard A. Dershimer

The American Educational Research Association is a national professional organization of educators and behavioral scientists who have an interest in basic research in education and in the improvement, development, and application of research to educational problems.

National Education Association (NEA)

NEA Records Division
1201 Sixteenth Street, N.W.
Washington, D.C. 20036

NEA is a non-profit voluntary non-governmental organization available to all professional teachers, school administrators, college professors and specialists. This organization cooperates with all groups who seek to improve education. NEA issues several publications: *Today's Education*—professional magazine with articles on psychology, methods of instruction, new publications, social implications of problems in education, etc.; *NEA Reporter*—containing news of professional and association developments; *NEA Handbook* [see "Directories and Indices" for a description of *NEA Handbook*] ; *Research Bulletin*; and several others.

XI. OTHER SCHOOL SYSTEMS

Valuable help can be given by other school systems. Because of their personal experience, other teachers and administrators can be the best sources of information about the practicability of an innovation. Title III of the Elementary and Secondary Education Act of 1965 "seeks to encourage innovative and exemplary programs." One way in which it does this is by charging those projects which it has funded as "innovative and exemplary" with a dissemination responsibility. Schools in which Title III projects are operating provide demonstrations and/or advice about their innovation to interested educators. Information about existing Title III projects can be obtained through state departments of education, and also *PACEsetters in Innovation*. [See "Directories and Indices" for a description of *PACEsetters in Innovation*.]

Appendix C

MAJOR WORKS ON CHANGE IN EDUCATION
An Annotated Bibliography

Appendix C

MAJOR WORKS ON CHANGE IN EDUCATION

An Annotated Bibliography

Compiled by:

Elizabeth A. Campbell
Mary C. Havelock
Ronald G. Havelock
Janet C. Huber
Shaindel Zimmerman

Originally compiled, 1969
Updated and Expanded, 1972

INTRODUCTION

This bibliography is designed for easy reference by practitioners, researchers, and instructors who are concerned with planned change, innovation, dissemination, and knowledge utilization. The focus is the field of *education*, but those concerned with similar processes in other areas of *social practice* should also find it useful. Work on the bibliography was supported under contract No. OEC-0-8-4535(010), U.S. Office of Education, Bureau of Research, as groundwork for a handbook for educational practitioners on the subjects of change planning and knowledge utilization: *A Guide to Innovation in Education*. We are grateful to the authors of the following three bibliographies for permitting us to draw material from their works:

Special credit is due to Norman Kurland and Richard Miller for their *Selected and Annotated Bibliography on the Processes of Change* (New York State Education Department and the University of Kentucky, 1966) which provided the basic material for some of the earlier citations. Material drawn primarily from this secondary source is credited by the symbol "[K & M]."

An Annotated Bibliography on Administering for Change (Administering for Change Program, Research for Better Schools, Inc., 1971) provided material for additional annotations. Annotations primarily based on this secondary source by Louis M. Maquire, Sanford Temkin, and C. Peter Cummings are credited by the symbol "[M, T & C]."

Additional citations were drawn from *A Selected and Annotated Bibliography: The Change Process in Education* (Columbus, Ohio: ERIC Clearinghouse on Vocational and Technical Education, The Center for Vocational and Technical Education, The Ohio State University, 1970). Material based primarily on this work by Gail J. Skelton and J.W. Hensel is credited by the symbol "[S & H]."

CRITERIA FOR SELECTION

We have selected references for inclusion on the following criteria:

1. general coverage of a range of topics relevant to educational change,
2. in book form, which is
3. published and available in education libraries, book stores, or by ordering from indicated sources.

For the most part we have excluded empirical studies and reports on specific research projects unless they cover a range of relevant topics, offer both research findings and implications for practice, and can be obtained as separate monographs. Hence, journal articles—unless they appear in collections—are not included. For a more exhaustive listing of approximately 4,000 references in this topic area see Havelock, R.G., *Bibliography on Knowledge Utilization and Dissemination*, Center for Research on the Utilization of Scientific Knowledge, University of Michigan, Ann Arbor, Michigan, 1968. Other extensive bibliographies are cited above; in addition we should mention Rogers, E.M., *Bibliography of Research on the Diffusion of Innovations*, Department of Communications, Michigan State University, East Lansing, Michigan, 1968; and *A Bibliography on the Process of Change,* Melbourne, Florida: Institute for Development of Educational Activities, Inc., 1968.

Abbott, Max G. and Lowell, John T. (eds.). *Change Perspectives in Educational Administration.* Auburn, Alabama: Auburn University, 1965, 87 pp.

Topics

- American education and technological change
- implications of a changing occupational structure
- the administrator's private and public responsibilities
- hierarchical impediments
- the organizational context

Contributing Authors

Max G. Abbott   Meno Lovenstein
Walter Buckingham   James E. McClellan
C.T. Hu   Matthew B. Miles

"Six papers are included which were given at a seminar on the change process held at Auburn University. The seminar dealt with: (1) the identifying and defining of basic forces in American society that impinge upon the educational institution, (2) the analyzing of specific implications of these forces on the educational institution, and (3) the discussion of different aspects of the change process itself." [K & M]

Bennis, Warren G. *Changing Organizations.* New York: McGraw-Hill Book Company, 1966, 223 pp.

Topics

- trends in organizational development
- scientific management
- leadership patterns
- models of social change
  - change agent
  - client system
  - collaboration
  - application of valid knowledge
- operations research (compared with planned change)
- implementation programs for planned change
- strategies for change agents
- laboratory (T-group) training to effect organizational change
- problems facing modern organizations

This book is a collection of essays which the author describes as approaching the problem of organizational change from many different angles. The essays are divided into two parts, the first of which describes evolutionary trends in organizational development. Democracy, science, and collaboration are suggested as the keys to adaptive organizations of the future. The second part of the book discusses how the behavioral scientist can help to direct the process of organizational change through action based on knowledge.

Planned change is described as the link between theory and practice in which a change agent collaborates with a client system to apply valid knowledge to the client's problems. Some strategies of planned change are outlined and the "risks and promises" of laboratory (T-group) training are aptly illustrated with examples of successes and failures.

This book puts the history, practice, and future prospects of planned organizational change into perspective. The focus of the book is not on education in particular; rather, the discussion is applicable to any complex human organization. Behavioral scientists concerned with the theory of planned organizational change will constitute its primary audience. Each essay is liberally documented with footnotes, and an index is provided.

Bennis, Warren G., Benne, Kenneth D., and Chin, Robert (eds.). *The Planning of Change. Second Edition*. New York: Holt, Rinehart and Winston, 1969, 627 pp.

Topics

- theories, strategies, and methods
- organizational change
- utilization of scientific knowledge
- application of social science
- helping relationships
- expert role
- consultant role
- defender role
- collaboration
- conflict resolution
- opinion change
- diffusion of innovations
- personal change and growth in adults
- socio-technical systems
- system models
- development models
- laboratory training
- cross-cultural training
- problem-solving
- sensitivity training groups
- mental health consultation
- survey feedback
- diagnosis of organizational problems

- the confrontation meeting
- resistance to change
- influence process
- predicting the future
- utopian-analysis
- manipulation of human behavior (ethics of)
- ethics in consultation
- values in social science

Contributing Authors

Chris Argyris
Louis B. Barnes
Raymond A. Bauer
Howard S. Becker
Richard Beckhard
Daniel Bell
Kenneth D. Benne
Warren G. Bennis
Max Birnbaum
Robert R. Blake
Paula H. Calder
Daniel M. Callahan
Gerald Caplan
Robert Chin
James V. Clark

Sheldon Davis
Charles K. Ferguson
Alvin W. Gouldner
Roger Harrison
Ronald G. Havelock
Richard Hopkins
Harvey A. Hornstein
Elihu Katz
George A. Kelley
Herbert Kelman
Donald Klein
Paul Lawrence
Ruth Leeds
Ronald Lippitt
Jay W. Lorsh

David C. McClelland
Margaret Mead
Matthew B. Miles
Jane Srygley Mouton
Carl Rogers
Edgar H. Schein
R. Steven Schiavo
Herber A. Shepard
Richard L. Sloma
E.L. Trist
Richard E. Walton
Goodwin Watson
Alexander Winn

Like the first edition (see Bennis *et al.,* 1961) this volume is the major general source on the subject of planned change in all areas of social practice, and would serve as a useful text for university courses in this area in social science departments and in various professional schools, e.g., business administration, social work, education, theology, nursing, and public health. Nine-tenths of the 1969 edition is entirely new material, most of it published in the mid-sixties. There is less emphasis on group dynamics and traditional social psychology, and much more on the emerging social technologies, and on knowledge utilization in planned change. A chapter by Chin and Benne offers an overview analysis of different general strategies in historical perspective. An index is provided.

Bennis, Warren G., Benne, Kenneth D., and Chin, Robert (Eds.). *The Planning of Change. Readings in the Applied Behavioral Sciences. First Edition.* (See also Second Edition described above.) New York: Holt, Rinehart and Winston, 1961, 781 pp.

Topics

- theoretical bases of change
- technologies

- planning
- helping professions
- social science, scientist, and policy
- human relations, human engineering
- evaluation
- values, ethics
- consultant role
- change agent role
- trainer role
- social therapy
- models and types of change process
- system linkage
- group dynamics and interpersonal relations
- conflict resolution
- force field analysis applied to school situations
- psychotherapy
- roles
- role conflict
- communities
- organizations
- power
- leadership
- influence
- attitude and opinion change
- training
- role playing
- T-groups
- resistance to change

Contributing Authors

John Arsenian
Howard Baumgartel
Alex Bavelas
Kenneth D. Benne
Warren G. Bennis
Robert R. Blake
Leland P. Bradford
Dorwin Cartwright
Robert Chin
George S. Count
Watson Dickerman
Ralf Dohrendorf
Cora DuBois
Lawrence K. Frank
John R.P. French, Jr.
George Geiger

Jacob W. Getzels
John C. Glidewell
Alvin W. Gouldner
Paul Grabbe
Ernest Greenwood
William Gruen
Robert G. Gunderson
Murray Horwitz
Elliot Jacques
David H. Jenkins
Helen H. Jennings
Gale Jensen
Herbert C. Kelman
Timothy Leary
Daniel Lerner
Max Lerner

George Levinger
Grace Levit
Kurt Lewin
Gordon L. Lippitt
Ronald Lippitt
Charles P. Loomis
Floyd C. Mann
Karl Mannheim
Alfred J. Marrow
Douglas M. McGregor
Robert K. Merton
Matthew B. Miles
Edward O. Moe
Barrington Moore, Jr.
Elting E. Morison
Arthur E. Murphy

Max Pages	William C. Schutz	Anselm L. Strauss
Talcott Parsons	Morris S. Schwartz	George Strauss
Thomas Parsons	Charles Seashore	Harry S. Sullivan
Faith Pigors	Elvin V. Semrad	Herbert Thelen
Paul Pigors	Herbert A. Shepard	James D. Thompson
David Riesman	Phillip E. Slater	Elmer Van Egmond
Carl R. Rogers	John P. Spiegel	Gwen Tudor Will
Irwin T. Sanders	William O. Stanley	Alvin Zander
Edgar H. Schein	Maurice Stein	

The authors bring together concept-realizations of different aspects of application and change processes, and tie these contributions together with extensive critical and theoretical introductions in each of the four major sections of the book: 1) the roots of planned change, 2) conceptual tools for the change agent: social systems and change models, 3) dynamics of the influence process, and 4) programs and technologies of planned change. The problems of various professions of social practice (including teaching) have been taken into account. The information in this text cannot be readily absorbed by the unsophisticated practitioner, since it is heavily embedded in a social-psychological context. An index is provided.

Benne, Kenneth D. and Muntyan, Bozidar (eds.). *Human Relations in Curriculum Change*. New York: The Dryden Press, 1951, 363 pp.

Topics

- conceptual tools for analyzing
- groups and group methods
- democratic ethics
- discipline for leadership

Contributing Authors

George E. Axtelle	Charles E. Hendry	Donald Nylen
Alex Bavelas	David H. Jenkins	R. Bruce Raup
Kenneth D. Benne	Irving Knickerbocker	Paul Sheats
Leland P. Bradford	Kurt Lewin	B. Othaniel Smith
Florence Cleary	Ronald Lippitt	Herbert A. Thelen
Alice Davis	Douglas McGregor	Helen G. Trager
Watson Dickerman	Arnold Meier	Alvin Zander
Paul Grabbe	Alice Miel	

This early work on the change process in education provides valuable conceptual background on the development of planned change and its application to the field of education. It does not rely heavily on research reports but the presentations are clear and might adequately serve to orient an educator to the basic discussions. Short introductions are provided for each major topic area. There is no bibliography, but an index is provided.

This is the forerunner to Bennis, Benne, and Chin, *The Planning of Change.* (See Bennis *et al.,* 1969; and Bennis *et al.,* 1961.)

Biddle, William W. and Biddle, Loureide J. (collab.). *Encouraging Community Development: A Training Guide for Local Workers.* New York: Holt, Rinehart and Winston, Inc., 1968, 224 pp.

Topics

- role of the community development volunteer: "encourager"
- what constitutes the community
- basic-nucleus and larger-nucleus process of community development
- necessity of trust, friendship and over-all sensitivity between "encourager" and citizen
- cultivation of emergent leadership
- building the sense of community
- "encourager's" working responsibilities: keeping the community action group going
- reconciling community conflict
- ethics of influence
- future of the process and of the "encourager"

This guide is both descriptive and prescriptive. In addition to detailing the practical mechanics of community development, the guide particularly emphasizes the personal dynamics of the involved relationships.

Although the Biddles suggest that the guide be primarily used by universities in the training of nonprofessionals (e.g., volunteers for the Peace Corps, VISTA, churches and clinic organizations), the guide's working format and readability lends itself to the use of a wide range of interested people. There are footnotes, and each of the sixteen chapters is followed by an Addendum for Social Science Students. An index is provided.

Brickell, Henry M. *Organizing New York State for Educational Change.* Albany: New York State Education Department, 1961, 107 pp.

Topics

- dynamics of educational change today
  - historical context
  - process on the local level
  - role of outside institutions and organizations
  - phases of instructional innovation (design, evaluation, dissemination)
- organizing to improve process of educational change
  - statewide coordinated design and evaluation
  - regional coordinated dissemination
  - roles of existing organizations

"A study of the dynamics of instructional change in the elementary and secondary schools of New York State with recommendations for improved organization. Elicits the background of how and why they change, the dynamics of change today, and suggests solutions pertinent for New York State." [K & M]

This study is popularly cited by researchers as an analysis of the problem and as a model for planning change which might be found useful by anyone concerned with long-range planning for change. It is clear and concise. No bibliography or index.

Burns, Richard W. and Brooks, Gary D. (eds.). *Curriculum Design in a Changing Society*. Englewood Cliffs, New Jersey: Educational Technology Publications, Inc., 1970, 353 pp.

Topics

- the need for curriculum reform
- future modes of education
- behavioral objectives; response vs. stimulus
- problem-solving and curriculum reform
- rigor in design of curriculum
- student readiness; implications for curriculum design
- student unrest and the curriculum
- student-centered curriculum
- curriculum design for special education
- curriculum changes implied in organizational changes
- reading curriculum for minority/disadvantaged students
- systems approach to curriculum change in secondary education
- curriculum reform in higher education
- general vs. specialized education
- impact of new materials and media on curriculum design
- impact of mass media on curriculum
- learning/information-processing models and curriculum design
- computers, instruction and the curriculum
- school accountability to students and public
- humanistic education
- administrative implications of curriculum reform

Contributing Authors

Max G. Abbott	William A. Deterline	G.L. Oliver
Alfred S. Alschuler	Terry L. Eidell	Henry J. Otto
Gary D. Brooks	Robert M. Gagné	Carl L. Rosen
Richard W. Budd	George L. Geis	Harold G. Shane
Richard W. Burns	John I. Goodlad	June Grant Shane
David S. Bushnell	Norris G. Haring	Edmund V. Sullivan
Robert C. Calfee	Max Jerman	Bruce W. Tuckman
Philip C. Chamberlain	Philip G. Kapfer	Abram W. VanderMeer
M.M. Chambers	Leon M. Lessinger	E.G. Williamson

The editors describe the authors of this set of papers as operating on one unifying premise: "They are agreed that the physical and administrative structure of the system of education should be derived from a prior determination of what is to be done about the curriculum, rather than the other way around." In the epilogue, Goodlad notes that there are more disagreements among the authors than there are agreements in how to approach the topic of curriculum reform. He emphasizes in particular that the papers start from widely divergent premises of what constitutes curriculum, and he therefore finds it difficult to provide a unifying summary of the contributions. We can however, note some common themes running through the papers. First, there is an emphasis on learning rather than on teaching; the implication for the curriculum is that it should become humanistic and student-behavior centered. Second, several authors are concerned that new technology should be exploited in the development of curriculum. They feel that we should develop curriculum worthy of modern technology, but that the basis for judging the resulting programs should be on the quality of the instruction rather than on the complexity of the hardware or the lack of it. Finally, we find the theme that the schools must be responsive to and accountable to society and that the learning experience should be relevant to the individual student's present and future role in society.

This book carries a message for anyone who is concerned with innovation in our school system, but it is particularly relevant for those who are responsible for curriculum design. There is no index, but there are bibliographic references at the end of each chapter.

Bushnell, David S. and Rappaport, Donald (eds.). *Planned Change in Education: A Systems Approach.* New York: Harcourt Brace Jovanovich, 1971, 223 pp.

Topics

- systematic strategy for school renewal
- coordinating human resources
- measuring the productivity of schools
- student performance
  - place in an accountability system
  - objectives and measurement procedures
- teacher performance
  - prototype of a practical system for appraisal
- yardstick project; charting pupil performance (the Growth Gauge)
- individualizing instruction; IPI
- characteristics of the multi-unit school; differentiated staffing approach
- performance contracting ("turnkey" approach) as means for school system reform
- procedures for developing and evaluating a computer-supported comprehensive guidance system of individualizing school guidance and counseling programs
- planning models for improved administration
- systems approach to planned growth
  - Education Planning System (EPS)
- implementing a results-oriented budgeting system

Contributing Authors

Charles Blaschke
C. Edwin Brewin
Mary V. Brown
Oliver Brown
David S. Bushnell
Desmond L. Cook
James Hardie

John Hayman
G. Brian Jones
Herbert J. Klausmeier
Dennis McFadden
Jack C. Merwin
Roland J. Pellegrin
Francis J. Pilecki

Fred Pinkham
Donald Rappaport
Robert G. Scanlon
Allen Schenck
Roger L. Sisson
Jack Stenner

The thirteen individually authored chapters are divided into four main parts: (1) Organizing for Change, (2) Making Schools Accountable, (3) The Instructional Process, and (4) The Planning, Allocation, and Management of Educational Resources.

Although educators in all roles will find at least some of this material of interest, the book is particularly appropriate for administrators who are concerned about instituting more systematic methods of planning and managing change in their schools. The majority of the chapters have a useful summary and a section of Suggested Readings (usually briefly annotated). There are footnotes and an abundance of figures, diagrams and charts. No index is provided.

Carlson, Richard O. *Adoption of Educational Innovations.* Eugene, Oregon: Center for the Advanced Study of Educational Administration, University of Oregon, 1965, 84 pp.

Topics

- educational innovation
- rate of adoption
- communication of new practices
- predictors of rate of adoption
- characteristics of innovations
- rates of diffusion

"This monograph traces portions of the life cycles of six innovations which have captured the attention of educators. Major attention is focused on the factors which bear on the varying rates of adoption and diffusion of educational innovations as revealed by research conducted among school superintendents in 107 school systems located within two states." [K & M]

No index is provided.

Center for the Advanced Study of Educational Administration, *Change Processes in the Public Schools.* Eugene, Oregon: The Center, 1965, 92 pp.

Topics

- barriers
- planned change and organizational health

- directed change
- characteristics of innovators
- the place of research

Contributing Authors

Richard O. Carlson   Matthew B. Miles   Everett M. Rogers
Art Gallagher, Jr.   Roland J. Pellegrin

These papers were originally presented at a seminar for school officials, and include an emphasis on organizational and systematic factors in the process, the relevance of research to practitioners, and Rogers' description of innovators.

An integrative summary is provided, as are footnotes and references, within the individual papers. There is no master bibliography or index.

A researcher's orientation is definitely the emphasis of these papers. It may not be very useful to practitioners with specific problems.

Center for the Study of Instruction, *Rational Planning in Curriculum and Instruction*. National Education Association, 1967, 203 pp.

Topics

- curriculum, its reform, and related issues
- instructional theory-building
- reorganizing the school and classroom
- change roles in education
- strategies for local school systems
- a model for action

Contributing Authors

Robert L. Brackenbury   Egon G. Guba   Robert M.W. Travers
Henry M. Brickell   Glen Heathers   Elizabeth C. Wilson
David L. Clark   Donald A. Myers
John I. Goodlad   Ole Sand

Most of the essays in this volume are products of a seminar conducted by the Center for the Study of Instruction in 1965. Each of the authors approaches the topic of educational reform and the concept of change in his own particular fashion, and thus there is a disparity in perspective and terminology. This volume does not make for easy reading for the unsophisticated practitioner. Although there is no index, there is an annotated bibliography and a list of related publications.

Centre for Educational Research and Innovation, *Innovation in Education.* Paris, France: OECD, 1971. Series of five technical reports, CERI/EI numbers 71.02 (55 pp.), 71.03 (58 pp.), 71.04 (69 pp.), 71.05 (67 pp.), and 71.06 (48 pp.).

Topics

- structure of national educational systems
- change strategies
- types of innovations introduced
- barriers to innovation
- innovative agencies
- needed reforms

Contributing Authors

Stuart Maclure — report on Sweden (CERI/EI/71.02)
Helga Thomas — report on Germany (CERI/EI/71.03)
Per Dalin — report on Norway (CERI/EI/71.04)
Leila Sussmann — report on United States (CERI/EI/71.05)
Anne Corbett — report on England (CERI/EI/71.06)

This group of technical reports is designed to give a descriptive overview of educational innovation in five OECD nations. A brief preface to the volumes notes some similarities in innovational concerns, such as structural and curricular reforms, running through all the reports. It also points out that some differences can be readily noted which can be largely traced to the size and political structure of the nations concerned and to their varying "national climates." Brief comparisons are made of the structure and innovation programs of the school systems in the five countries, but these volumes would benefit from a more comprehensive comparative analysis.

These reports should be of particular interest to planners of educational policy at the national level. Although they give only brief accounts of a very large area of concern, they do include some illustrative examples of innovations and planning. However, only two of the volumes (Germany and United States) contain bibliographic references, and none is indexed.

Centre for Educational Research and Innovation. *The Management of Innovation in Education.* Paris, France: O.E.C.D. Publications, 1971, 67 pp.

Topics

- the process of innovation in education
    - centralization and decentralization
    - entry points for innovation in the educational system
    - characteristics of innovative systems
- management of the process
    - policy decisions and planning
    - construction and development of an innovative project

- evaluation and dissemination
- training for innovation management
- finance
- innovation in practice: organizational, technological, and curricular
- the role of CERI
  - expertise on planning, policy, strategy, and mechanisms
  - international training

Contributing Authors

Per Dalin
James Scotland
David Thomas

This volume was prepared on the basis of an international conference, sponsored by CERI, which was held in 1969 at Cambridge, England and which brought together fifty educators from the eleven member-nations of the Organization for Economic Co-operation and Development. Listings of the participants and the working papers of the conference are given in the appendices.

The book is directed towards managers of innovation in education, that is, "those who have the task of directing the innovation and making it operational." The aim of this book is to report on the existing state of practical knowledge concerning the establishment of effective mechanisms for educational innovation. Some comparisons are made of the innovative context, problems and achievements of various OECD member nations.

A recommendation is made that an international program be developed for the training of educational innovation managers, and the possible role which CERI might play in such a program is discussed.

This volume does not go into great detail on any of the topics listed, but the papers listed in its appendix should provide extensive additional information on the state of educational innovation planning and management in several Western countries. No index is provided.

College Entrance Examination Board, *The Challenge of Curricular Change.* **Princeton, New Jersey: College Entrance Examination Board, 1966, 151 pp.**

Topics

- current state of curricular reform
- changing tasks of the high school
- three dimensions of curricular change
- quantity and quality
- effect on student maturity
- the value of education for Americans
- a flexible college plan
- the liberal arts curriculum
- teaching, need for effectiveness

- educating to structure experience
- the learning revolution outside educational institutions
- training for responsible citizenry
- faculty's goals for students
- a commission on general education

Contributing Authors

Stephen K. Bailey
Robert F. Byrnes
Harold F. Clark
William G. Cole
John I. Goodlad
M. Jacqueline Grennan

Douglas H. Heath
Stanley J. Idzerda
William L. Kolb
Thomas C. Mendenhall
Lloyd S. Michael
Richard Pearson

Fillmore H. Sanford
Henry Scattergood
Gene L. Schwilck
Sidney Sulkin
Ellsworth Tompkins

These papers were presented at a colloquium co-sponsored by CEEB and the National Association of Secondary School Principals. They are interesting discussions of the topics listed. However, no index or bibliography is provided, and footnotes are rarely used. A good introduction summarizes the works.

Specific program recommendations are not the purpose of these papers; many of the themes are philosophical. Case material is, however, abundant. The educator may not find this source useful for efficient data retrieval, but many of the authors' ideas are thought-provoking.

Eastern Regional Institute for Education, Inc. *How to Get New Programs into Elementary Schools.* **Englewood Cliffs, New Jersey: Educational Technology Publications, Inc., 1972.**

This is a series of five booklets designed for use by administrators who are considering curriculum changes in their schools. Each booklet is described individually below.

Mahan, James M. and Gill, F. Jean. *How to Install a New Curriculum* (Book Number One), 50 pp.

Topics

- phases in curriculum installation
  - readiness
  - selection of innovation
  - preparation for installation
    - equipment
    - workshops
    - inservice education
  - expert assistance in implementation
  - implementation guidelines
  - assessment
  - maintenance

- dissemination/demonstration

Each of the phases which are described as making up the process of innovation installation is treated in a separate brief chapter. A checklist following each chapter gives a quick overview of the steps involved in carrying out that phase. Particularly useful are listings of references and resources which follow each chapter.

Gill, F. Jean and Harty, Harold. *Administrator's Plan Book for Curriculum Change* (Book Number Two), 32 pp.

This book consists of a diagram and a record sheet for each phase of curriculum installation described in Book Number One above. It is therefore designed to be used in conjunction with Book One, and is intended to provide the administrator with a handy workbook for keeping track of his actions and the results of those actions.

Bickel, Robert F. and Gill, F. Jean. *How to Select a New Curriculum* (Book Number Three), 57 pp.

Topics

- the search/selection committee
- needs survey, program objectives, and search criteria
- the search: information collection; committee tasks; curriculum-criteria matrix
- narrowing the choice
- making the selection
- major information sources in education

This book is to be used only after the need for a new curricular program has been firmly established. It is intended to be used during the phase of innovation selection as described in Book One. Brief guidelines are provided for carrying out the steps of this phase, and the appendix* ("Major Information Sources in Education") provides the reader with references to many more detailed resources.

Renker, Marcia M., Andrulis, Richard S., Heffernan, Thomas P. and Bush, Steven J. *How to Use Data to Make Curriculum Installation Decisions* (Book Number Four), 38 pp.

Topics

- procedures to follow in data-based decision-making
- case histories
- resources for readiness

*The appendix to the booklet was developed by Havelock and associates and used with his permission; it is an earlier edited version of Appendix B of this edition of the *Guide.*

This book has been developed for use during the readiness phase of curriculum installation, as described in Book One. The decision-making procedures are presented only in very brief form, but again the resource references will provide the reader with broader information on this topic. The case studies provide interesting accounts of individuals involved in curriculum installation.

Renker, Marcia M. and Bush, Steven J. *How to Develop a Pupil-Assessment System for a New Curriculum* (Book Number Five), 28 pp.

Topics

- administrator preliminary activities
- administrator-teacher interaction; workshops and in-service education
- model for scheduling activities
- resources on pupil-assessment system development

This book illustrates in brief fashion how an administrator may work to develop an assessment system to measure pupil attainment of instructional objectives in a new elementary school program. It stresses that all school personnel should be involved both in the development and in the implementation of such a system. The resources listed should be helpful in following up on the suggestions contained in this volume.

Eidell, Terry L. and Kitchel, Joanne M. (eds.). *Knowledge Production and Utilization in Educational Administration.* Eugene, Oregon: University Council for Educational Administration, and Center for the Advanced Study of Educational Administration, University of Oregon, 1968, 184 pp.

Topics

- knowledge production and utilization
- development, diffusion, and evaluation
- dissemination and translation roles
- organizational influence on innovative roles
- training programs and change

Contributing Authors

Norman J. Boyan	Egon G. Guba	Sam D. Sieber
Launor F. Carter	Ronald G. Havelock	
Keith Goldhammer	Richard Schmuck	

This volume deals with seven problems inherent in the application of knowledge to practice. Some of these papers view the problems of applying new knowledge to practice quite generally in the context of the broader society while others focus more sharply on strategies for implementing the utilization of knowledge in the context of educational organizations. No real attempt has been made to integrate the papers into a unified document. The book would be of use primarily to researchers and administrators, rather than to practitioners, due to its technical language and its scarcity of case studies. There are many references to informative research findings. There is no general bibliography, but specific bibliographies follow each chapter. No index.

Evans, Richard I. and Leppman, Peter K. *Resistance to Innovation in Higher Education: A Social-Psychological Exploration Focused on Television and the Establishment.* San Francisco: Jossey-Bass Inc., 1967, 198 pp.

Topics

- resistance to innovation in higher education
- theories of innovation
- research case history: instructional television
- profile of a university faculty
- Pro-ITV and Anti-ITV professors
- changes in attitude toward innovation
- views on innovation from nine universities
- major variables in the process of innovation and future research possibilities

This book examines the problem of traditional resistance to change in the American academic community by drawing a variety of information from the investigation of the case history of instructional television. The examination successfully integrates different levels of analysis. Information about the personality structure of a faculty and its pattern of attitudes toward innovation is provided, as are social psychological theories about the formation and change of attitudes. A resulting methodology emerges as well as a broad theoretical model of innovation.

There are three appendices, occasional tables, a bibliography, and an index.

Frymier, Jack R. *Fostering Educational Change.* Columbus, Ohio: Charles E. Merrill Publishing Company, 1969, 209 pp.

Topics

- forces affecting educational change
- previous efforts at educational change: six kinds of hypotheses and reasons for their failures
- education as a social system
- five theoretical dimensions of American systems
- propositions for educational change

Frymier feels that the need for educational change in America has not been met to date. In considering why the various hypotheses designed to bring about change have failed, he finds that the fundamental problem is that education has not been adequately appreciated in conceptual terms.

Frymier contends that education is a social system, and that one of its basic shortcomings is not having a group of persons to assume the evaluating role who are separate from those persons who are executing the *planning* and *doing* roles. There is inadequate feedback. He believes that a comparison of education as a social system with American democracy, science, and free enterprise suggests the crucial dimensions enabling the "success" of the latter and leading therefore to a theoretical model of educational change. The dimensions are those of "goal," "domain," "function," "confidence," and "record."

Although of some interest for its conceptual breadth, practitioners might not find this work very useful in providing concrete guidance on the day-to-day management of change. The eighty-two pages of text are divided into five chapters, each of which is concluded by a summary. Included as one of the four appendices is an annotated bibliography of over 250 research reports. There are footnotes and an index is provided.

Gideonse, Hendrik D. *Educational Research and Development in the United States.* National Center for Educational Research and Development. Washington, D.C.: U.S. Government Printing Office, 1970.

Topics

- research
- development
- dissemination
- dependency models
- decision-oriented models
- linkage models

"The author attempts to portray the past history and current status of educational research and development in the United states. Three major activities are viewed as being associated with research and development: (1) research, the objective of which is to discover, reinforce, or refine knowledge; (2) development, the objective of which is to produce materials, techniques, processes, hardware, and organizational formats for instruction; and (3) dissemination, the objective of which is to make information about research and development available in usable and effective forms. Three types of models on the relationship of research to development, or development to research, or the relationship of both to the improvement of education are described. The first type, called linear or dependency models, tends to view the goal of educational improvement as being dependent upon adequate diffusion mechanisms which in turn require the invention and development of tested innovations to diffuse, which in turn depend upon the adequacy of the research base. The linear or dependency model is likely to be used by a student of institutional change or of the larger process of the diffusion of innovation through a social system. The second type, called decision-oriented models, sees essential differences and disconnections between the research, development, and dissemination functions, and draws attention to the different rules of evidence and sources and types of data input to decision making in each function. These models tend to be more impressed by the current decision-making requirements than by patterns which may emerge from somewhat longer-term historical analysis of change or from the apparent logical dependence of one function on another. Decision-oriented models are likely to be used by a sponsor of educational research and development who stands midway between the research and development process and the educational system and is confronted by demands for immediate effects as well as long-term benefits. The third type of research and development model, called linkage models, stresses the close interrelations of research, development, and dissemination. Linkage models tend to be performer-oriented and stress the importance of individuals in a research-development-dissemination continuum. Linkage models are likely to appear to be much more realistic to the researcher or developer. The author emphasizes that each type of model is relevant from the particular perspective of the one who uses it and each must be in some sense compatible with or sensitive to the requirements of the others." [M, T & C]

Goldhammer, Keith and Elam, Stanley (eds.). *Dissemination and Implementation, Third Annual Phi Delta Kappa Symposium on Educational Research.* Bloomington, Indiana: Phi Delta Kappa, 1962, 200 pp.

Topics

- electronic data processing for storage and availability of research data
- role of private philanthropy in dissemination and implementation
- role of school study councils and local school districts
- role of USOE and the state departments of education
- use of inter-institutional agencies
- use of the communications media

Contributing Authors

Roald Campbell
David Clark
Charles R. Foster

John Gauge
Keith Goldhammer
Andrew W. Haplin

Paul B. Jacobson
Allen Kent

These papers are primarily descriptive. Some review of research is included for evaluation. Each paper is followed by a transcript of the symposium discussion of the material. The collection has no integrating introduction or summary. No bibliography or index is included.

Its discussion of the roles of education-related agencies may be of particular interest to the educator. The explanation of computer uses in storage and retrieval is technical, but clear.

Goulet, Richard R. (ed.). *Educational Change: The Reality and the Promise.* New York: Citation Press, 1968.

"This is the report on the National Seminars on Innovation, held in Honolulu from July 2-23, 1967. The papers are divided into five sections: Into the Future with Our Changing Schools; Systematic and Effective Innovation; Creative Directions for Innovation by Government,

Universities, and Industry; and State of Technology in Education and Its Further Development and Implementation.

"There are abstracts of each paper in the publication at the beginning of each section." [S & H]

Gross, Neal, Giacquinta, Joseph B., and Berstein, Marilyn. *Implementing Organizational Innovations: A Sociological Analysis of Planned Educational Change*. New York: Basic Books, Inc., 1971, 309 pp.

Topics

- review and appraisal of literature on planned organizational change with reference to the problem of implementation
- case study of educational innovation; research methods used and methodological problems encountered
- external and internal climate for change at the case study school prior to announcement of the innovation in November, 1966
- degree of innovation implementation in May, 1967
- five factors explaining the minimal implementation of the innovation
- two fundamental deficiencies in the director's strategy
- theoretical and practical implications of the case study

It is the authors' perception that the *implementation* of organizational innovations is the most critical and unappreciated aspect of the process of successful organizational change. The authors find that too often the failure of an innovation to achieve its intended effects is simplistically ascribed to the inability of a change agent to overcome the initial resistance of organizational members to change.

The authors determined that there was no initial resistance to change on the part of the members of the inner-city elementary school they selected for case study. On the contrary, they were receptive to the educational innovation of the "catalytic model role" of teaching as introduced to them in the fall of 1966. Nonetheless, by May of the following year the innovation had not been substantially implemented.

Five factors were isolated as reasons for the minimal adoption of the innovation: (1) teachers' lack of clarity about the innovation; (2) teachers' lack of needed capabilities; (3) the unavailability of required instructional materials; (4) incompatability of organizational arrangements with the innovation; (5) lack of staff motivation (as developed after the announcement). The existence of these obstacles lies with two fundamental deficiencies in the strategy used by the director: (1) it failed to identify and bring into the open the various types of difficulties teachers were likely to encounter in their implementation attempts, and (2) it failed to establish and use feedback mechanisms to uncover the barriers that arose during the period of attempted implementation. These findings highlight the need for leadership in management of the innovation process.

The authors' approach to organizational implementation is detailed and thorough. Both social scientists and educational practitioners should find the work useful. The eight chapters proceed logically in their presentation, and are clearly subdivided to make their content easily accessible.

Each chapter is concluded by a summary. There are footnotes, four particularly helpful appendices, a listing of over a hundred references, and an index.

Harris, Seymour E., Deitch, Kenneth M., and Levensohn, Alan. *Challenge and Change in American Education.* Berkeley, California: McCutchan Publishing Corporation, 1965, 346 pp.

Topics

- government and education
- state vs. federal power
- lobbies and legislation
- federal government and university research
- manpower development in underdeveloped countries
- planning
- learning ability
- social values
- the teacher shortage
- state and local investment
- economic productivity
- management of higher education
- roles and responsibilities
- academic quality and financial aid
- role of the liberal arts college
- graduate education
- tenure and academic freedom
- the challenge of growth

Contributing Authors

Vernon R. Alden	John J. Corson	Robert W. Merry
James E. Allen	Adam Curle	Rexford G. Moon
Homer D. Babbridge, Jr.	Andre Daniere	John F. Morse
Charles S. Benson	John S. Dickey	Donn K. Price
Bernard R. Berelsen	Otto Eckstein	Robert Rosenzweig
Clark Byse	Seymour E. Harris	Elliot Richardson
Theodore Caplow	Francis Keppel	John M. Stalmaker
John B. Carroll	Charles V. Kidd	George R. Waggoner
John Chase	Glen A. Lloyd	Eugene S. Wilson
James S. Coles	Dan C. Lortie	Montagne Yudelman
Herbert S. Conrad	John S. McCauley	

Dealing primarily with issues of educational policy and management, these seminar papers were originally presented at the Harvard University Graduate School of Public Administration.

There is a substantial integrative introduction by Harris which is referenced. However, there is no index or bibliography and most authors do not use footnotes or research data. Although policy is an issue of general interest to educators, these articles may be found more valuable by those directly involved in policy-making or changing.

Havelock, Ronald G., in collaboration with Guskin, Alan. *Planning for Innovation Through the Dissemination and Utilization of Knowledge.* Ann Arbor, Michigan: Institute for Social Research, The University of Michigan, 1969.

Topics

- the emerging discipline, state of the art
- basic concepts and models
- social systems of knowledge transfer
- the individual
- interpersonal linkage
- knowledge flow in organizations
- organizational barriers
- linkage and linking roles
- taxonomy of knowledge flow
  - one-way and two-way media
  - strategies and tactics
- phases in change processes
  - dissemination process
  - utilization process
  - problem-solving process

Contributing Authors

Mark Frohman
Alan E. Guskin
Mary Havelock

Ronald G. Havelock
Marjorie Hill
Janet C. Huber

This is a report to the Office of Education on a "comparative survey and theoretical analysis of the literature in several fields," including mental health, agriculture, medicine, public health, law, business management, and technology, and with a special emphasis on the field of education. Concepts for the analysis are drawn from social psychology, sociology, and communications science.

It includes a bibliography with about 4,000 entries. Research evidence is presented, as well as theoretical concepts. The final chapter offers a synthesis and draws implications for research, development, practice, and policy related to dissemination and utilization.

The work is most relevant to researchers or scholars concerned with the change process in the several fields represented.

Author and subject indices are provided.

Havelock, Ronald G., and Havelock, Mary C., in collaboration with the Staff and Participants of the Michigan Conference on Educational Change Agent Training, CECAT. *Training for Change Agents: A Guide to the Design of Training Programs in Education and Other Fields*. Ann Arbor, Michigan: Institute for Social Research, University of Michigan 1972, 206 pp.

Topics

- our contemporary knowledge of the change process: assessment of four major perspectives
- goals of training: four approaches to the issue
- summary statement of fifteen principles of good training design
- framework for training designs: analysis of eight elements which can be used as an evaluation checklist
- alternative training models
  - programs to train school systems to develop a self-renewal capacity
  - programs for change agent linkage of school systems to resources
  - programs to effect political and structural changes in school systems
  - programs to improve the effectiveness of other educational agencies
- ideal model for a fully developed training design: program for change agent training for state education agencies

Havelock relates the new concept of "planned innovation" to the development of a professional discipline concerned primarily with the *process* of change. The author sees the need for a coherent strategy if change is to lead to real progress. The concept and role of the change agent is central to formulation and implementation of strategy.

This work contains a number of items, suggestions, frameworks, principles, and tactical details at several levels of specificity applicable to a wide range of change agent skills and situations. It should be a useful aid and reference source to trainers and training program developers. There are numerous tables and clarifying schematic diagrams, a bibliography, and index.

Leeper, Robert R. (ed.). *Strategy for Curriculum Change*. (Papers from the First ASCD Seminar on Strategy for Curriculum Change.) Washington, D.C.: Association for Supervision and Curriculum Development, 1965, 75 pp.

Topics

- contrasting strategies
- roles and processes
- diffusion of research in agriculture and in education
- relevance of community power structure

Contributing Authors

Ralph B. Kimbrough   Ronald Lippitt
Herbert F. Lionberger   Kimball Wiles

These papers are generally technical analyses of "strategies" from an organizational viewpoint. They do present some case material as well as quantitative research evidence. Bibliographies are provided by Lionberger and Wiles, but none is given for the entire publication. A summary of major issues is presented. There is no index.

Lin, Nan, Leu, Donald J., Rogers, Everett M., and Schwartz, Donald. *The Diffusion of an Innovation in Three Michigan High Schools: Institution Building through Change.* East Lansing, Michigan: Institute for International Studies in Education and Department of Communication, Michigan State University, December 1966.

Topics

- factors associated with innovation assimilation
- study of schedule modification
- four dependent variables
- numerous independent variables

"The main purpose of this study was to examine the factors that might be associated with various degrees of innovation assimilation in a school.

"The study was conducted in three Michigan high schools in which the teachers were asked to complete a questionnaire in a meeting arranged for that purpose. The innovation selected for study was schedule modification.

"Dependent variables were:
1. Times of awareness of innovation
2. Time of adoption of innovation
3. Innovation internalization (defined as the extent to which a member of an organization perceived the innovation to be relevant and valuable to his role performance)
4. Change orientation (defined as an individual's degree of general predisposition toward change)

"In addition, a large number of independent variables were selected for study in the following categories: demographic variables; institutional variables such as perception of one's superior, perception of peers, perception of school procedural consequences; communication behavior variables; psychology and personality variables.

"For each of three independent variables, it was hypothesized whether its relationship with the four dependent variables would be positive or negative.

"Findings are summarized in detail in a separate chapter and are summarized generally at the beginning of the monograph. Correlation of each independent variable with the dependent variables is presented.

"An extensive bibliography and all measuring instruments are included." [S & H]

Lippitt, Ronald, Watson, Jeanne, and Westley, Bruce. *The Dynamics of Planned Change.* A Comparative Study of Principles and Techniques. New York: Harcourt, Brace and World, Inc., 1958, 312 pp.

Topics

- orientation of planned change
- diagnostic orientations toward:
  - internal relationships
  - external relationships
- motivation of the client system
- role of the change agent
- phases of planned change
- initiating planned change
- working toward change
- transfer and stabilization of change
- the training of change agents

The fundamental ideas of this volume are centered around such terms as *change agent, client system, change forces, resistance forces, phases of change* and *methods of change*. It is a comparative study of the principles and techniques used by various professional agents concerned with change. Though there are no definitive answers, this book is suggested reading for anyone, practitioner as well as researcher, interested in the *process* of planned change and in the various roles of the change agent. The bibliography is sectioned according to major topic areas. An index is provided.

Lurie, Ellen. *How to Change the Schools: A Parents' Action Handbook on How to Fight the System.* New York: Vintage Books, a Division of Random House, 1970, 293 pp.

Topics

- how to make a school visit
- how to evaluate the curriculum
- how to get good teachers and supervisors
- how to get rid of bad teachers and supervisors
- how to evaluate and change report cards and homework
- how to get the most out of a parent-teacher conference
- how to be sure that the students' rights are being represented
- how to use a public hearing on schools
- how to organize against the system

This book fulfills its objective of providing a handbook for parents who would like to improve their children's schools. The author has spent fifteen years working in community action groups and on school boards in New York City, and it is her observation that in general "schools exist for the sake of the system; children are barely tolerated." She feels that all parents want to see the schools changed and the approach she advocates for them is cooperation with other parents. She stresses that although different parents and different groups of parents may have different grievances, all grievances are legitimate, and no objectives will be achieved if community groups fight each other. If this happens, the author cautions, only the school system wins.

A wide range of problem situations are illustrated with anecdotes, and "action checklists for parents" are provided which suggest ways of approaching each problem area. Although the material is drawn from the author's experiences in the city of New York, parents all across the country will be able to identify many similar situations in their own children's schools; this book will provide stirring reading for any parent.

There are no footnotes and no index, but an extensive appendix is included which lists "Things to Read and Do." This list not only includes scholarly reference materials, but also lists information such as places to visit, organizations which can provide materials and assistance, and information on how to obtain materials on federal programs.

MacKenzie, Norman, Eraut, Michael, and Jones, Hywel C. *Teaching and Learning: An Introduction to New Methods and Resources in Higher Education.* Paris, France: UNESCO and the International Association of Universities, 1970, 209 pp.

Topics

- expansion in mass higher education
- crisis in teaching: inadequacy of methods, preparation of teachers and theoretical frameworks
- new technological resources for learning
- uses and ideology of media
- clarification of objectives: deciding what to teach
- role of evaluation: finding out what one has taught
- teaching methods
  - classification of methods
  - quality vs. quantity of student-teacher contact time
- research in educational technology
- systematic course development
- management of resources: investing in new learning materials
- organizing support systems
- management of innovation

This book is directed towards the managers of innovation in higher education. Its task is described as being "to indicate ways in which institutions of higher education . . . can begin to reconsider their methods of teaching and learning, not to offer neat or immediate remedies." The text is organized into four main parts: (1) Expansion, (2) the Impact of New Media, (3) Systematic Approaches to Teaching and Learning, and (4) the Management of Resources. The book successfully carries out its intent to proceed logically from "an immediate concern with the problems of teaching, through the repertories of resources and procedures which are relevant to them, to the innovations in management which are required to apply those resources effectively."

This book is unusually well organized and written. There is no index, but extensive listing of bibliographic references follows each chapter.

This book is one in a series of books on The Development of Higher Education.

Meierhenry, Wesley C. (ed.). *Media and Educational Innovation.* University of Nebraska, Extension Division and University of Nebraska Press, 1964, 445 pp.

Topics

- models of and ideas about change
- the role of the advocate
- a sociological consideration of acceptance
- leader characteristics for the promotion of change
- diffusion research in rural sociology and its relation to the field of education
- innovations in the Air Force
- the role of the media
- generalizations about educational change
- the role of new media in state organization
- the role of newer media in planned change

Contributing Authors

Henry Brickell	Art Gallagher	Matthew B. Miles
Robert Chin	Herbert Lionberger	Gabriel Ofiesh
Wayman Crow	Paul Meadows	Truman Pierce
Jack Edling	Wesley C. Meierhenry	

Reactors

C. Ray Carpenter	Charles F. Hoban	Robert W. Wagner
George Gerbner	Kenneth D. Norberg	Paul Wendt

These symposium papers were presented from several different fields and express viewpoints from both theory and practice. Thus, they are loosely linked by "education" and "media," though the variety of approaches to these topics is interesting.

Use of bibliographic citation varies among the authors proportionately with their concern for research data. A brief introduction explains the rationale of coordination of the presentations. There is no index.

These papers provide interesting information to educators about media, their problems and potentialities, but it is not in a format that facilitates retrieval of specific data.

Michigan Department of Education, *Research Implications for Educational Diffusion, Major Papers Presented at the National Conference on Diffusion of Educational Ideas, East Lansing, March 1968.* Lansing: Michigan Department of Education, 1968, 181 pp.

Topics

- summary and critique of existing research
- needed research on utilization

- needed research within educational organizations
- innovative research methods
- implications for practice

Contributing Authors

Richard O. Carlson   Nan Lin   Everett M. Rogers
Ronald G. Havelock   Ronald Lippitt
Nemi Jain   Richard I. Miller

These papers are primarily conceptual or interpretive summaries with the exception of Nan Lin's contribution on research methods, which is a report of his work. There is an introduction, but no index. Bibliographies are presented with each paper.

The focus on research evaluation and on research goals suggests this publication's relevance to practitioners involved in planning for change.

Miles, Matthew B. (ed.). *Innovation in Education.* New York: Teachers College, Columbia University, 1964, 690 pp.

Topics

- nature of educational innovation
- small-scale administrative change
- collaboration in teaching and learning
- Utopia and rebellion
- Title III and educational change
- innovation at the state level
- technologies
- programmed instruction
- innovation of classroom mental health practices
- resistance to adoption of audio-visual aids
- educational innovation from the Institute of Administrative Research
- school superintendents and modern math
- experimental program in medical education
- progress report on the teaching of reading
- curricular change
- administrative theory and change in organization
- temporary systems
- support of educational innovation
- educational innovation and the masses
- structural features of American education

Contributing Authors

Part I. *Case Studies*	Part II. *Research and Theory*	Part III. *The American Educational System*
M.S. Atwood	Allen H. Barton	Theodore Brameld
Jan E. Clee	Richard O. Carlson	Henry M. Brickell
Richard Colvard	Gerhard Eichholz	James M. Cass
Thomas H. Eliot	Robert S. Fox	John H. Fischer
Donald C. Flesche	Daniel E. Griffiths	Frank G. Jennings
Louis Forsdale	Patricia Kendall	Joseph C. Kiger
Leo S. Goldstein	Ronald Lippitt	Martin Mayer
Lassar G. Gotkin	Gordon Mackenzie	Matthew B. Miles
Donald W. Johnson	Matthew Miles	Sloan R. Wayland
Paul E. Marsh	Paul R. Mort	Benjamin C. Willis
Nicholas A. Masters	Everett M. Rogers	
James B. Reswick	David E. Wilder	

"In this volume, change processes are given close study by an assembly of persons—educators, sociologists, psychologists, and writers—who have worked in the midst of educational change. They deal with a wide range of questions: What causes resistance to change? Why is a particular strategy of innovation so effective? What principles can be used to plan and guide educational change efforts? The volume begins with a general introduction on the nature of educational innovation. In the book's first section, nine case studies illuminate what happened when specific innovations were introduced. Each case is analyzed to uncover the underlying factors which determined success or failure. A second major part of the book presents nine separate studies of research and theory in educational innovation. A third section is devoted to studies of the American educational system as a setting for change. In conclusion, the generalizations about educational innovation made in the book are reviewed and discussed." [K & M]

This volume would be equally valuable to both researchers and practitioners. Research findings are well referenced. The bibliographic information and the index provide easy access to particular areas the reader may wish to investigate.

Miller, Richard I. (ed.). *A Multidisciplinary Focus on Educational Change.* Lexington, Kentucky: Bureau of School Service, College of Education, University of Kentucky, 1965, 83 pp.

Topics

- current developments
- human relations
- sociological perspectives
- early childhood education
- political realities
- needed research and development

Contributing Authors

David A. Booth
Robert Chin
C. Milton Coughenour

Albert J. Lott
Richard I. Miller

These papers presented at a conference for elementary school principals exemplify one valid approach to defining the problem of change in education. No summarizing section is included, but a 23-item selected bibliography is provided, as are references from the individual chapters.

Most of the presentations are quite scholarly and would be most useful as resources for the research-oriented educator. No index is given.

Miller, Richard I. (Director). *Catalyst for Change: A National Study of ESEA Title III (PACE) Reports of Special Consultants.* Washington, D.C.: United States Government Printing Office, 1967, 557 pp.

Topics

- background on the Elementary and Secondary Education Act of 1965 (Title III)
- curriculum development
- community participation
- rural schools
- urban and metropolitan schools—civil rights
- role of the state
- individualized instruction
- pupil personnel services
- the gifted and the disadvantaged
- handicapped students
- the arts and cultural enrichment
- the sciences
- educational facilities
- teacher education
- evaluation
- educational technology
- computer technology

Contributing Authors

William M. Alexander
George E. Bair
Paul F. Brandwein
Don D. Bushnell
Howard Conant
Don Davies
Elliot W. Eisner

James D. Finn
Harold B. Gores
Egon G. Guba
Glen Heathers
Arthur A. Hitchcock
Samuel A. Kirk
Norman D. Kurland

A. Harry Passow
Thomas F. Pettigrew
Everett M. Rogers
Ira J. Singer
Harold Spears
Hilda Taba

These papers were presented before the U.S. Senate Subcommittee on Education. The first section is the study report of Richard I. Miller's research on ESEA Title III in its first year. The other papers are by consultants in areas which dominated Title III funding to that time. Summaries of the recommendations in both sections are provided.

The analyses are stimulating, quite informative, and not too technical. However, there is no index or bibliography.

Miller, Richard I. (ed.). *Perspectives on Educational Change.* New York: Appleton-Century-Crofts, Division of Meredith Publishing Co., 1967, 392 pp.

Topics

- overview of educational change
- change at the elementary level
- change at the secondary level
- role of local school systems in change
- effects of outside funds on school districts
- role of State Education Department in change
- process of change in educational TV
- summer elementary school for underachievers
- new math in elementary school
- case study of educational innovation
- the teacher as innovator
- curriculum change

Contributing Authors

William M. Alexander	Robert Chin	Hollis A. Moore
Robert H. Anderson	Ann R. Edson	Jack W. Pattyson
Wailand Bessent	Richard A. Gibboney	Ruth W. Radcliffe
Henry M. Brickell	Glen Heathers	J. Lloyd Trump
Evelyn Carswell	Ronald Lippitt	Harold E. Wigren
Ruth E. Chadwick	Richard I. Miller	Raymond A. Wilkie

This book may serve school administrators and state department officials interested in the process of innovating, especially with respect to team teaching and non-gradedness. It should also interest those planning graduate courses in education. Specialists in educational change may find some chapters quite interesting. A balance has been sought between theoretical and research aspects of change and those relating more directly to actual situations through case studies. Miller begins with an overview of educational change and ends with some very lucid observations and suggestions on this topic. There are many figures and diagrams to illustrate concepts discussed in the text. There is an appendix which lists some of the on-going activities across the United States that are being directed toward educational change. There is no formal bibliography and no index.

A Model for Innovation Adoption in Public School Districts: Research on the Characteristics of Selected School Systems as They Relate to the Need for Appraisal, Acceptance, and Use of Innovations. Final Report. Cambridge, Massachusetts: Arthur D. Little, Inc., March, 1968.

Topics

- inadequate change models
- innovation adoption model
- initiating mechanism
- sustaining mechanism
- performance information

"Several change models are reviewed and found to be inadequate in defining the process of innovation as it is encountered in local school districts. The report describes a model which purportedly adequately defines this process. The model is only for a local school district and assumes that design and evaluation stages of research and development models are completed. The model is one of innovation adoption. It assumes that an initiating mechanism and a sustaining mechanism must be simultaneously present in some force exceeding a very modest threshold value before an innovation adoption can occur. An initiating mechanism is defined as an activity by means of which information about innovations designed elsewhere is brought into the school district. A sustaining mechanism is defined as a characteristic of the school district which acts primarily to establish a climate within which initiating mechanisms can be effective. Performance information about the effects of an adoption and readiness for further adoptions and about overall performance of the school district's educational system is related to the model." [M, T & C]

National Association of Secondary School Principals. "Changing Secondary Schools," *The Bulletin*, Vol. 47, No. 283, May 1963, 168 pp.

Topics

- premises
- anatomy of change
- ingredients of change
- dynamics
- role of the principal
- organizational changes
  - team teaching
  - non-graded
  - flexible scheduling
- technological changes
- curricular changes

Contributing Authors

Dwight W. Allen
Henry M. Brickell
B. Frank Brown
Robert Bush
Joseph M. Cronin

James D. Finn
Douglas W. Hunt
John F. Kourmadas
Lloyd Michael
Richard I. Miller

Ole Sand
B. Othaniel Smith
J. Lloyd Trump

The first section of this issue is devoted to conceptual analyses of change in schools. The second contains descriptions of *types* of changes (e.g., curriculum) or of specific innovations (e.g., flexible scheduling) followed by lists of high schools attempting that change and a description of the program of each.

No summary, index, bibliography or footnotes are provided, but if the innovation is relevant, contact with a school that has already adopted it might be very useful.

Netzer, Lanore A., Eye, Glen G., Dimock, Marshall E., Dumont, Matthew P., Homme, Lloyd, Kast, Fremont E., and Knezvich, Stephen J. *Education, Administration and Change: The Redeployment of Resources.* New York: Harper & Row, 1970, 207 pp.

Topics

- roles involved in innovation adoption
- professionalism: new orientations
- motivation, reinforcement, and change
- administration: bureaucracy and participatory management
- organizations as complex systems
- organizational planning
- Tension-Penetration-Interaction Model of change
- research possibilities

This book, directed primarily at researchers in the fields of organizational and professional change, contains a collection of papers which were prepared for a seminar. The approach is interdisciplinary and each contributing author has developed his own topic in a distinct manner. However, there is some cross-referencing between chapters, and Netzer and Eye, in the final chapter, relate the contributions of each scholar to the "Tension-Penetration-Interaction Model" of change.

The authors state that "the purpose of the TPI Model . . . is to provide a systematic way of thinking about the conversion of ideas into performances or other types of outcomes and products." The model focuses in particular upon the range of forces which bear upon each element in a change situation. In the final chapter the concepts presented in each of the foregoing papers are analyzed in terms of the "interaction potentials" which may result from the interplay of such forces as environmental, institutional, and personal tensions. Numerous research hypotheses based on these interactions are proposed.

This is a scholarly work, with an index, a bibliography and numerous footnotes.

Oettinger, Anthony G. with Marks, Sema. *Run, Computer, Run: The Mythology of Educational Innovation.* Cambridge, Massachusetts: Harvard University Press, 1969, 302 pp.

Topics

- systems analysis
- goals of education
- educational technology: devices and processes
- language laboratory
- computers in education

The author discusses the misconceptions and misuses of educational technology which have tended to discourage or counteract the constructive development and use of potentially beneficial technological aids. He describes a variety of technological devices and analyzes their use in contemporary school settings, noting the fact that present schools and teachers seem designed to resist change. Although his conclusion is that vast institutional changes must take place before the new technology can make a significant contribution to American education, he remains optimistic that this can be accomplished. He describes a rational plan of progress in terms of setting meaningful educational goals and allocating far greater amounts of time and money to the development of a fewer number of new technological devices and processes.

This book should be of interest to educators concerned with the new technology, and it is of particular importance to planners of educational policy at all levels. A number of case illustrations are presented in the text, and footnotes are provided. There is no index.

Ontario Institute for Studies in Education, *Emerging Strategies and Structures for Educational Change.* Toronto: The Institute, 1966, 177 pp.

Topics

- current picture in the United States
- types of strategies
- R and D Centers in the United States
- curriculum reform (England)
- aspects of social change (Quebec)
- problems and issues in implementing
- relationship to the social sciences
- concepts, structure, and program of OISE

Contributing Authors

Daniel E. Berlyne
S.C.T. Clarke
W.G. Fleming
George E. Flower
Burkhart Holzner

R.W.B. Jackson
R.S. MacArthur
David Munroe
Ewald B. Nyquist
K.V. Parkhurst

Kenneth F. Preuter
Sam Sieber
Philip Taylor

These papers, along with the reactions to them and group discussions, were part of the first anniversary conference of OISE. Authors often use case examples from experience, but no quantitative research is reported. A 17-item bibliography on R and D Centers is provided, but there is no footnoting, index, summary, or other bibliography.

Pellegrin, Roland J. *An Analysis of Sources and Processes of Innovation in Education.* Eugene, Oregon: University of Oregon, 1967.

Topics

- sources of educational innovation
- conditions fostering or discouraging innovation
- conditions for translating knowledge into practice

"This publication reviews existing and potential sources of educational innovation, the conditions under which innovation occurs, and the changes which must be made to tie together knowledge and practice. The author considers a number of sources of current educational innovation, including: (1) classroom teachers; (2) school administrators; (3) school board; (4) the lay public; (5) state departments of education; (6) education faculties of colleges and universities; (7) other federal agencies; (8) textbook publishers; (9) scientists, technical specialists, and other experts. Certain conditions fostering or discouraging innovation are discussed, along with conditions for translating knowledge into practice in educational settings." [S & H]

Postman, Neil and Weingartner, Charles. *The Soft Revolution: A Student Handbook for Turning Schools Around.* New York: Dell Publishing Co., 1971.

A soft revolution is described as one that accomplishes reform without contributing to the destruction of society or the revolutionaries. Although this handbook is always entertaining—and filled with "advice, maxims, homilies, metaphors, models, case studies, rules, commentaries, jokes, sayings, and a variety of other things"—it carries out its serious intent. Among other topics, the handbook advocates understanding the structure of the system, diagnosing its problem before trying to implement solutions, and the acquisition of resources.

Both "young radicalized militants" and concerned educators could be interested in this handbook.

The Principal. Melbourne, Florida: Institute for Development of Educational Activities, Inc., 1968.

Topics

- principal as change agent
- knowledge a principal must have
- guiding questions a principal might answer

"It is suggested that the principal can direct change by controlling the ebb and flow of forces within his organization. A principal's moves to bring about change must be made with complete knowledge of the nature of the group with which he is working, the value of the goal he is seeking, and the impact of the change which he desires. It is suggested that a principal who is interested in effecting change answer the following questions:

1. Exactly what kind of change do I, as a principal and a change agent, desire to see made?
2. What factors favor introduction of change and what factors oppose it?
3. What is known about change in organizations that directly bears upon what I, as principal, am trying to get my staff to do?
4. What alternative modes of action are available to me as I initiate the change process?" [M, T & C]

Rogers, Everett M. *Diffusion of Innovations.* New York: The Free Press, 1962, 367 pp.

Topics

- introduction to diffusion of innovations
- traditions of research on diffusion
- culture, norms, and diffusion
- the adoption process
- characteristics of the innovation
- adopter categories
- innovators as deviants
- opinion leaders and the flow of ideas
- role of the change agent
- predicting innovativeness
- toward a theory of diffusion and adoption of innovations

The author reviews more than 600 publications principally in sociology, but also in such fields as anthropology, economics, education, speech, industrial engineering, and history. Findings in these areas are synthesized into an intelligent discussion on the nature of the spread and adoption of innovations. Rogers begins with a brief introduction on the topic and concludes with some generalizations in the form of one-line statements and hypotheses on the nature of diffusion. Each section contains a concise summary section. The comprehensive bibliography is subdivided into general and diffusion research studies. An index is provided. Although this book is not aimed at the educational practitioner, it remains an interesting extracurricular piece of reading material in terms of its perspective on the spread of innovation.

Rogers, Everett M. with Shoemaker, Floyd F. *Communication of Innovations: A Cross-Cultural Approach.* New York: The Free Press, 1971.

Topics

- overview of the elements of diffusion
- emerging diffusion research traditions: the middle-range analysis
- the diffusion-decision process

252

- perceived attributes of innovations and their rate of adoption
- adopter categories
- opinion leadership and the multi-step flow of ideas
- the change agent
- communication channels
- collective innovation decisions
- authority innovation decisions and organizational change
- consequences of innovations
- generalizations about the diffusion of innovations

This new book is the second edition of Rogers' *Diffusion of Innovations*. The author's stated theme in this revision is that "social change is an effect of communication."

Rogers' approach in this book breaks from traditional diffusion research (including his own), which has always emphasized the "individual" adopter of innovations. Here his focus is on the informal social group and the formally organized system, assessing their influence on the adoption behavior of their members. In doing so, he achieves the important integrative objective of relating the concepts and theories of diffusion research to those of organizational change.

This edition also contains a substantial bibliography, but does not have a subject index. Nevertheless, because of its focus on relevant organizational issues, *Communication of Innovations* will probably be more directly valuable to the educational practitioner than was the first edition.

Rogers, Everett M. and Svenning, Lynne. *Managing Change*. San Mateo, California: Operation PEP, 1969, 94 pp. [Prepared under contract to USOE, Title III, ESEA 1965].

Topics

- communication principles and process
- diffusion principles and process
- process of social change
- educational change as a type of social change
- steps in managing change
- change strategies in education

This short book is designed to serve as a useful tool in assisting the managers of change to use what is known about the processes of change, communication, and diffusion in formulating their own strategies for change. It describes steps involved in the management of change: determination of objectives, analysis of the target audience, employment of communication and diffusion principles, integration of the innovation into the educational system, evaluation of the innovation, and dissemination of the results to other educational systems. Some strategies are suggested for various change objectives, such as the free flow of ideas within and between educational systems, staff participation in decision-making and planning, and the use of change agents; it is stressed, however, that managers of change must design their own change strategies based on each specific situation confronting them.

The focus of the book is on managing change in education, but it is suggested that the same strategies may be used in most other change situations. The first chapter is a summary which is designed to serve as a quick reference source for practical application of the textual content, and it should serve this purpose adequately even though no index is provided. There is a bibliography.

Rossi, Peter H. and Biddle, Bruce J. (eds.). *The New Media and Education: Their Impact on Society*. Chicago: Aldine Publishing Company, 1968, 417 pp.

Topics

- recent and projected technological developments (instructional media, simulation and games, programmed instruction and teaching machines)
- impact on school systems (economic, social organization, physical plant)
- impact on other aspects of American education (higher education, adult education)
- implications for society

Contributing Authors

Neal Balanoff
Bruce J. Biddle
Nelson N. Foote
Morris Janowitz
Malcolm S. Knowles

Charles F. Lehmann
Henry F. McCusker, Jr.
H.J. McKeachie
James A. Robinson
Peter H. Rossi

Philip H. Sorensen
Lawrence M. Stolurow
David Street
Martin Trow

These papers review quantitative research in media usage for the prediction and prescription of the future of educational media. The editors' introduction provides an overview of the topics, and an orientation to the issues involved in the utilization of media for education.

The book would be a useful reference for educators in evaluating media policies or programs. The bibliography, containing approximately 300 items, includes numerous reports of experimental and empirical research on specific media and media usages. An index is provided.

Rubin, Louis J. (ed.). *Improving In-Service Education: Proposals and Procedures for Change*. Boston, Massachusetts: Allyn and Bacon, Inc., 1971, 284 pp.

Topics

- relationship of pre-service and in-service education
- deficiencies of present in-service education
- the need for continuing professional growth: the self-evolving teacher
- setting standards for performance
- performance observation and assessment
- specialization and differentiated staffing
- attitudes and values of teachers
- group learning and sharing of experiences
- making adequate time and resources available for in-service education

Contributing Authors

Dwight W. Allen
Robert N. Bush
Mario Fantini
Louis Fischer

Abraham S. Fischler
Robert Fox
Philip W. Jackson
Ronald Lippitt

Edward J. Meade, Jr.
Louis J. Rubin
Herbert A. Thelen
Ralph W. Tyler

Each chapter in this book considers a different aspect of teacher professional growth, and although each chapter is authored by a separate contributor, the flow of ideas from one concept to another is smooth and the chapters are organized into sections which build successively on one another. The editor has provided a summary of "operational implications" and a commentary at the conclusion of each chapter; these are helpful in pointing out areas of agreement as well as differences in viewpoint among the contributing authors.

This book stresses the necessity of revising current in-service training of teachers both to meet the needs of changing educational systems and to provide teachers with the opportunity for continuing professional growth. In discussing the relationship between pre-service and in-service education, it is pointed out that there are many skills which teachers can acquire only after a period of exposure to schools, students, curricula, and their own teaching behavior.

There is general consensus among the authors that performance standards for teachers *can* be set. Some authors suggest the use of clinical observers and video-tape equipment as an aid in developing desirable teacher behaviors. Other authors stress a problem-solving approach to teacher-training, with heavy emphasis on group training sessions and the sharing of experiences among teachers.

All authors stress the importance of providing a wide range of training support, which should include technical equipment, training specialists, community and educational resources, and, above all, ample time.

The editor suggests that this book should be of value to teacher supervisors both in training institutions and in the public school, to school principals and to curriculum designers. We might add that teachers themselves will find a wealth of ideas. In addition to discussing the theoretical aspects of in-service education, this book also suggests some alternative training program models which are designed to meet a variety of desired outcomes. It should thus be of use to anyone who is concerned with any aspect of the design of in-service training programs for teachers. An index is provided.

Sarason, Seymour B. *The Culture of the School and the Problem of Change*. Boston, Massachusetts: Allyn and Bacon, Inc., 1971, 246 pp.

Topics

- outsiders' difficulties in relating to the school culture
- universities' relationship to the school culture
- modal process of change: a case report
- requirements for a theory of change
- relationships between programmatic and behavioral regularities
- ecological approach as an alternative to individual

- principal in a critical role for which he is not prepared
- principal's self-conception
- teacher's role and dilemmas
- the Dewey School

Sarason finds that the more things change, the more they remain the same because of an assumption of the separation of means and ends, i.e., a lack of appreciation of the change process. In contrast to the stance of viewing the situation in terms of individuals, Sarason stresses the need to appreciate the school culture as a complex social system. He deplores the lack of awareness about existing structures and inherent traditions and laments the deficiency of actual descriptive information. He feels that to instigate change, not only should one be a neutral observer, but one should also use an ecological approach in making his observations. This requires one "to suspend one's values, one's conception of right and wrong, good and bad, and instead to describe what is 'out there.' " It is Sarason's belief that in seeking to implement change by changing attitudes, it is the principal who is crucial.

Footnotes, a bibliography, and an index are provided.

Sieber, Sam D. with the collaboration of Lazarsfeld, Paul F. *The Organization of Educational Research in the United States.* New York: Bureau of Applied Social Research, Columbia University, 1966, 364 pp. plus appendices.

Topics

- value climates and arrangements for research
- recruitment policies, joint arrangements with other departments, and substantive areas of research
- research units in schools of education
- research directorship
- relations with service
- career training

This report of a study conducted among administrators of educational research units is lengthy and rather technical. However, it is an interesting analysis of leadership and its influences on educational research *in the university setting.*

The report contains no index or bibliography and is probably of limited value to educational practitioners in general. It would be most informative to policy makers in educational research or professional training programs.

Trow, Wm. Clark. *Paths to Educational Reform.* Englewood Cliffs, New Jersey: Educational Technology Publications, 1971, 239 pp.

- evolution of our school system
- current educational approaches
- false assumptions about education
- means for fostering change
- education of teachers
- need for new criteria for assessing teacher competence
  - learning vs. letter grade
  - proficiency vs. credit hour
- student behavioral objectives
- measuring student performance
- implications of programmed instruction
  - curriculum
  - personnel
  - evaluation
- instructional television
- psychological issues in automated teaching
- psychology in the school curriculum
- an educational model for social learning
- educational renovation
  - teachers' roles
  - grading and marking systems
  - methods
  - objectives

In his foreword to this book, Wilbur J. Cohen states that American educators must teach today's students to be adaptable to the dramatic changes in our society. Trow feels that successful renovation of our educational system cannot take place without taking into account its complexity and without a careful analysis of what is right with the present system as well as what is wrong with it. Although he feels that schools today are doing a better job of educating our children than they have ever done in the past, he sees a need for sweeping educational renovation to prepare children for the complexities of life in our present and future society. To bring about a broad program of reform, Trow sees the need for adequate financial support, professional collaboration, and automation of instruction. The form which Trow feels renewal efforts should take is based upon his observation that successful schools can be characterized as meeting at least three important conditions: "there is high morale; instruction is well adapted to the students' needs; and teaching is competent, with learning appropriately rewarded or reinforced." To bring about these conditions in other schools, Trow recommends sharp revisions in four areas: "concepts of the teachers' roles, of grading and marking systems, of methods employed, and of the nature and use of educational objectives."

This book is written in a clear and thought-provoking style, and it has implications for educators in all areas and at all levels. Considering the scope of the reforms which the author advocates, however, the target audience would most appropriately be educators in policy-making positions. There is no index, but bibliographic references are included for most chapters.

Watson, Goodwin (ed.). *Change in School Systems.* Washington, D.C.: National Training Laboratories, NEA, for the Cooperative Project for Educational Development 1967, 115 pp.

Topics

- the nature of COPED
- schools viewed as systems
- socialization
- organizational development
- orientation and strategy for changing school systems
- the role of the trainer change agent

Contributing Authors

Paul C. Buchanan	Ronald Lippitt	Goodwin Watson
Robert Fox	Dorothy Mial	
Charles C. Jung	Matthew B. Miles	

This book is one of two volumes produced by COPED for "the exploratory development of models of planned change in education." The attention is focussed on the properties and processes of schools and on strategies intended to test and develop the core ideas of the COPED program. There is no index, yet the bibliographic material at the end of many chapters may be quite valuable for the practitioner. There are many useful references to case studies throughout this book. However, the information is presented in a scholarly fashion as opposed to a more practitioner-oriented form.

Watson, Goodwin (ed.). *Concepts for Social Change.* Washington, D.C.: National Training Laboratories, NEA, for the Cooperative Project for Educational Development, 1967, 115 pp.

Topics

- nature of COPED
- organizational development
- resistance to change
- the role of the defender
- collaborative action-inquiry
- knowledge utilization

Contributing Authors

Kenneth D. Benne	Dale G. Lake	Herbert A. Thelen
Paul C. Buchanan	Ronald Lippitt	Goodwin Watson
Ronald G. Havelock	Dorothy Mial	
Donald Klein	Matthew B. Miles	

This book is one of two volumes produced by COPED for "the exploratory development of models of planned change in education." It attempts to develop the core ideas about planned change with emphasis on resistance to innovation and strategies for planned change. No index is provided, yet many of the chapters contain bibliographies which may prove helpful. The information in this volume is aimed primarily at the scholar studying the change process rather than the practitioner.

Woods, Thomas E. *The Administration of Educational Innovation*. Eugene, Oregon: Bureau of Educational Research, School of Education, University of Oregon, 1967, 61 pp.

Topics

- preparation for change
- adoption process
- diffusion process
- characteristics of innovation
- personnel administration
- barriers to change
- strategy for change

Woods describes the process of planned change from the point of view of the school superintendent. It is presented in a style that is easy to comprehend; yet, despite its simplicity, it is a complete description of the change process. There is no index, but the bibliography is geared specifically to the practitioner. There are many references to quantitative research studies. The concluding chapter consists of a series of one-liners which summarize the points made throughout the monograph, which may be used as a framework for change plans.

INDEX

development—246
evaluation—241
installation—230-231
sex education—27-31
social science—33-35
See also specific curriculum areas

D

Dalin, Per—228, 229
Danger signals—58-60
Daniere, Andre—237
Data
evaluative—91
use of in decision-making—231
Davies, Don—246
Davis, Alice—222
Davis, Sheldon—220
Decentralization—228
Decision-makers—48, 72
Decision-making—33, 36, 69, 231, 234-235, 253
Decision-oriented models—234-235
Defenders—*See* resisters
Deitch, Kenneth M.—237
Demonstration—56, 92, 104, 108, 116, 123, 126, 161, 163, 164, 169, 174, 231
Dentler, Robert A.—205
Dependency models—234
Derivation conference—158, 168, 169, 174
Deriving implications from research—97-98, 100-103
Dershimer, Richard A.—211
Design
of instructional innovation—223
of training programs—239
Deterline, William A.—224
Deutsch, M.—180*n*
Development—232, 234
of products—161, 162, 163, 164, 171, 175
models—219
needed—245
Dewey School—256
Diagnosis—13, 23, 26, 27, 33, 35, 36, 38, 63-75
as pattern of avoidance—73
for destructive confrontation—73-74, 75
imposing a favorite—74
of organizational problems—219
of system—66-69
acquiring resources for—81-87
stage of change process—63-75
strategies and tactics for—174-175

too much—73
Diagnostic
instruments—86
inventory—69-72, 83
monitoring—86-87
orientations—74, 241
pitfalls—72-75
research team—86
resources—*See* resources for diagnosis
Dickerman, Watson—221, 222
Dickey, John S.—237
Differentiated staffing—225-254
Diffusibility of innovation—98-108
Diffusion—128, 163, 232, 252
natural—160, 169, 174
network—160, 170
of innovation—240, 252
process—119, 122-123, 159, 161, 252, 253, 259
projects—162
rate of—226
research—239, 243, 252
See also dissemination
Dimock, Marshall E.—249
Directories of educational information—199-204
Directory of Educational Information Centers—199
Directory of Federally Supported Information Analysis Centers—200
Directory of Information Resources in the United States: Social Sciences (1965)—200-201
Directory of Special Libraries and Information Centers—201
Disadvantaged—16
curriculum for—224
students—246
Discipline, for leadership—222
Discussion—127-128, 219
Disengagement of change agent from client—133, 138-139
Dissemination—161, 223, 229, 231, 234, 235
mass media—160-175
process—238
roles—232
strategy—34-35
See also diffusion
Division of tasks—33, 35, 70, 161
Documentation
of diffusion—163
of innovation—162, 163
Dohrendorf, Ralf—221

Programmed instruction—244, 257
Project Social Studies—34
Proximity of resources—95
P-S strategic orientation—155-157
Psychology, in curriculum—257
Psychotherapy—221
Public
    hearing on schools—241
    relations ability—45

R

R & D centers—209, 250
R, D & D strategic orientation—161-163, 165
Racial tension—36
Radcliffe, Ruth W.—247
Rappaport, Donald—225, 226
Raup, R. Bruce—222
RBS—206
Readiness for Curriculum installation—230, 231-232
Reading
    curriculum for disadvantaged students—224
    the teaching of—241
Rebellion and Utopia—244
Reciprocity—55
Recording information
    in brainstorming—105
    information—83
Recycling—98
Redundancy—129
Reference books—204
Reflection—83, 84, 157, 171, 175
Reform in education—228
    See also change in education
Regional educational laboratories—93, 162, 205-206
Regional Information System (RIS)—192, 197
Reinforcement—*See* reward
Rejection
    of change efforts—59
    of innovation—117
    the gaining of—24-26
Relating
    to client—44-45
    to client's environment—45-47, 58
Relationship
    between change agent and client
        building—13, 23-24, 27, 33, 35, 37, 38, 83
            stage of change process—43-61
            strategies and tactics for—174-

175
    groups—52
    ideal—55-58, 61
    indicators of difficulty—59-60
    initial—47-50, 153-154
        blank slate—48
        redefining an existing one—49-50, 51
        reestablishing a good one—48-49
        reestablishing an uncertain one—49
    helping—219
    maintenance of—61
    sizing up—60-61
    between change agent and community citizen—223
    between client subgroups—52, 67, 84
Reliability of innovation—107
Renewal in schools—225
    See also self-renewal
Renker, Marcia M.—231, 232
Report cards, evaluating—241
Research—161, 163
    and development centers—209, 250
    and development unit—175
    deriving implications from—*See* deriving implications
    development and diffusion—175
    development and diffusion—strategic orientation (R, D & D)—161-163, 165
    educational—234, 256
    evaluation—171, 175
        See also evaluation
    goals—244
    in public schools—227
    information
        implications for action—100, 103
        reformulating—100, 101-102
        relevancy—100, 102,
        utilizing—100
    methods, innovative—244
    needed—245, 249
    on diffusion—252
    on utilization—243
    team—33, 34, 100
Research and Development Center for Teacher Education—209
Research and Information Service for Education (RISE)—192, 197-198
Research Centers Directory, 1968—204
Research for Better Schools, Inc. (RBS)—206

NOTES